A DICTIONARY OF OLD TRADES, TITLES AND OCCUPATIONS

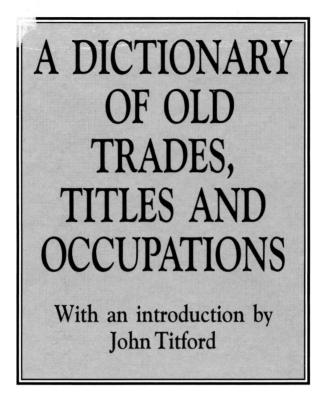

With an introduction by
John Titford

COLIN WATERS

COUNTRYSIDE BOOKS
NEWBURY · BERKSHIRE

First published 1999
This new expanded edition 2002
Text © Colin Waters 1999, 2002
Illustrations © The Colin Waters Collection 1999, 2002

COUNTRYSIDE BOOKS
3 Catherine Road
Newbury, Berkshire

To view our complete range of books,
please visit us at
www.countrysidebooks.co.uk

ISBN 1 85306 794 6

for Marie

Produced through MRM Associates Ltd., Reading
Typeset by Techniset Typesetters, Merseyside
Printed by J. W. Arrowsmith Ltd., Bristol

INTRODUCTION

O let us love our occupations,
Bless the squire and his relations,
Live upon our daily rations,
And always know our proper stations
      (Charles Dickens, *The Chimes*, 1845)

Not all of us love our occupations, but in a very real sense they
define who we are. As a conversational gambit, 'What do you
do?' follows quickly on the heels of 'How do you do?'; keen as
we are to pigeon-hole people and to understand what makes
them tick, we often feel more at ease once we know what a
person does for a living – or even what a retired person *used to
do* for a living.

'I'm a doctor', 'I work in the media', 'I'm an electrician down
the pit'; what a wealth of social information these innocent
little phrases contain! I had a great-great grandfather who
worked in London as a pawnbroker's assistant, later becoming
a commercial clerk, a general salesman and a shopkeeper. It
was typical enough of a Victorian husband and father to turn
his hand to a series of different jobs to earn enough to support
his family, but whenever Benjamin Titford was asked to state
his occupation on any formal document, he declared that he
was a 'silversmith' – the trade to which he had initially been
apprenticed but one which he had never actively practised as a
way of making a living. To his ears and those around him, the
occupation of silversmith would have conferred a certain social
cachet which would determine his ranking within the artisan
class to which he belonged. Benjamin's eldest son would
become a schoolmaster – the first person in his family to have a
'career' as such, where to move job and location would ensure
a crab-like progress up a ladder of social status. Most of our
ancestors had no such pretensions: an occupation was something they learned in their early years and practised until they
dropped. Not for them the luxury of pursuing the path of
ambition which was afforded to those in the law, the church or

the military. You hewed stone or drew water because that was what was needed to keep the wolf from the door; indeed, you probably did both, since dual or multiple occupations have often been the norm in English society, as is evidenced by many a seventeenth century 'shoemaker and alehousekeeper' or a nineteenth century 'collier and grocer'.

Not all occupations followed by our ancestors in time past were as straightforward as 'silversmith' or 'schoolmaster', both of which were terms used nationally with little variation. By contrast, a man whose job it was to finish cloth would usually be referred to as a 'fuller' in the east and south-east of England, as a 'tucker' in the south west, and as a 'walker' in the north. These regional variations are reflected in the surnames derived from such terms, and Colin Rogers' *The Surname Detective* (1995) includes maps showing their distribution. The same author points out the fascinating fact that the surname 'Carpenter' had a strong presence in the south-west of England but was much less common elsewhere – principally because a man doing the same job was known in other parts of the country as a 'wright', not as a 'carpenter'.

Some trades and occupations came and went, as did the terms associated with them. Sedan carriers ceased to exist once sedan chairs had passed out of fashion; ecclesiastical lawyers known as proctors, practising an occupation known for its rampant nepotism, disappeared once their monopoly had been broken and their function taken over by common-law attorneys in the late nineteenth century, and a warrener was no longer required once Lords of Manors had ceased to keep their rabbit or hare warrens. In more recent times, type founders who cast type in hot metal have passed into history with the advent of modern printing technology. Even a few decades after a trade or occupational term has ceased to have daily relevance, it may well slip into history and will eventually be understood only with the help of a dictionary. This is why a dictionary such as the present one is of such importance to the family historian, the social historian, the local historian – and the reader with a general interest in such things. Some may well use Colin

Waters' book in the process of compiling a learned thesis; others may find that it helps them defeat their sworn enemies in a game of *Trivial Pursuit*.

Those writers, editors and others who work for *Family Tree Magazine*, as I do, have long found that certain sorts of queries exercise the minds of readers more than others; so it is that we have always had a constant stream of questions about occupational terms and the meaning of surnames, both of which are reflected from time to time in the content of the magazine itself. Very often these two topics are connected. If you have a surname such as Cooper, Mason or Thatcher, the meaning speaks for itself in the context of words still used today. If your name is Wainwright you may have to think rather more carefully; if it is Farmer you may have to eschew the obvious derivation and think in terms of an ancestor who was a tax collector; if it is Pinfold you may have to use a dictionary, and if it is Billiter (from a bell mould maker) you'll probably fly to such a dictionary in some desperation.

My advice to those who are perplexed about the meaning of a trade or occupational term has always been to refer to the enormous and comprehensive *Oxford English Dictionary*, available in print and on CD-ROM, or to find a copy of Joseph Wright's magnificent six-volume work, *The English Dialect Dictionary* (1898–1905). This is no easy solution to those who cannot easily get access to such works, however, and in recent years one or two useful but comparatively modest publications have helped fill the gap, such as *An Introduction to Occupations: a preliminary list* by Joyce Culling (Federation of Family History Societies, 1994) and *Dictionary of Old Trades and Occupations* by Andrew and Sandra Twining (Woodcroft, South Australia, second edition 1995).

Twentieth century reprints of two classic earlier works, *The London Tradesman* by R. Campbell and *The Book of English Trades or Library of the Useful Arts* offer fascinating historical detail on a select number of trades, and the illustrations in the latter are particularly appealing. Stuart Raymond, meanwhile, has produced two very useful and relevant bibliographies on the subject: *Occupational Sources for Genealogists* (Federation of Family History Societies, second edition 1996) and *Londoners' Occupations: a Genealogical Guide* (Federation of Family History Societies, 1994). Yet still a really comprehensive dictionary of old trades, titles and occupations was lacking, until the publication of the present work by Colin Waters. Only a work as substantial as the present one can do justice to its subject; it matters not to the reader how many other terms are defined in such a book, if the one that he or she seeks is lacking. There should be very few disappointed readers in this instance, but if you do find a term which is lacking and which you think merits inclusion, do please write to the publisher in the hope that it may be featured in a later edition.

Meanwhile, consider whether the trade of the genealogist or the whore is the oldest in recorded history, or whether flint-knapping can lay claim to such a distinction, as Colin Waters suggests. And enjoy revelling in a forgotten world of alectoromachers, buddle boys, claquers, dobbers, hokey pokey men, knock nobblers, rogue spotters and sperviters.

John Titford

AUTHOR'S NOTE

The entries in this guide are taken on the whole from English sources of many periods dating back to before the Norman conquest. Other entries from English speaking countries abroad (e.g. Australia & U.S.A.) have also been included when found. Many of the old trades which are self explanatory e.g. 'milk seller' have been omitted unless there is other supplementary information of an historic nature to impart. A large number of old terms and titles from Victorian London have been extracted from, or verified with, 'London Labour and the London Poor' by Henry Mayhew, which appeared in serial form in the *Morning Chronicle* in 1849. This has been published in book form on a number of occasions and is an excellent reference source for those who wish to study the lifestyle of tradesmen and London residents in greater detail.

Though in some cases, dates have been included, there has been no real attempt to date any of the names and titles used. In many cases the reader's own document or source in which the name occurs will be sufficient to date the term being used.

Latin occupations and titles vary in spelling to some degree as do Old English terms. The main variations are shown in brackets e.g. Aromatar(ius) – Grocer. However, if an entry cannot be found, it may be worth searching for other spellings or variations (including words with different endings).

Some terms still in modern use are included, either because the name or trade is dying out; because it is only used regionally; to give historical information; or to show any changes that may have taken place in the tasks undertaken by people using that title. Similarly, some job descriptions were used by various (often unconnected) trades. These have been described where appropriate.

The use of the forward-slash / simply indicates 'and/or' (e.g. barrel maker/repairer).

AUTHOR'S NOTE TO SECOND EDITION

This second edition of old trades, titles and occupations contains over one thousand new entries. Some entries that appeared in the first edition have been revised if new or alternative meanings have come to light. In addition, dates have been given in some cases as guidance as to when the term was in use, though it should be remembered that in some areas, at least, certain titles would be in use long before or after that quoted.

A number of foreign terms which were once in common usage by the English speaking nations have been included as these were either invented, absorbed, retained, or used by British colonials both when abroad and at home. In response to requests, a selection of criminal titles has also been included from both sides of the Atlantic. Acknowledgement is given to the excellent publication, *Dictionary of American Underworld Lingo*, Editor in Chief, H. E. Goldin – Constable & Co Ltd, London, 1950, which is an invaluable reference source for those wishing to study this aspect of the subject in extended detail.

Finally, I would like to extend my thanks to all those who have contacted me with suggestions and additions for this second edition.

A

abbess. Female version of an abbot. Though the term is often used to describe a female head of a priory, the more correct term in that situation would be prioress.

abbey lubber. Someone who relied on an abbey for his living (without working), e.g. a lazy monk or a pensioner.

abbot. Head of a monastery with powers similar to lord of the manor. Except in smaller abbeys it was often largely an executive rather than just a religious position. The abbot would have his own separate residence together with his own cook and other staff. He was elected by the monks with the approval of the archbishop and the King.

abbot commendatory. A non serving monk who acted as a guardian and executive of the abbey.

abbot regular. An abbot who was a serving monk.

abbot's cook. Private servant cook of an abbey's abbot. His wages were paid for privately by the abbot.

abbot's proctor. An abbot's representative at Parliament and religious gatherings.

abbrocarius, abbrocator. General broker.

abecedarian. Someone who taught (or was learning) the alphabet.

ablaster. Crossbow operator (soldier).

able seaman. Seaman more highly skilled than an ordinary seaman or a landsman.

abra. Maidservant.

academic(ian). Member of a learned academy.

academy proprietor. Owner of a private school (often with the principal as the only teacher).

acater. Food buyer and supplier (often to ships).

accipitrary. Falcon trainer.

accompant, accomptant. Accountant.

accouchereuse. Midwife.

accoucheur. Male midwife or women's doctor.

accoutrea(ment)er. Supplier to the military.

acicularius. Comb maker. Also a maker of decorative pins for holding clothing together.

ackerman. Cowkeeper.

acreman. Cowman/ploughman.

acrographer. Engraver on metal (for printing purposes).

actuary. Accountant specialising in documentation especially concerning insurance.

acupictor. Embroiderer.

Adamite. Member of a religious sect who went about naked.

addle-plot. A name given to someone who farmed his land so badly that he ruined it.

adjutant. Originally someone who passed on orders from his leader to other men.

administratrix. Any woman in charge.

admirilis. Admiral.

adventurer. A member of the Merchant Adventurers who dealt in wool. Also a term given to a shareholder in tin mines.

advertisement conveyancer. Man who advertises carrying a 'sandwich board' consisting of two large noticeboards (one at the front of him and one at the rear) strung over his shoulder by straps.

advocate. Lawyer.

advocate depute. Law officer in Scotland.

advowee. A person with rights to appoint a clergyman (advowson) to a parish.

aedificator. Builder or architect.

aegyptianus. Gypsy (literally 'Egyptian').

aerobat. Pilot of a plane performing stunts at airshows and carnivals.

aeromancer. Ancient name for a weather forecaster.

aeronaut. Balloonist, also a trapeze artist.

affeerer. Manorial officer (usually one of two) who set fixed court penalties.

African brocade weaver. Specialist weaver of floral/geometric patterns.

after chromer. A person who fixed colour in dyed cloth.

ag. lab. Abbreviation for agricultural labourer.

aga. A chief, officer or dignitary.

agent. Someone who acts on behalf of another (varied trades).

aggillarius. Hay maker.

agister. Royal forest official who received payment for pig foraging. Also in charge of other animals in some cases.

agmatologist. Physician who specialised in broken bones.

agnate relative. A family relation on the father's side.

agonist. An athlete or athletic combatant.

agrestic. A common, rustic or rude person.

agricola. Farmer.

agricultural labourer. General farm hand (often shortened to ag. lab.).

agriculturist. Farmer or land worker.

aid canvas weaver. Weaver of open woven material used in needlework/embroidery.

air raid warden. See under warden.

alabar weaver. Operator of a very large and fast weaving loom.

alabasterer. Carver of alabaster work.

aladinist. English name given to a free-thinker, particularly among foreigners.

alarum maker. Specialist clock maker who constructed the clock almost entirely of wood. To this was attached the 'alarum' bell, (i.e. he produced the ancestor of our modern alarm clocks). Most alarum makers (also known as wooden clock makers) in Britain were of foreign extraction. Alarum clocks were plentiful in the early 1800s and were considered cheap and inferior.

Alaska yarn spinner. Spinner of mixed cotton and wool cloth.

albalasterea. Same as balista.

Albert twill weaver. Weaver of lining materials.

Albert weaver. Overcoat cloth weaver.

Albigensey. 12th century protestant branded a heretic by the Pope.

Albigensian. Medieval member of a group of religious reformers allied to the Cistercians & Knights Templar. They were at one time branded heretics. The name comes from Albi, Languedoc (France), where the movement is said to have started.

alchemist. Ancient scientist/chemist/physicist.

alderman. Public official higher than a councillor but lower than a mayor. He was usually a senior local official, elected by councillors, not the public. The title dates back to Anglo-Saxon times.

aldis (light) signaller. Signalman using light flashes to pass messages.

ale conner. Public ale tester similar to an aletester.

ale draper. Publican (see illustration opposite).

ale tunner. Brewery worker who filled casks known as 'tuns'.

alectoromacher. Someone involved in alectomachy (i.e. the sport of cock-fighting).

alectryomaker. Same as alectoromacher.

aletester, ale founder, ale taster. Official position dating back to 1200s to test quality of ale being sold.

alewife. Female publican.

algerine. Pirate.

algerino. Seaweed gatherer. (This Latin based term is still used colloquially as a name given to a resident of Scarborough [Yorkshire], by a resident of nearby Whitby.)

alien. In medieval times a foreigner who could not inherit land.

alien monk/prior/nun. Member of a British religious order which held allegiance to a foreign monastery. Many alien

A 17th century woodcut featuring an ale draper. The ale draper got his name from the old practice of selling ale by the 'measure', a term still in modern usage. Some old inns still display 'yard of ale' and 'half yard of ale' containers which consist of long metal or glass trumpet-shaped funnels with a bulbous bottom. Though in modern times, bets are taken to see if anyone can drink from a yard of ale glass without spilling a drop, it was never intended as a drinking glass, more as a measure from which to pour. Other modern left-overs from the custom of selling ale by the yard are the expressions a 'long drink' and a 'short'.

monasteries appeared after the Battle of Hastings under the influence of William the Conqueror.

alienee. Someone to whom a right has been legally transferred.

alley dasher. Factory worker who would sweep up between the machines.

all hot man. Street seller of hot potatoes or pies.

allopathist. Physician who treated a disease with its opposite cure (directly opposite to homeopathy).

allottee. A person who had obtained shares in, or part of, a grant of land.

allspice(r). Grocer.

alluvial miner. Surface miner who works for minerals deposited by mud washed down a river course. Also called a placer miner (especially in the U.S.A.).

all-wise. Village wiseman or woman.

almanac man. Street seller of calendars (see illustration). Also a specific Lincolnshire officer who warned of high tides near the Trent.

almoner. Giver of charity to the needy or a person in charge of petty cash (in a college etc). In an abbey he was in charge of all charity functions both internally and externally. He was forbidden to associate with women when on his travels outside the abbey 'lest those visits of mercy should be employed to cover intrigues of love'. The almoner was provided with a horse, equivalent of the latter day 'company car'.

almsman, almswoman. Receiver of charity or a pension (male).

almsperson. In Victorian times paupers, prisoners and lunatics were officially designated almspeople.

alnager. Official who stamped cloth as a sign of quality in market places.

alum worker/miner. Worker/miner involved in obtaining the mineral alum, used in the chemical industry. (See also slopseller.)

alumnus. Tanner of animal hides. Also a university student.

alutarius. Leather tanner.

A 19th century woodcut showing an almanac man displaying his wares. Almanac men were not confined to selling calendars. Their stock in trade included tide-tables, astrological predictions, theatre programmes, coach time-tables and any publication giving information about events happening in the future. Such items were not generally sold by bookshops, so the almanac man found a steady trade for his wares throughout the year. Like all other street traders, he would be known by his own distinctive cry to help potential customers locate him in the busy town or city streets.

amanuensis. Secretary or recorder of transactions etc. (Also spelt ananuensis.)

ambassadress. Wife of an ambassador (i.e. not a female ambassador).

amber cutter. Jewellery maker from amber, a fossilised resin.

ambergris merchant. Someone who dealt with the whale fishermen, buying ambergris (found in the intestines of sperm whales) and selling it to perfume makers, who used it as a scent fixative.

ambler. Horse breaker.

ameer. A prince or similar ruler.

amen clerk. Parish clerk.

amen man. Same as amen clerk.

amoroso. A wanton woman or prostitute.

Anabaptist. Member of a religious group who believe that baptism should only take place by total immersion of adults.

ananuensis. See under amanuensis.

anchor smith. Anchor maker.

anchoress. Female religious hermit.

anchorite. Male religious hermit.

ancilla. General female servant.

androchia, androgia. Dairy maid or cow-girl.

angela. A female messenger.

angel(us). Anciently, as angelus, a male messenger. Later, as angel a patron of theatrical productions.

angle smith. A kind of blacksmith who specialises in working with flat iron bars making brackets and similar items.

anilepman. Small land-holding tenant of a manor.

animal preserver. Taxidermist.

ankle beater. Child employee who drove cattle to market.

ankle biter. Colloquial version of ankle beater or any young person.

annatto maker. Yellow dye maker.

annotina. Any child who had reached the age of one year.

annuitant. Someone who receives an annual pension.

antigraphus. Secretary or scribe.

antigropelos maker. Maker of waterproof trousers/leggings.

antisabbatarian. One who opposed the keeping of Sunday as a special Holy day.

anvil smith. Maker of anvils and blacksmiths' accessories.

apiariana. Bee keeper.

apiarist. Modern form of apiariana.

apothecarius. Usually a dealer in drugs, but sometimes used for a simple shopkeeper.

apothecar(y). Drug dealer. The Society of Apothecaries was founded in 1617. They were the lowest of the medical profession in status, after physicians (the highest), doctors and surgeons.

apparitor. Official of a church court who summons witnesses to appear.

appellee. Defendant in a court of appeal.

apposer. Someone appointed to question or examine others.

appraiser. Valuer of property, buildings, quality of materials, etc.

apprentice. Originally someone who paid (or worked for nothing as an assistant) to learn a trade under contract. In ancient times, a man could not move from apprenticeship to craftsman until he was 23 years old.

approprietary. A lay person who obtained the benefits normally given to a member of the clergy.

apron man. Mechanic or 'black collar' manual worker, usually skilled or semi-skilled.

aproneer. Shopkeeper.

Aquarius man. Water seller.

aquavita seller. Whisky/spirit seller.

arab. Apart from the meaning as a native of Arabia, the term was once generally used to indicate an orphan or outcast.

arbalistarius. Same as balista(rius).

arbiter. Someone who made a judgement in a civil dispute (i.e. an arbitrator).

archarchitect. The head architect.

archbishop. Church leader in charge of a diocese.

archdapifer. High ranking ceremonial servant.

archdeacon. Bishop's deputy who had his own court which dealt with licences, fees and probate.

archdiaconus. Archdeacon.

archer. Originally a soldier with bow and arrow, later anyone who could use those weapons with skill.

archiator. Physician.

archical. A first officer or chief official.

archiereyist. Member of the higher ranks of the clergy.

archil manufacturer. Maker of a violet textile dye from lichen.

architect, architectus. Designer of buildings. In ancient times he would also be described as a builder.

architector. A thatcher of houses. Also a builder but rarely an architect.

arconarius. Wool trade worker.

arcubalista. A crossbow man.

arcularius. Cabinet maker specialising in large boxes and trunks.

argentarius. Silversmith. Also a banker.

argoist. A professional thief. (From 'argot', a slang jargon used by them.)

argolet. An archer on horseback.

argus. A watchman or lookout.

Arien. Originally a follower of Arius, who denied the holiness of Christ. The term is sometimes confused with 'Aryan'.

ariolator. A soothsayer or fortune teller.

aristarch. Term given to describe a severe critic.

arkwright. Joiner/carpenter who specialised in 'ark' (box/chest) making.

armentarious. Animal herdsman.

armiger. Originally the carrier of arms for a knight, later a general term for a person of high status who is entitled to bear arms.

Armorican. A resident of ancient Brittany.

armorist. A person skilled in heraldry.

armourer. Originally a maker of armour. Later a gunsmith.

armourplate glass worker. Worker in a factory producing an early type of reinforced glass known as 'armourplate'. (See illustration.)

armurarius. Armourer (including the supply of weapons).

aromatar(ius). Grocer.

aromatopola. Grocer.

arpenteur. Land surveyor.

arquebusier. A soldier equipped with an 'arquebus' (a kind of musket which was rested on a forked metal stick).

arrant. Any infamous or notorious person.

arrowsmith. Manufacturer of arrows or of the constituent parts of an arrow.

art silk worker. Same as artificial silk worker.

articifer. Skilled mechanic. In military terms a soldier involved with explosives. In the 16th century the term was used to describe an apprentice. (See also artificer.)

artifex. Craftsman (of any kind).

artificer. A soldier mechanic . (See also articifer.)

artificial seller. Street seller of artificial flowers.

artificial silk worker. A worker in the rayon industry making artificial silk from cellulose etc.

artillator. Same as attilator.

artillerist. A skilled gunman.

artisan. See artizan.

artist of fireworks. Firework manufacturer and/or display organiser.

artizan. Craftsman who is educated in his trade or has served an apprenticeship.

asbestos weaver. Maker of fireproof cloth.

ascian. English term for someone who lived in the tropics.

ashman. Dustbin/dry toilet emptier.

asphalter. Road builder or surfacer.

assay master. Assayer who specialises in precious metals.

assayer. Tester of metals, ores or precious metals for quality or value.

Armourplate glass workers are seen demonstrating the quality of their product in this picture taken around 1940. The glass they are standing on is only about a quarter of an inch thick and measures only four feet by two feet in size.

assessor. Property tax calculator.

assizer. Weights and measures inspector. (See also assizor.)

assizor. A juror. (See also assizer.)

assurer. Insurance agent or underwriter.

astronomer. Weatherman who assisted mariners who were going on long voyages to try and predict what weather conditions they might encounter.

asylum keeper. Attendant of a refuge for the homeless, poor or insane.

atheling. Title used by Anglo Saxon royalty and large landowners.

attilator. Medieval officer responsible for all of the weaponry kept in a castle.

attire man/woman. Same as tireman/woman.

attornatus (ad legem). Attorney (at law).

attorney. Law official and/or representative.

aubobulcus. Herder of oxen.

aucker. Goose seller (the word auca is medieval Latin for goose and the term hawker to denote a travelling salesman may well derive from this term).

auctionarius. Term used for both a retailer and a general broker whether an auctioneer or not.

auf. A fool or simpleton.

auger. A fortune teller.

auger maker. Maker of tools used for boring holes of any kind.

Augustinian monk. A monk who belonged to an order which was designed to draw together into a monastic order, priests who formerly served non-monastic churches. They were also known as Black Canons.

Augustinian sister. A nun who specialised in nursing of the sick.

aulnager. Official who stamped cloth as a sign of quality in market places.

aurifaber. Same as aurifex.

aurifex. Goldsmith.

aurist. Someone skilled in the treatment of ear problems.

auspex. Fortune teller who used the movement of birds as his divinatory means.

author. Originally someone who brought any plan to fruition.

autochton. An old term similar to 'aborigine' meaning a native of any particular country.

autogiro pilot. Pilot of an early form of helicopter.

autographic artist/printer. Producer of printed pictures from designs drawn on printing blocks.

automath. Title given to a self taught person.

autoplater. Newspaper industry worker operating an autoplate press for making curved moulds for printed pages.

auto-typist machine operator. Operator of an early machine that typed multiple letters, leaving spaces where necessary for hand-typing of individual details.

auxiliary. Anyone assisting or carrying out a trade or job they are not fully qualified for, under the direction of someone who is qualified.

avant courier. A person employed to go ahead and announce someone's arrival.

avenator. Hay and feed merchant.

avener, avenor. Officer of the King's stable.

avowry. Manor holder.

axeman. Woodman or logging worker.

axle tree maker. Maker of axles for wheels.

axle tree turner. Same as axle tree maker (especially using wood).

ayah. A servant. The term was first used for native Indian servants by the British who occupied India.

azo dyer. Dyer using synthetic dyes.

B

babu. A Hindu term once used by the British aristocracy as a term of respect for a gentleman.

baccalaureate. Bachelor (sometimes Bachelor of Arts).

bacchante(s). Pagan priest/priestess.

bachelor. (see under **banneret**.)

bachinator. Medieval officer who inspected castles and their accounts.

back end man. Textile factory worker who operates a machine which stretches the fabric being woven.

background artist. A painter of scenery for stage shows etc. Later someone who did the same job for animated films.

bac(k)us boy/girl. A general unskilled help.

back washer. Wool washer.

backmaker. Another name for a cooper ('backs' were tubs).

backster. Same as baxter.

badger. Also **badge-man**. In Tudor times a licensed beggar or receiver of alms. Later, in the 17th century a receiver of poor relief who was required to wear a badge and could not beg anything but 'broken victuals' at fixed times. Later a pedlar (originally of food). Also a corn dealer.

badgy fiddler. Army boy trumpeter.

bagasse dealer/agent. In the days when sugar cane was the only source of sugar, bagasse, a by-product obtained from the outer casing of the cane was used to manufacture paper and as fuel. Bagasse dealers were the middle men between supplier and customer.

bag collector. Man who collects up empty sacks from farms, shops etc for return to the supplier.

bag wig maker. Maker of short half-wigs which sat below the back brim of a hat in the 18th century.

bagman. Travelling salesman.

bagnio keeper. The term means 'public baths attendant' but was also used to describe a brothel keeper.

bagpipe boy. Victorian street musician generally using the English or Irish, rather than Scottish bagpipes.

bailee. See under bailor.

bailetus. Medieval valet.

bailie. Bailiff.

bailiff. Guardian or an officer of the lord of the manor below the rank of steward. (A water bailiff was a guardian against fish poaching.)

bailor. Legal term. An owner who gives up possession of something he owns on a temporary basis to a bailee with an intent to retrieve them at a cost. E.g. owner of a pair of shoes (the bailor) who gives them to a cobbler (the bailee) to repair.

bairman/woman. Same as bareman/woman.

bajan. Scottish equivalent of fresher (see under that heading). The term is from the French 'bec jaune' meaning 'yellow bill'.

bajulus. General term in medieval times for an 'officer' of any kind.

baker. A position not a job in abbeys; he was in charge of all outlying abbey bakeries, and income from them. Maker of bread, cakes etc (see illustration).

This picture shows a 19th century baker alongside his large brick built oven. He is kneading dough, ready to be made into loaves for general sale. In the days before household ovens, it was the practice of householders to take their own baking to the bakehouse and to pay a fee for it to be cooked.

bakestone maker/cutter/firer etc. Specialist stonemason or quarryman who prepared stones for bakers and household ovens.

bal captain. Underground manager of miners in Cornish tin mines.

bal maiden. Same as buddler.

balaclava knitter/maker. Person who made a type of headgear consisting of a hood with a round or oval hole for the face. They got their name from the fact that they were originally issued to soldiers at the Battle of Balaclava. Balaclavas can be of chain mail, leather or more commonly in modern times, knitted wool.

balancer. Coal miner who operated a coal truck pulley.

baldrick fixer. Man who manufactured, assembled and repaired the leather hanging straps and the clapper for church bells.

baldrick maker. Manufacturer of richly ornamented shoulder belts.

baler. Person in a factory or on a farm who makes up bales.

balista(rius). Soldier in charge of the large catapult machine used for throwing rocks at city walls. Also a crossbowman. (See illustration.)

balister. Same as balista.

balius/balivus. Bailiff.

ball miller. Process worker in the cement industry.

Balistarius. Known variously also as a Balista, Balister and Arbalistarius. This ancient soldiers' job was to act as a crossbowman or man a large catapult for throwing rocks at enemy city walls. The illustration above was carved in stone and shows a balistarius carrying his crossbow and a variety of bolts.

ball thrower. A potter who moulds clay by hand.

ballad seller/monger. Street seller of sheet music.

balladeer. Same as ballardeer.

ballard master. Man in charge of loading the ballast into the hold of empty cargo ships.

ballardeer. Travelling singer/poet or teller of stories (street entertainer).

ballast heaver. Loader of ballast into empty ships' holds.

baller. Worker in a ropery.

baller (upper). Potter's assistant (makes up balls of clay).

bam. A cheat.

band filer. Metal worker (often in a gun factory).

band miller. Sawmill worker operating machinery that saws logs into planks.

bandster. Someone who 'banded' the hay in sheaves or tied it onto stacks or ricks after harvest on a farm.

bang beggar. Parish official responsible for ensuring beggars moved on (colloquial).

bank man(ager). Person in charge of a coalmine lift cage. Also, manager of a financial bank.

banker. Originally a ditch digger. Later a term given to anyone who would lend money at interest. (See illustration.)

banker mason. Stonemason who works carving stones directly after removal from a stone quarry. Originally they worked in the quarry itself, but with the coming of the railways were often situated in a shed at the end of a railway line leading from the quarry, often in a nearby town.

banksman. Same as bank man.

Banlieue watch. A guard or watchman who patrolled the 'Banlieue' (city limits outside of the city walls).

banneret. A knight whose knighthood had been conferred on the battle field and who was entitled to lead his men into battle under his own banner, as opposed to a Knight Bachelor (otherwise known as a Bachelor) who could not.

Banker. Banking developed from a more informal system of money-lending. Later wealthy men would lend from their homes (banking houses) where they kept impregnable safes. From these early banking houses developed the first formal banks (as illustrated here). Security features were minimal as the risk of robbery was relatively small and 'gentlemanly conduct' was not only expected, but was very much a feature of the times.

banqueter. Broker or banker. Also one who organised banquets.

bantling. A term applied to any young child.

banyan. Strictly a native Indian merchant but used during the British occupation of India to describe any merchant.

barege weaver. Weaver of barage cloth, a thin gauze made from a mixture of silk, wool and cotton and used for ladies' dresses.

bar keeper. Tollbar operator. (It was rarely used to describe a publican before 1900.)

bar master. Lead industry worker.

barber. Men's hair cutter. Up to 1745 they were also surgeons.

barber chirurgeon. Same as barber(us).

barber surgeon. Same as barber(us). See illustration.

Barber surgeons were considered a 'jack of all trades' in earlier times. They would undertake everything from cutting hair and pulling teeth to veterinary work and surgery. Though many would carry out amputations using herbal narcotics in order to stupefy their patients, others simply used the old tried and tested method of getting the patient extremely drunk. The ancient illustration above shows a barber surgeon removing the leg of a man in very primitive conditions whilst an assistant stands by to catch the man when he faints from pain.

barber(us). Originally a surgeon, haircutter and dentist.

barbitonsor. Barber/dentist in an abbey.

bard. Poet (sometimes a travelling minstrel).

bareman/woman. Beggar or pauper.

bargee. Private/naval or merchant barge operator. (Also a carrier of goods on a canal.)

bargeman. Same as bargee.

barilla maker. Burner of the plant saltwort to obtain crystals used in the glass industry.

barker. He owned a 'barking house' where nets were steeped in a solution made from oak bark, the tanning of which helped to preserve the nets from salt water. Also a leather tanner. Also someone who shouts to the crowds at a fair, circus etc (see bawker).

barking house keeper. See barker above.

barkman. Barge operator or a sailor on a bark (ship).

barleyman. Manorial court official in charge of bylaws.

barm maker/brewer. Yeast manufacturer.

Barnado boy/girl. A child who spent a period of their lives in one of the 'Dr. Barnado's homes'. These were orphanages set up in the late 1800s for distressed children. The organisation still exists.

baro. Baron.

baro fisci. Baron of the exchequer.

baronettus. Baronet.

barrastorius. Law barrister.

barracoon attendant. Someone who worked in the slave trade.

barrel filer. Files the barrels of guns during manufacture.

barrel filler. Labourer (generally in a brewery).

barrel organ man. Street musician with an organ carried on wheels.

barrista. Barrister.

barrman. Gate keeper, usually in a medieval city, but often used in other senses where a barrier was involved.

barrow boy. A street salesman (boy or man) working from a barrow or stall.

barrowman. Coal barrow pusher in a pit.

barton(er). Man in charge of a farm attached to a monastery.

baseborn. Illegitimate.

bashaw. A tyrannical leader. Also describes a proud man.

basil(er) worker. Worker with goat or sheep skins.

basket maker. A term which is wider than its literal meaning. In ancient times, basket makers were employed in the making of boats, buildings and other large objects where their skill at 'weaving' wood was at a premium.

basket man. One who fills or empties baskets (especially in coal mining). Also a basketmaker.

bass dresser. Fibre mat worker.

bast worker. Same as bass dresser.

basyle. A political radical.

batellagius. Boat hirer.

bater. See courage bater and master bater.

bathing machine proprietor. Operator of changing huts on beaches. Common in Victorian times.

bathorse man. A carrier who used a pack horse.

bath stone quarryman. Stone quarry worker who worked with bath stone, a kind of easily worked oolite stone similar to sandstone in appearance, but differing in structure. It was originally discovered close to Bath.

batman. A military officer's personal attendant.

batt maker. Wadding maker for quilts and padded furniture. Also a wool industry worker who prepares wool for the fulling process.

battledore maker/stringer. Manufacturer of cane or wooden carpet beaters and paddles. Also manufacturer or stringer of tennis and similar sports raquets once known as 'battledores'.

bauer. A Teutonic word meaning 'builder' but generally used in Britain to mean a peasant.

bauer man. Same as boreman.

bauge weaver. Weaver of a coarse cloth known as 'bauge' used as a substitute for carpeting.

bavin seller. Seller of brushwood (known as 'bavin') for firewood.

bawd(er). 'Pimp' or agent for a brothel.

bawker. Also known as a barker. A kind of town crier or public announcer.

baxter. Baker.

bay yarn spinner. Spinner of knitting wool.

bayadeer. A dancing girl.

bayweaver. Weaver of baize fabric.

beachcomber. Originally one who made a living from what he could gather on the beach.

bead piercer. Person who drilled the holes in beads.

beadle. Parish officer whose duties varied in different areas, from that of churchwarden to town crier. Other establishments (e.g. banks) sometimes employed beadles as a kind of security official. Beadles were often in charge of the town's workhouse and were renowned for their lack of compassion in many areas. (See illustration.)

beadman. Originally an inhabitant of a hospital or poorhouse. Also a religious person. Also used in the sense we use the word 'employee' in modern times.

beadsman. Same as beadman.

beamer. Textile worker who handles materials before weaving. (See also warper.)

beamster. A tannery worker.

bearer. Coal carrier in a mine. Also a professional coffin carrier.

bear-ward. Travelling entertainer with a live performing bear.

beat sweeper. A street cleaner with his own particular area of coverage in one locality (see also gang sweeper).

beater. Cloth cleaner in the textile trade. Also one who beats the ground to disturb game birds for shooting.

beater room worker. Worker in a paper mill.

beatster. Person who mended herring nets on shore.

A 17th century woodcut showing a beadle with his 'staff'. The office of beadle had different duties and powers with it, depending upon which town he was employed in. Some beadles carried out purely church duties, whilst others had extensive powers like a policeman or town guardian. Though the beadle above carries a long staff shaped like a cudgel, others would carry a decorative long staff complete with silver knob and gold embellishments. Virtually all beadles wore livery or a uniform of some sort.

beau. Colloquial term for a 'ladies man'. Also for a boyfriend. Sometimes used for a well dressed man.

beaux esprit. Same as bel esprit.

beaver. Felt maker (for hats etc).

bedder. Bed maker. Also a stable worker. Also an upholstery worker.

bede. Same as beadman. Also same as bedman.

bedel(l). Same as beadle.

bedesman. Same as beadman.

bedlam worker. Worker in a lunatic asylum.

bedman. A sexton.

bedral. Scottish minor official equal to a clerk, sexton or beadle.

bedswerver. Colloquial term for an adulterer.

bedwagon maker. Manufacturer of a large oak contraption designed to hold a pan of hot ashes and used for warming beds.

bedweaver. Quilt maker or webbing maker.

bee master. A person who keeps bees for honey.

bee skep maker. Maker of beehives from plaited straw. Skeps were generally dome shaped and not square like the modern beehive.

beefeater. Yeoman of the Royal Guard.

beestie. Title used in colonial India for people who supplied water to the British residents.

beetle finisher. Same as beetler.

beetler. Embossing machine operator in the textile or leather trade. Also a worker in the textile bleaching processes. Also someone who prepared flax for spinning. Also a laundress who beat the clothing with a 'beetle' (large flat paddle).

beg. A governor of a town or district.

beggar banger. Same as a bang beggar. A sort of constable or beadle.

Beguine. Female devotee to a religious order dedicated to doing charitable acts.

bel. Same as beldam.

bel esprit. A man of wit.

beldam. An old haggard woman.

Belgravian. An aristocrat.

bell boy. A boy in a hotel who attends to residents, being summoned by a bell.

bell founder. Bell maker.

bell host. Same as a host.

bell reaper. Operator of a revolutionary mass produced reaping machine introduced in the 19th century. The machine was *pushed* by two horses with the farmer guiding them from behind. It was very successful and proved a great advance on traditional cutting by scythe.

bell ringer. Town crier. Also someone who rings church bells.

bell swagger. A bully. Also used to describe a lewd man.

bell wether. Colloquial term for a shepherd. The bell wether was actually the leading sheep in a flock which was fitted with a bell.

belle. A fashionable lady.

belleyetre. Same as bellyster.

bellhanger. Installer of bells in churches.

bellman. Town crier or messenger who announces his presence by a bell.

bellow farmer. Repairer of church organs.

bellow maker. Maker of bellows for fire lighting or operating organs.

bellow man/boy. Low grade servant whose duty was to keep a fire going by using bellows (often found in castle kitchens).

belly builder. Piano maker who makes the shell and interior of the piano.

bellyster. Bell maker/hanger.

below stairs maid. A maid in a large house who never entered the 'upstairs' living quarters.

belter. Bell maker.

bencher. Senior member of a society of barristers.

bender. Leather cutter.

Benedictine monk. A monk who followed the rule of St Benedict.

benefactor. A class of worker who assisted people to better themselves (e.g. teacher or trainer).

benshi. Narrator in an early cinema who commented to an audience during the days of silent films.

BEPO worker. Worker at the early experimental nuclear reactor plant at Harwell, Oxfordshire.

bercar(ius). Shepherd.

bergmaster. A bailiff or chief officer (especially among Derbyshire miners, where he made judgements in a miners' court).

berner. Person in charge of a hound pack.

bersar(ius). Forester.

besayle. Great grandfather.

besom manufacturer. Brush maker.

bespoke tailor, framer etc. Someone who would make an item to your own measurement or other requirements.

bess warden. Similar to a pinder. A town official responsible for stray animals.

bessant. Manufacturer of coins in a regional or Royal mint (various spellings, e.g. bezant, besent, etc).

bessemer process worker. Steel industry worker.

Bethlemite. A lunatic. Also a kind of monk (probably one who worshipped in a 'Bethal' dissenting chapel).

bever(er). Drink maker/seller (non alcoholic).

bey. The governor of a province known as a 'beylick'.

bibber. Habitual drinker.

biblicist. A teacher of the bible who was not a member of the clergy.

bibliopeg(us). Book binder.

bibliopola. Bookseller.

bibliothecary. Book seller or librarian.

bid stand(er). Highway robber. Also someone who puts up money for a financial venture.

biddy. Colloquial term for female farm worker/servant, especially if Irish.

bijou man. Jeweller.

bijouxler. Jeweller.

bilker. A fraudster. Also a colloquial term for someone who never paid their debts.

Bill Barlow. Street clown who dressed in a standard fashion.

bill deliverer. Person who travels around to various bill posters with the posters which are to be put up.

bill poster. A man who puts up signs and notices.

bill sticker. Same as a bill poster.

billier. Cotton spinner.

billiter. Bell mould maker.

billy piecer. Wool mill worker who collects broken yarn and joins it.

billy roller operator. Cotton spinner.

billyman. Cotton spinner.

binder. Bookbinder. Also used in other trades for someone who binds materials together (e.g. hats). Prior to 19th century books were sold un-bound. The purchaser would then take them to the binder of his or her choice.

Bioscope projector. Operator of an early cinema projector. The 'Bioscope' was a travelling film show which toured the country in a van pulled by four horses.

bird boy. A kind of human scarecrow who would patrol fields to keep birds off crops or seeds. This was often a man not actually a boy.

bird catcher. Someone who catches wild birds and sells them.

bird nester. Someone who collected birds' eggs, either for food, for collections, as a novelty in cities where they were considered rare, or to hatch and sell as pets.

birds' nest seller. Same as bird nester.

birleyman. A patroller of grounds as a kind of warden.

biscuit baker. There were five grades of biscuit baker, each involved with a different part of the manufacturing process. (See under moulder, marker, splitter, chucker and depositer.)

biscuit glazer. Pottery process worker who glazes 'biscuit ware'.

bishop. Apart from its religious context, a bishop was a man who was paid to make an old horse look young prior to a horse sale.

bizzy. Colloquial name (especially in Liverpool) for a policeman.

black borderer. Maker of black-edged stationery for use during mourning.

Black Canon. See under Augustinian monk.

black collar worker. Colloquial term for someone in a dirty job.

Black Friar. A friar who followed the rules of the Dominican order.

black jack maker. Leather worker who made black leather jugs known as 'black jacks' which were used both in the home and in public houses.

Black Maria man. Colloquial term for a policeman who drove around in a large black police van equipped to carry multiple prisoners.

Black Monk. Benedictine monk.

black profile cutter. See under profile cutter.

Black Rod. Parliamentary office, same as Gentleman Usher of the Black Rod.

black tray maker. Someone who made trays as a japanner.

blackguard. Someone running a protection racket (from the words 'black guardian'). Also a menial servant who did dirty work.

blacking manufacturer. Polish maker.

blacklead worker. Graphite worker (e.g. making pencils).

blackleg. Originally a gambler or swindler.

bladarius. Corn seller.

bladesmith. Specialist maker of knife and sword blades.

blanch farmer. A farmer who paid rent in silver when it was normal to pay in livestock.

blank cutter. Worker in the first stages of many industries who cuts out the 'blanks' ready for manufacture.

blaster. Person in charge of setting off explosions in a quarry etc.

blaxter. Owner of a bleaching house or bleaching grounds.

bleacher. Same as blaxter.

bleaching garth worker. Exterior worker who attended to the cloth that was bleaching in the sun.

blemmer. Plumber.

blencher. A worker whose job is to shrink cloth or garments.

blimp pilot. Airship pilot.

blind tooler. A leather worker who engraved designs on wet leather leaving a black impression.

blindman. Same as blindsman.

blindsman. Post office worker dealing with mis-addressed mail.

bloater seller. Seller of whole cured fish (unlike herrings which are split before smoking).

block cutter. Maker of printing blocks. An engraver of the same. Also a shipyard worker.

block maker. Maker of block and tackle in the shipping trade. Also a printing block engraver.

block ornament salesman. Seller of pieces of cheap off-colour but edible meat bought from butchers who would previously have displayed them on a block until such time as they were unsaleable to their normal customers. Hence the term 'block ornament'.

block printer. One who prints with blocks as opposed to type.

blocker. Hat trade worker. Also a block maker and a shipyard worker.

blood letter. Doctor or vet who used leeches to draw blood from patients in order to lower blood pressure.

blood man. Dealer in blood from carcases (e.g. to make black pudding or fertilisers). Also a blood letter (i.e. a 'letter of blood' for medicinal purposes).

Bloomer. Victorian term for a woman who wore a fashionable over-skirt, trousers and head-dress in the style popularised by a Mrs. Bloomer.

bloomer(y worker). Maker of iron from raw ore. (See illustration.)

blower. Glass blower. Also a textile worker. Also someone who operated bellows in any trade.

blowfeeder. A textile worker.

blowze. An old term for a fat faced, ruddy cheeked woman (often a farmer's wife).

blue(y). A term used to describe a child in custody at a Borstal who was ready for release. (See also Borstal boy.)

Blue Coat. Colloquial name for someone who attended a charity school. Their uniform was always blue.

Blue Devil. Colloquial name given to Britain's first police in 1829 when they first appeared on the streets.

Workers at an 18th century ironworks. The term bloomery worker dates back at least to monastic times when abbeys and priories obtained much income from iron mining and production. Bloomery workers were involved in the first stages of making iron from ore. The picture above shows 18th century bloomery workers engaged in a number of tasks involved in the making of this rough iron ore.

blue dyer. A person who whitens clothes using blue dyes.

blue jacket. A sailor. (See illustration.)

blue maker. Someone who makes the dyes used for whitening laundry.

bluestocking. Secretary, female writer, librarian etc. (Originally a mocking term in the days when women were not expected to have 'brains'.)

bluffer. Publican.

Boanerges(s). A preacher, particularly one who preached in the 'Hell and Damnation' style.

boarding officer. Customs inspector of ships.

boardman. A rent paying tenant. Also a school truancy inspector. Also a street advertiser.

boardwright. Specialist carpenter who made tables and other objects requiring boards.

boatman. Same as boatswain.

boatswain. Small boat operator. Also a petty officer in charge of deckwork aboard a ship.

bobber. Metal polisher. Also someone who unloads fish from boats.

bobbin carrier. Spinning/weaving mill worker.

bobbin winder. Someone who winds thread onto bobbins in the textile trade (usually a child).

bobbinet maker. Machine operator making fine netting.

BLUEJACKET - DRILL-LEADING SEAMAN

A British Royal Navy Blue Jacket or Bluejacket shown in the uniform he would have worn around 1900.

bobby. An English policeman without rank. 'Bobby' comes from the Christian name of Robert Peel, the then Home Secretary who instituted Britain's first real police force in 1829. (See illustration.)

bocher. Butcher.

The last of the Old Charlies.
Born 1785.

C

The last of the " Peelers."
Sir Robert Peel's Act, 1829.

D

Bobby. The British policeman, colloquially known as a 'bobby' developed from the medieval 'circa' or patrolling guard (A). Later came the 'wakeman' or 'night-watchman' (B), who patrolled the streets with his familiar cry 'All is well. It's five o'clock on a cold frosty morning', or whatever fitted the scene at that time. Most residents of towns and large cities drew comfort from his cry despite the obvious interruption to their night's sleep. Many relied on him for getting up for work in the morning. The last of the watchmen known as 'Charlies' is pictured above (C), together with one of the uniformed policemen who replaced them and who themselves became popularly known as the 'bobbies' (D).

bod(e)ys maker. Maker of bodices.

bodger. Forest worker making chairs, spars, spindles etc from un-cured wood.

body maker. Car assembly plant worker who fixed the car body to the chassis. (See illustration.) Also a bodice maker in the female garment trade.

bog trotter. Colloquial term for a farmer or countryman.

Bohemian. A Victorian who ignored conventional social and moral rules.

Bohemian brother. See under Moravian.

boiler firer. Person in charge of lighting boilers.

boiler maker. Industrial worker of metal (not necessarily making boilers).

boiler palter. Rolled iron worker making boiler cases.

boiler plater. Same as plater.

boiling house keeper. Used specifically for those who rendered down whale blubber, but also for other trades where fats were boiled down.

Body makers assembling cars in the days before mechanisation.

boll(er). Textile industry worker operating a powered loom.

bolter. Someone who sieves something. Also a person who rolls up bolts of cloth.

bombazine weaver. One of many 16th century Flemish weavers who settled in England. They produced bombazine, a mixture of silk and cotton.

bombmaker. Maker of 'bombs' for fumigation purposes. Also a military bomb maker.

bondager. A farm worker tied to his farm, not a freeman.

bondman. A worker tied by contract or custom to a master.

bondsman. Someone who supplies a bond (often a money lender). Also a bondman.

bone (button) turner. Button maker from bone.

bone lace maker. Maker of lace used for edging pillows etc.

bone man. Same as a rag and bone man.

bone mould maker (or turner). Button industry worker.

bone picker. Rag and bone dealer.

bone setter. Specialist in setting bones (not always a doctor or surgeon). Also a brush maker who made large household brushes using the 'bone setting' technique of anchoring each set of bristles with tar.

boniface. Keeper of an inn.

Bonstromme monk. A monk who was a member of a sub-Augustinian order (with only two religious houses in Britain).

book gilder. Someone who decorates book spines with gold leaf.

bookies runner. Someone who acts as assistant or messenger to a bookmaker.

bookmaker. Someone who gives odds and takes bets on horse races etc.

booky/bookie. Same as bookmaker.

boom defence man. A person in charge of wartime sea defences during World War 2. Boom defences consisted of strong metal anti-submarine and anti-torpedo mesh nets suspended in the water by large spherical metal floats.

boonmaster. An official surveyor of highways.

boot catcher. A kind of cloakroom attendant in old inns who took off and looked after customers' boots.

boot closer. Shoe manufactory worker who stitches the upper parts of the shoe.

bootbinder. Shoe manufactory worker who binds the soles to the uppers.

bootboy. A shoe cleaner. Applied to adults as well as boys.

boothman. Corn merchant.

bootlegger. Originally a smuggler known for wearing thigh length boots in which he could carry smuggled merchandise. (Hence 'booty'.)

bordar. Same as a border.

border. An ancient subsistence cottager of a low order.

boreman. Farmer.

borler. Maker of coarse fabrics.

borsholder. General officer or parish constable.

borstal boy/girl. A term given to any young offender who had served a sentence in a Borstal (children's prison). Borstal was seen as the 'hard option' when sentencing children. The 'soft' option involved being sent to an approved school.

bort dealer. Dealer in rough uncut diamonds.

boscar(ius). Woodsman.

bosh hand/attendant. Railway worker who cleans and maintains railway rolling stock.

bostarius. Common grave digger.

bostio. Cattleman (especially a drover).

botcher. Unskilled stitcher (e.g cobbler, tailor etc).

botellis. Butler.

botescarlus. Boatman.

botham(er). Farm worker.

botteril. Same as bottler.

bottiler. Same as bottler.

bottle boy. Publican's or pharmacist's boy assistant.

bottle maker. Originally a leather worker who made leather bottles for holding liquids. (See also harvest bottle maker.)

bottler. Leather (not glass) bottle maker.

bottom knocker. Pottery worker who assisted the sagger maker.

bottom man. See topman.

bottomer. Miner who worked at the bottom of the pit shaft.

bound servant. A servant bound by a contractual indenture. The term was often used to describe an apprentice.

bouquet seller. A poor woman who visited public houses etc selling tiny bouquets or posies for money. Sometimes called a posy woman.

Bow Street Runner. One of a small band of men employed as police in London in 1749. The name comes from Bow Street Magistrates Court, where the magistrate, Henry Fielding (novelist and playwright) first appointed them. Other courts later also had their 'runners'.

bowdler. Iron ore worker.

bower maid. Chamber maid or personal maid.

bowker. Butcher. Also a bleacher of yarn and wool.

bowler. Maker of bowls. Also person who made spoon bowls in cutlery manufacture.

bowlman/woman. Crockery seller.

bowlminder. Wool process worker.

bowyer. Maker/dealer of bows. A livery company (guild) for bowyers was established in 1371.

box mangler. Operator of a large contraption to press clothes or cloth. It was operated by large stone filled rollers, pressing upon a flat surface.

bozzler. General officer or parish constable.

brabener. Weaver.

brachy(o)grapher. Shorthand writer.

braider(er). Maker of leather cord and laces. Also same as a strawplaiter and a net maker (usually women's work when not making fishing nets).

braie maker. Manufacturer of men's trousers in the 12th century. Later the term was used for underclothes in the form of loose breeches.

brailler. Girdle maker.

brake machinist. Person who passed bread or biscuit dough through a machine.

brake(s)man. Operator of a brake on a train, in a pit shaft etc.

Brandt drill operator. Workman who used a Brandt hydraulic drill for use in mines and tunnels.

brasiar(ius). Malt maker/seller(sometimes a brewer).

brasiator. Same as brasiar(ius).

brasiatrix. Ale-wife (female publican).

brasil(ier). Dyer of cloth.

brass cutter. Copperplate engraver.

brass finisher. Polisher of brass objects after manufacture.

brass founder. Maker of cast brass objects.

bratt. A term given to a medieval peasant. The name comes from the coarse clothing worn by them.

braucher. Medical healer who used plants and other natural medicines.

brayer. Someone who breaks or hits objects or reduces something to powder (bray means to hit).

brazier. Brass worker, later any metal worker.

breach maker. Maker of gun parts.

breaker. Anyone who breaks up or dismantles anything (used in many trades).

breaker-up. Railway worker who breaks up and recycles railway parts.

breakman. Operator of any kind of breaking mechanism. Also used in place of brickman.

brenner. Medieval term meaning burner used in a number of trades but particularly in potash manufacture.

breeker. Maker of britches (trouser maker).

brew farmer. Collector of taxes paid to a lord of the manor by brewers and inns.

brewer. In an abbey this was a position not a job. He was in charge of all abbey-owned inns and their staff.

brewster. Brewer.

brick burner. Brick manufacturer.

brick dust seller. One of the 18th century street tadesmen who made his living by selling brick dust manufactured from old broken house bricks.

brick moulder. Maker of hand-made bricks using clay and moulds.

brickman. Brick maker/bricklayer.

brideman. Groom at a wedding.

bridewell keeper. Strictly the keeper of a county gaol but was also used for a local 'lock-up jailer'.

bridgeman. Originally a collector of bridge tolls but also a moveable bridge operator.

brieze seller. 'Brieze' was strictly cinders, but was a term used for all goods collected by dustmen/scrap dealers which could be re-sold.

brightsmith. White metal worker who polished his wares to a high degree. Many were also bell-hangers or locksmiths.

brilliander. Polisher of diamonds and other precious stones used in the jewellery business.

Bristol board maker. Worker in the paper manufacturing industry making a kind of smooth paste-board, often with a glazed surface.

britzka hirer. Someone who hired out a small 'britzka' carriage pulled by one or two horses.

broad cooper. Wholesaler of alcoholic beverages.

broadcaster. Agricultural worker who sows seeds by throwing them with both hands in a rhythmic motion. Also a radio or TV announcer.

broadcloth weaver. Weaver on an extra wide loom.

broderer. Embroiderer.

brogger. Wool dealer.

brogue maker. Shoe maker.

broiderer. Embroiderer.

broker. When used generally, another name for an agent. Also an iron worker.

broom dasher. Cleaner. Also a broom maker.

broom seller. A street salesman with his own distinctive cry, 'Buy any broom, old shoes buy any broom'. He would accept a pair of old shoes in exchange for a broom, due to the resale value of the leather. (See illustration.)

broom squire. Broom maker.

brother. A monk who if not serving in a monastery was titled as such, being a member of a religious order. Knights Templars and Knights Hospitallers were two such groups.

brotherer. Embroiderer.

brouge maker. Shoe maker.

brow girl/lass. Same as buddler.

" Buy a Broom?"

An unusual 1820 sketch of Dutch female broom sellers in London. The girls known as 'Flemings' arrived each summer with their identical traditional dresses and hairstyles and became models for unpainted penny wooden dolls sold in toyshops throughout the country.

browderer. Same as brotherer.

brown collar worker. Colloquial term for someone who works in a manual or dirty trade in a minor executive capacity (e.g. an office worker at a coal mine).

brownsmith. Copper or brass worker.

brueria. Brewer.

brush filler. Labourer who mended holes in roads by filling with brushwood and then topping with stones and mud.

buck. An unlicensed cab driver (see also rubber up).

buck giver. Same as rubber up.

buck man. Same as rubber up.

buck washer. Laundress.

buckle smith. Caster of buckles.

buckle tongue maker. Bucklemaking worker.

buckler. Buckle maker.

buckram maker. Clothing worker who made stiffening materials.

buddle boy. Ore washer at a tin or copper mine.

buddler. A female surface worker at a Cornish tin mine who assisted tin dressers. Also called a bal maiden.

budge maker. Person employed in the skin or leather industry who processed lamb pelts with the wool attached.

bulldog. Assistant, protector and enforcer of a proctor's authority at a university. This is the origin of the term 'school bully'. Bullers (or bulldogs) wore a 'uniform' of a traditional suit with a top or bowler hat. It was part of their duties to patrol university towns in the evening to act as a kind of university police.

buller. Same as bulldog.

bullock team leader. Someone who leads a cart etc towed by bullocks rather than horses.

bullwhacker. Colloquial term for an oxen drover.

bully. Same as bulldog.

bumboat man. Local trader with vessels anchored offshore. Also used as a term for a smuggler.

bummaree. Same as bummer.

bummer. A middleman.

bunter. Rag and bone man.

bureis. Medieval title given to those with civil rights under the protection of a town or city. It was the origin of the term burgess meaning a town or city official.

bureler. Maker of coarse cloth such as 'borel'.

burey man. Grave digger.

burgess. A town official similar to a councillor today. Originally a townsman representing an important town in Parliament.

burgomaster. Mayor or town official.

burl. A cup bearer.

burler (mender). Skilled textile finisher.

burler. Cloth finisher.

burleyman. Enforcer of bylaws for the lord of the manor. Secondary constable. Same as barleyman.

burmaid(en). Chambermaid or personal maid.

burn man. Brewery worker.

burnisher. A polisher (many trades).

burriar(ius). Dairyman, also donkey keeper.

bursar. Originally an abbey accountant. As this was a position of extreme trust he was well respected and took charge of all receipts and payments, collecting taxes and distributing money. He also visited all synods and meetings. He had his own horse for this purpose.

bury man. Grave digger.

bus conductor. A person employed on passenger buses to collect fares and ring a bell to signal the driver to start or stop.

bushel maker. Barrel/container maker.

busheler. Assistant to a tailor.

bushranger. Originally escaped convicts who roamed illegally in Australia. Some became robbers and gave their name to the second group of bushrangers, namely those who were notorious for robbing gold-prospectors as well as committing other robberies.

busker. Originally a travelling hairdresser who would work in the street as opposed to in his own premises. Later applied to anyone who plied their trade in the street.

busman. Driver of a horse drawn omnibus.

buss maker. Maker of blunderbuss guns.

busy. See bizzy.

buticularius. Private butler.

butler. Servant with widely diverse duties depending on the size of the household. He could either act as house steward, head waiter, or personal assistant to the householder. (For under butler, see footman.)

butner. Button maker.

butter carver. Carver of decorative butter moulds.

button burnisher. Someone in the button making trade who polished the finished goods.

button turner. Bone or wood button maker.

buttoneer. Button maker.

butty. A contract negotiator and supplier of labour.

butty boat man. Same as dumb boat man.

bylawman. Enforcer of the lord of the manor's bylaws. Secondary constable.

C

cab driver, cabbie, cabman. Originally a horse drawn taxi-cab driver. Later a motorised taxi-cab driver. See illustration.

cab yard owner. Someone who was paid to allow his ground to be used for the parking of horse-drawn cabs.

cabbage net seller. Itinerant salesman of small low quality hand-made nets.

cabinet maker. Originally a maker of boxes and box-like structures (e.g. a cabin). The trade later became skilled in manufacturing furniture.

cable layer. Electrical contractor (usually on a large building site) who lays out the electric cable system. Also someone working on a ship laying undersea cables between two separate countries or land points. Also a rope manufacturer of a rope consisting of many separated twisted strands.

cad. Traveller selling small items he carries. Also colloquial name for a horse-drawn omnibus conductor.

cada(man). Same as ostler.

cadaver. In ancient records the caduc and cadaver were the injured and the dead respectively. (See also under **caduc**).

caddy/caddie. Assistant or runner of errands (later a golfer's companion).

caddy butcher. Horse meat butcher.

caddis dealer. Dealer in rags or pieces of a new rough cloth alternatively called caddis, cadach or cadas.

cadet. Trainee (usually for some uniformed trade or service). Also used in heraldry to signify a younger son.

cadger. Anciently, a seller of hawks or other birds in cages. Also a dealer or pedlar in small items. Also used later to describe a beggar.

caduc. Sick or infirm person (usually mentioned in hospital or battlefield documents), as opposed to cadaver, a dead person. (See also under cadaver).

"WOT D'YER CALL THAT?"

THE VICTORIAN CAB-DRIVER

In his articles published in the Morning Chronicle *in 1849, the writer and journalist Henry Mayhew gave a rare and detailed insight into life in Victorian London. His descriptions of the cab-drivers of the city show us that far from being a hum-drum job, the profession was as complex as the maze of streets, alleys and lanes upon which the drivers plied their trade. Cab drivers he tells us, were drawn from all walks of life, ranging from criminals to a baronet. Many of them described as 'fancy men' used their vehicles in the course of another trade, prostitution, and lived on the earnings of the 'ladies of the night' they 'managed'. This fact alone is perhaps the reason why there was a clear distinction between 'day cabmen' and 'night cabmen' for few of the respectable owner drivers would work other than daylight hours. Respectable cab drivers, we are told, worked from cab-yards in the better part of the city, whilst the less respectable presumably sought their customers elsewhere.*

caedis quaesitor. Coroner.

caementarius. Building mason.

cafender, cafener. Carpenter.

caffler. Rag and bone man.

cage man. Man responsible for the lift used for transporting miners from the surface to the workface.

cainer. Maker of woven chair seat material. Also walking stick maker. (See also caner.)

caird. Same as cad.

caitiff. Strictly a prisoner, but also used during the 18th century for anyone in a wretched condition.

calamanco weaver. Weaver of a chequered glazed cloth.

calamander merchant. Dealer in a fine hard black wood similar to ebony originally obtained from Ceylon (Sri Lanka).

calcarius. Spur maker, also shoe maker.

calcearius. Shoe maker.

calciar(ius). Same as calcarius.

calciner. Bone powder grinder. Also someone who roasted iron ore in order to improve its quality by driving off moisture prior to smelting.

calculator. Medieval tax assessor.

calenderer. Textile industry worker. Rarely someone who works with account documents.

calico glazer. Production worker in the making of calico cloth.

calico man. Printer/dyer/dealer of calico cloth.

calico printer. Printer of a linen-like cloth made from cotton. The first calico printing began in London in 1676.

caligarius. Hosier/stocking maker.

calker. Fortune teller/astrologer/magician.

calligrapher. Specialist clerk who wrote up decorative official documents.

cambist. Money changer/banker.

cambric maker/weaver. Cloth worker.

camerarius. In an abbey he was also known as a chamberlain.

The dark interior of a Lancashire calico printing factory. Calico printing was a branch of the cotton industry. In areas such as Lancaster where textile mills were common, a large range of supplementary processes such as this took place in surrounding factories. Most factories would be dark and noisy, though those involving the textile industries were clean work-places compared to other factory situations. In the above illustration the large wooden printing contraptions, complete with wooden cog wheels, used for the printing process can be seen. Each machine would have its own 'minder', whilst elsewhere supplementary workers, including children, would carry out the other jobs such as cutting the cloth, wrapping it in brown paper ready for delivery, and preparing unprinted cloth ready for printing.

This was a responsible position in charge of the abbey's wearing and sleeping apparel, provision of shoes (including horse shoes) and all travelling arrangements.

camerist. Personal maid.

camister. Cleric.

camlet merchant. Salesman of camlet cloth used to make cloaks, petticoats, etc.

campanarius. Maker of bells in a bell foundry.

campanologist. Bell maker/ringer.

campsor. Banker.

cancellarius. Chancellor.

candelarius. Candle maker.

candidarius. Cloth bleacher.

candler. Egg trade worker who checked eggs by holding them up to a candle. Also candlemaker.

candyman. Colloquial name for an official. Also a seller of sweets etc. See illustration.

caner. Same as cainer but specifically one who makes chair seats from any woven material other than cloth.

cannes a voltaire manufacturer. Maker of a high class walking cane with gold top, used by magistrates, gentlemen and those of high status.

cannifex. Butcher.

Candyman. A street seller with his tray of Fry's candy. The word candy, though associated with the U.S.A. is in fact an English one. Candy sellers once sold 'sweetmeats' made of honey and eggs. Later as sugar became cheap and popular, a whole new range of candy became available. Chocolate coated sweets were the last to arrive on the scene.

cannonicus. Solitary monk or clergyman attached to an abbey or cathedral but not living there. (A canon.)

canon. A solitary monk or other clergyman attached to a cathedral. (See also regular canon and secular canon.)

canter. Vagrant. Sometimes a singer. Sometimes a canting caller.

canteen lady. Woman in a works or school who served meals etc in a room provided for the purpose.

canting caller. Auctioneer.

canvasser. Originally a canvas cloth worker. Later anyone who carried out research.

cap money collector. Minor official who collected a fine of three shillings and fourpence from each 'common person' who failed to wear an English woollen cap on Sundays as laid down by a statute of 1574.

Cape cart hood maker. A specialist hood maker (see hood maker).

Cape merchant. Chief merchant.

caper. Same as capper.

cap(p)ilair(e) manufacturer. Maker of orange syrup.

capistrius. Maker of horse bridles, halters etc.

capitalis. Head man/manager.

capitaneus. Captain.

cappelan(ius). Chaplain in charge of a chapel.

capper. Cap or hood maker.

captain. Apart from use as a rank in the navy, army etc, a foreman.

car driver. Short for carriage driver in the days before motor cars.

carabineer. Soldier armed with a 'carabine' (a short gun).

carbonado dealer. Dealer in rough uncut clusters of diamond crystals.

carbonar(ius). Charcoal maker, rarely a coal miner or dealer.

card cutter. Puncher of cards for loom weaving etc.

card maker. Maker of cards used by card cutters. Rarely a playing card manufacturer.

card match seller. Seller of an early form of phosphor-coated matches which consisted of a long strip of card, coated on one edge and split into individual strips, ready for tearing off.

card nailer. Machine maintenance worker in a cloth mill (often self employed).

card roomer. Cloth mill worker.

carder. Textile industry process worker (usually female).

cardinal. Originally one who advised the Pope and who was in line to be Pope himself.

cardinal maker. Specialist tailor who manufactured high class long red-hooded cloaks (of the type associated with Little Red Riding Hood). It later became the fashion to change the colour of the cloak to denote political allegiance.

carding engine worker/minder. Cotton industry worker.

carecar(ius). Butcher.

caretarius. Carter or carrier of goods by oxen, mule, horse etc.

carl(ot). Same as ceorl (also used sometimes as a substitute for clown).

carle. General worker. Also a strong, rough or rude man.

carlock supplier. Supplier to the brewing and wine industry of carlock, a substance used to clarify wines.

carman. Same as carter.

Carmelin. Member of the Carmelite religious order.

Carmelite. Member of an order of monks and nuns. The monks were known as White Friars.

carnarius. Butcher.

carner. Keeper of a granary.

carnifex. Butcher (often also a slaughterer of cattle etc).

carpentar(ius). Carpenter.

carpet planner. Person who plans how to build up a certain design when manufacturing carpets.

carpet weaver. Operator of a heavy weaving loom, producing carpets, at first operated by hand but later using automation.

carpetor, carpetrix. Wool worker.

carrier. A man who carried either his own or other people's goods from place to place by horse and cart, or by donkey/mule/horse.

carrier off. Someone at the end of a sorting process who 'carries off' the sorted goods to different storage areas.

carseatrix. Cheese maker.

carter. Man in charge of a cart (sometimes a stable).

Carthusian monk. Member of a strict order of monks who led austere lives like the original hermits (though they were not solitary). Their accommodation was a single bare cell within a larger community called a charterhouse.

cartographer. Originally a hand-drawer of maps.

cartomancer. Card reader for telling fortunes.

cartridge maker/filler. Maker of gun cartridges/bullets.

cartwheeler. Maker/mender of cart wheels.

cartwright. Maker/mender of carts.

cas chromer. Farmer or crofter who uses a 'cas chrom' hand-plough (without use of animals). Especially common in the Hebrides.

caseman. Same as compositor.

cashmarie. Travelling fish seller.

cask gauger. In the brewing industry, someone who measures the amount of liquid in barrels. See illustration.

cask manufacturer. Barrel maker. A cooper.

casmarie. Same as cashmarie.

casque maker. Manufacturer of an ornamented metal helmet with ear and cheek protection but with no visor.

cassimere weaver. Weaver of a cloth made from rough wool cross woven with fine wool or silk.

castaway. Originally someone rejected or abandoned.

castellan. The person in charge of a medieval castle. The position was either awarded by the king, or was purchased from him. Castellans obtained many powers, benefits and taxes from the position.

caster. Metal worker using moulds.

castor. Hat maker.

castor maker. Maker of salt cellars and sugar shakers.

castrato. A singer who had been purposely castrated in order to improve his singing voice.

castrator/castrater. Someone who castrates farm animals.

casuist. A lawman or judge who ruled on moral rather than written laws.

cat/dog meat seller. Buyer and seller of low quality meat for the consumption of animals.

catabaptist. Member of a religious movement opposed to baptism.

Cask Gauger. The cask gauger generally worked for the brewery and spent his time inspecting the barrels and their contents for both quality and quantity. Sometimes the term is applied to official weights and measures men who did the same job on behalf of local authorities or government.

catagman. A cottage dweller.

catamite. A boy kept for immoral purposes.

catchlove. Wolf catcher. (From Catch loup.)

catchpole/catchpoll. An early local authority officer with varying duties. A debt collector. Also a person who hunted wildfowl.

catechist. Religious teacher, usually a clergyman, who taught using question and answer sessions, together with repetition.

catellar(ius). General pedlar.

cater cousin. Strictly a quarter cousin but used for any distant relative.

cateran. Irregular soldier of Ireland and the Scottish Highlands who fought as a freedom fighter or mercenary.

catherege/catherick. Maker of carts.

catour. Caterer.

cattager/catageman. Small holder or small farmer.

catterick. Maker of carts.

cattle float driver. Man who delivered cattle using a cart made for the purpose.

cattle jobber. Cattle dealer.

caulker. Shipworker (filling cracks in timber planks to make them water-tight).

caupo. Same as cauponar(ius).

cauponar(ius). Inn keeper.

causeway builder. Similar to a lath bridge builder.

causeway man. Same as causey man.

causey builder. Same as causeway builder.

causey man. Road official or worker.

causidicus. Barrister or advocate.

cavalier. Strictly a knight or gentleman soldier, but generally used also for a soldier on horseback. Also a 'ladies man', particularly if he was a soldier.

cavener. Same as cafener.

ceapian. Stall holder or seller of inferior or cheap goods in Anglo-Saxon times.

ceapman. Another spelling for chapman.

ceiler. Ceiling builder/decorator. Also used in place of the term cellarar.

celanese worker. Textile worker making 'celanese', a rayon-type artificial silk from cellulose acetate. This process was developed by Camille Dreyfus who with his brother had earlier developed a process for treating First World War aircraft wings with a similar substance.

celebrant. Priest.

celesta manufacturer. Maker of celestes (keyboard instruments).

celibate. Originally applied to anyone who was not married.

cellar dweller. Colloquial term given to poor families, considered 'lower class', who in many cases actually lived in family groups, often in one room, in the cellars of city buildings.

cellar man. Person in a public house responsible for stocks and maintenance of equipment.

cellarer. In an abbey he was next in rank to a sub prior. A high ranking position similar to an estate manager. He dealt with all land matters and had a large number of staff under him. (See also kitchen cellarer.)

cellerarius coquinae. Same as kitchen cellarer.

Celt. Originally it referred to the inhabitants of Gaul, Britain, Spain or Italy. A 'forest dweller' ('ceiltach').

cementarius. Building mason.

cemmer. Same as comber.

Cenobite. Member of a religious group living together either in a monastery or in a community.

censarius. Common farmer. See illustration.

centesimate. Title given to one who was selected under an ancient wartime punishment where one man in a hundred was chosen for execution.

Soŵing seed

A censarius was a common farmer who would carry out any of the many tasks on a medieval farm. In the above illustration from an old manuscript, we find one such farmer sowing seeds using the hand broadcasting method. This ancient method of planting seeds dates back into antiquity and continued in some areas right up until the 20th century.

centurio. General term for an officer.

ceorl. Ancient term for a free peasant who had military obligations.

cerecloth manufacturer. Maker of a kind of waxed cloth.

cereographer. Either an engraver on wax, or someone who painted using wax colours.

cerevisiae coctor. Brewer.

cericus. Wax dealer. Also candle maker.

ceromancer. Someone who told fortunes using drops of melted wax on water.

ceroplastic modeller. Carver of wax objects.

certified child. Name given to a child worker who was registered and issued with a certificate under the Factories Regulations Act 1836.

cervisarius. Publican.

cervisior. Brewer (often also a publican).

cess man. Tax collector.

cest manufacturer. Maker of ladies' girdles.

chafery worker. Ironworks production worker.

chafewax. Formerly an assistant to the Lord Chancellor who dealt with the sealing of documents.

chaff seller/dealer. Straw chaff dealer.

chafferer. Same as chaffman. Small time merchant, especially in a market. (Old English.)

chaffman/maker. One who works with straw.

chain loom weaver. Cloth machine worker.

chain twister. Textile worker.

chainman. Operator of a chain-driven machine/winch etc. Also, a surveyor's assistant. Also in the 1800s, a term for a pickpocket of watches and watch chains worn on the outside of coats and waistcoats.

chair bottomer. Maker of the woven seat of wooden chairs.

chair mender. Man who would travel the country from village to village mending cane or raffia chairs.

chaisemaker. Carriage maker.

challis maker. Maker of a fine cloth of mixed silk and wool.

challoner. Blanket maker/cloth seller.

Chair mender.

chamber counsel. An advisor to a court or meeting who did not have the power personally to make a judgement or decision.

chamber maid. Female who tidies and makes the beds.

chamberlain. In monastic terms, another name for a camerarius. A steward of the household. Anciently a eunuch employed to look after the bedchamber or household. The terms were interchangeable.

chambermaster. Shoe and boot maker.

champion. One who fought or undertook combat as an individual on someone else's behalf.

chancellor. A high ranking official in various sectors of society (e.g. Chancellor of the Exchequer), sometimes honorary (e.g. Chancellor of a University). Originally a person who was of high enough rank to take his place in the chancel of cathedral churches.

chandelarius. Candle maker.

chandler. Strictly a candle maker but also a seller of candles and groceries.

changeling. A baby who was wilfully and secretly swapped for another. This may have been done for political reasons (e.g. a deformed child born as heir to a throne).

chanter. Travelling ballad singer.

chantor. Same as precentor.

chanty (man). Professional singer or a lead singer in a group.

chaperon. Originally a matron who attended a young lady in public places (a chaperone).

chaplain. Originally a church minister in charge of a chapel. Later a minister who was attached to a group of men (from varying religious backgrounds) such as in the army, navy etc.

chapman. Travelling seller of magazines known as chap books. Later any pedlar.

chappeler. Hat seller/dealer.

chapter member. A member of an order, monastery, or other group who excluded others from their meetings (e.g. Knight's Chapter).

char. A general cleaning woman.

char-a-banc driver. Driver of a multi-seated holiday or excursion passenger coach which was often referred to as a 'sharavan' or 'shara'.

charcoal burner. Usually a woodcutter who made charcoal as a sideline.

chare. Someone who is paid by the day (e.g. chare sweeper). (See also chare cleaner.)

chare cleaner. Cleaner or sweeper of a 'chare' (a small street or courtyard).

charlatan. The term originally meant someone who boasted continuously.

Charlie. A forerunner to the 'bobby'. This was the popular name for the old night watchmen who guarded the streets at night.

charman. A carrier of goods. Rarely a tea-maker.

charnel house attendant. Someone who looked after a mortuary. Also a meat store worker.

Charon. Strictly the mythical ferryman who took the souls of the dead to heaven, but used colloquially to describe any ferryman.

charterer. See under tramp owner.

Charterhouse monk. See under Carthusian monk.

Chartist. Member of a movement in the mid 1800s to reform agricultural and social life by the presentation of charters to Parliament. Most, but not all, Chartists were working class.

chartmaster. In industry, one who negotiated workers' contracts and supplied manpower.

chartographer. Map maker.

charwoman. Same as char.

chaser. Decorative metal beater. Also a cloth worker. Rarely an engraver who finishes off work done by another.

Chatham pensioner. A wounded or distressed sailor who received the 'Chatham pension'. This was set up in 1590 and was maintained from deductions from the pay of all seamen.

chattelane. A key holder (usually to a castle). This could mean an actual key holder or the lord of the castle. Later 'chatelaine' referred to the mistress of a household.

chatwood seller. Firewood seller.

chauffer stoker. Keeper of a small furnace.

chauffeur. Private driver (usually in uniform). Though the term is used for both male and females, the female version is strictly called a chauffeuse.

chauffeur mechanic. A chauffeur who also undertakes to repair his employer's vehicle.

chauffeuse. See under chauffeur.

chaunter. Same as chanter.

chauvin. Title given to a person who admired Napoleon to the point of worship.

cheap-john. Wholesaler or retailer of damaged or inferior goods.

cheapman. Market stall holder. Also chepe man.

check weaver. Weaver of chequered materials.

checker. A woman employed in the days of the horse-drawn bus to check that the driver was declaring the correct number of 'inside' and 'outside' fares. She travelled incognito as a well dressed passenger. Term used in a number of trades for anyone whose job it was to check items either for quality or quantity. Also a railway clerk who daily checked whether wagons were available for despatch or re-allocation.

cheese moulder. Cheese maker.

cheese weaver. Weaver of cheesecloth.

cheese winder. Cloth worker.

cheeseman. Cheese dealer.

cheirothecarius. Glove maker.

Chelsea pensioner. Receiver of the Chelsea pension, set up to cater for those who had served in the army. Chelsea pensioners are still known by their distinctive red uniform.

chemist. Originally someone who mixed chemicals in a laboratory (i.e. not a pharmacist). (See alchemist.)

chequer brat. Out of work weavers who went to London and other large cities to beg by singing in groups. They received their name from a kind of uniform they wore consisting of a paper cap, white apron, white bib, and a chequered pinafore.

chessle maker. Manufacturer of moulds and presses to be used in the cheese industry.

cheval-glass manufacturer. Maker of full length mirrors on a swivel contraption.

chevalier. Same as cavalier.

chickweed seller/gatherer. Collector and seller of chickweed plants for feeding to domestic fowl and cage birds.

Chief Baron. President of the court of the Exchequer.

chief pledg(er). A parish or town constable.

chiffonni(e)r. Wig maker. Also sometimes a worker in a rag factory.

childe. The eldest son of a nobleman who had not yet attained knighthood.

china (clay) miner. Same as kaolin miner.

Chinese shade. Chinese street entertainer in Victorian times.

chingler. Same as shingler.

chipper/chipa. Shipwright. Also another version of 'chippy'.

chippy. Carpenter, particularly aboard ship.

chirognomist. Fortune teller who read the palms of people's hands.

chirologist. Person employed to translate or transmit messages by the use of hand signals and gestures. Later used to describe anyone who taught or practised 'signing' for the deaf.

chiromancer. Same as chirognomist.

chirothecarius. Glove maker/seller.

chirrugus, chirugeon. Surgeon/dentist.

chocolate house proprietor. Owner of a kind of cafe similar to coffee houses where hot chocolate was sold as a drink.

chop house proprietor. Owner of a 17th/18th century eating house where the customer chose his own chop which would be cooked to order.

chopper. Though used generally for someone who chops something, the term is particularly used for a stone quarry worker who chops blocks of stone using an axe weighing fourteen pounds.

choragus. Musical conductor.

chorepiscopus. Any member of a congregation or group.

choriator. Surveyor.

Christadelphian. Member of a religious group set up in the mid 1800s by an Englishman, John Thomas, who lived in the U.S.A. Though mainly an American movement, branches were set up in the U.K.

chronicler. Same as chronologist.

chronologist(a). Documenter of events. Rarely a clockmaker.

chrysographer. A sign writer or illustrator who specialised in using gold lettering.

chubb. An unskilled rustic worker. Also used to describe any strong or rugged person.

chucker. Biscuit baker who supplied the oven man with the unbaked biscuits on a 'peel'.

chuff. A clown. Also used to describe someone rough in appearance or manners.

church hayman. Any churchyard worker (e.g. grass-cutter, grave digger, etc).

church master. Churchwarden.

church railman. Person with the responsibility of maintaining the fence around church lands or a graveyard.

church reeve, churchman. Churchwarden.

churchwarden. Originally a complex high position of trust involving acting as treasurer of a church. Later they acted as general managers of a church's activities and financial affairs.

Most churches had two or four churchwardens, depending upon the size of the congregation. Their election took place at Easter under the control of the vestry committee.

churl. Same as ceorl. Also a countryman, someone who was rough in appearances or manners.

churn driller. Quarry machine operator.

chymist. Same as alchemist.

cid. A leader, commander or chief.

cimeliarch. Ancient name for the keeper of a church's silver plate and other valuables.

cinder carrier. In the Victorian refuse collection trade, cinders and old bricks were the property of the master. The cinder carriers (usually the master's children) sorted and moved them in baskets to a separate storage area.

cinder man. Someone who emptied dry toilets. Also the male equivalent of the cinder wench.

cinder wench, cinder woman. Female who collected industrial cinders and re-sold them.

cinema organist/pianist. Employed in the days of silent movies to provide background music for the film being shown.

cipharius. Maker of drinking cups.

cippius. Person in charge of the public stocks, pillory, etc.

circa. Watchman or patrolling security guard.

circuit judge. A travelling judge who usually had a fixed circuit which he travelled, hearing court cases along the way. Also called an eyre judge.

circuiteer. Anyone who travels a circuit in order to carry out their job or profession.

circulating library proprietor. Owner of a private library.

circulator. Barrel maker or wood turner.

cissor(ia). Tailor.

Cistercian monk. Member of the Cistercian order (founded 1098) which was formed because of dissatisfaction at the Cluniacs' inability to achieve their stated purposes.

cit. Literally a citizen.

cives. Citizen. A trade usually follows (e.g.. Cives et aurifex = Citizen and goldsmith). Denotes a freeman of the town or city.

civilist. A lawyer skilled in civil law.

clapman. Town crier.

claquer. Someone who was specially hired to applaud in a theatre and so encourage others to applaud.

Clare. See under Poor Clare.

clarence carriageman. Driver of a four wheeled horse-drawn carriage carrying four passengers.

clark/clerk. In early days a clergyman, later a clerk. (See also clerk in holy orders.)

class man. Out of work labourer.

classic. Originally a highly rated author (living or dead).

clavifaber. Nail maker.

clavigarius. Maker of horse bits (and other horse tackle).

claviger. General worker.

clawback. A term used to describe a flatterer or 'yes man'.

clawer. Same as clower.

clay digger. Labourer in a clay pit who cuts large blocks of clay ready for transportation to a pottery, etc.

clay man/carrier. Pit or quarry worker who worked with clay. Also someone who specialised in waterproofing ponds, buildings etc with layers of clay. Clay carriers in brickworks were always children up to the 1880s when compulsory schooling was introduced.

cleaver. Man who makes fencing poles by splitting wood.

clemmy clearer. Someone employed to clear a field of 'clemmies' (rocks and stones). This was often undertaken by farmworkers' wives and families.

cleric(us). In early days a clergyman, later a clerk.

clericus parochialis. Parish clerk.

clerigh. Found in Celtic records and meaning clerk or cleric.

clerk. Same as cleric. (See also clerk in holy orders.)

clerk in holy orders. Always a clergyman, never a clerk in the sense of dealing with non religious documents.

Clerk to the Signet. High ranking Scottish law attorney who attended to royal documents. Also called Writer of the Signet.

cleromancer. Fortune teller who used dice for divination purposes.

cley man/worker. Same as clay man.

clicker. Shoe trade worker, also leather trade worker. Printer's assistant. Also a tallyman.

clicus. Same as clericus.

client of the fishhouse. In an abbey he dealt with all fishery rights and income. This was a uniformed position, not just a job. He would live outside the abbey with his own family and would have a range of staff under him.

cliff climber, cliff climmer. Someone who would climb down cliffs on a strong rope to obtain seagull eggs for sale to the public for food.

climber. Same as cliff climber.

climbing boy. A boy engaged by a chimney sweep to climb chimneys.

climbing sweep. Chimney sweep who worked without long rods and specialised in climbing large chimneys. It was this type of sweep who employed boys to climb up chimneys.

clip mat maker. Same as clippy mat maker.

clipper (on/off). Coal mine worker.

clippy. Colloquial term for a bus conductor/conductress who clipped used tickets.

clippy mat maker. Maker of rugs and carpets using 'clips' of cloth from old clothing etc. Once a cottage industry.

cloacal worker. Sewer worker.

cloakroom attendant. Someone who looks after guests' coats and belongings whilst at a function.

clobberer. A low untrained cobbler who roughly and cheaply patched up old boots and shoes.

clocker. Night watchman or guard who punches one or more time clock cards at set intervals on his rounds.

clod. Once a common colloquial term for a rustic simpleton.

clod hopper. Colloquial term for a farmer.

clog iron maker. Maker of the iron studs used in clog manufacture.

clog maker. Interchangeable with the term clogger in some cases, but clog makers were often specialist cobblers who made factory shoes with leather tops and steel studded wooden soles.

clogger. Wooden shoe maker who often worked from a wood where he collected his raw materials.

cloistress. A nun.

closer. Worker in a glove factory. Also used for other finishing processes in other industries e.g. shoe-making.

cloth lapper. Same as lapper.

cloth linter. Same as linter.

cloth man. Textile worker.

cloth picker. Same as linter.

clothes prop maker. Unskilled man who makes long wooden poles with a V shaped end to hold up washing lines.

clothesman. Dealer in clothing.

clothier. General clothes seller.

clouter. Either a clothier, a nail maker or a shoe repairer.

clower. Nail maker.

clubbist. An old term for any member of any club.

clumps. Same as clod.

Cluniac monk. A member of an order founded around the 10th century as a movement to restore the strict rule once observed by Benedictines which had become lax.

cnight. Anglo Saxon term for a knight.

coach driver. Holder of the reins of any horse-drawn vehicle.

coach trimmer. Someone who finishes the trimmings etc on coaches (both horse-drawn and motorised).

Coachman.

coachman. Usually the person in charge of the coach and coaching staff. Sometimes just a coach driver.

coaid. An assistant.

coal backer. Carrier of coal (manually on the man's back).

coal burner. A maker of charcoal.

coal carrier. Same as coal backer but also someone who traded in coal.

coal drawer. Pit worker who pushed or pulled carts of coal.

coal getter. An early term for a coal miner (generally in open cast mines).

coal heaver. Same as coal backer.

coal higgler. Household coal seller and deliverer. A coal man.

coal meter. Weigher/sorter/measurer of coal (usually in a mine).

coal runner. Underground coal mine worker.

coal whipper. Unloader of coal from ships and barges using baskets and winches. Also a man who would steal coal or other items from ships. They usually worked in pairs, one knocking large lumps of coal into the water, another 'finding' the coal when the tide receded. (See also mudlark.)

coalman. Man who delivers coal, coke etc to the customer's door for fuel.

coaly. Colloquial term for anyone who works with coal in any way.

coast waiter. Customs man.

coastal surveyor. Customs officer.

cob man/builder. Craftsman builder specialising in building house walls from layers of a mixture of soil, straw and water which proved very durable. (Surviving ancient thatched houses are generally made of cob.)

cobble fisherman. Fisherman in Yorkshire who fishes from a small clinker-built boat called a cobble.

cobble layer. Someone who makes road or pavement surfaces using rounded stones.

cobbler. Shoe maker/repairer.

cocarius. Cook.

cockfeeder. In cock fighting pits, the person in charge of the birds.

cock-laird. A Scottish yeoman.

cockle gatherer. Professional gatherer of wild cockles for selling at markets in the Victorian and Edwardian periods. (Also known as a cockler, cockle fisher and cockle hunter). See also scurtionist.

cockney. As well as indicating a resident of London who was born within the sound of the bells of Bow church, the term was also once used in contempt to describe an effeminate man.

coco(a) meat dealer. Person who bought the fruit extracted from coconut shells by those using the 'coir' fibre (coir dealers).

coctiliarius. Charcoal burner. Sometimes used to describe a baker or cook who used a charcoal oven.

cocus. Cook.

cocuus. Cook.

cod placer. Pottery worker.

codger. Originally applied only to an eccentric old man.

codman. A fish seller or fisherman.

coelebs. Bachelor.

coffee roaster. Though this can be a shopkeeper who sells coffee, it is more likely to indicate one of many workers in a large coffee producing factory.

coffer dam constructor. Someone who works building temporary dams.

cofferer. In former times an assistant to the Controller of the Royal Household.

coffey distiller. Whiskey distiller (named after the type of still used).

cog maker. Maker of wooden (or metal) cogwheels. Also a weaver/seller of coarse 'cog' cloth.

cogger. A cheat.

cogman. Same as a cog maker.

cognate relative. A family relative through the mother's side.

cognizee. A legal term indicating a person to whom a fine or damages was due.

cohen. Rabbi.

coiler. Used in many trades for someone in charge of coiling rope, springs etc.

coiller. Collector.

coillor. Same as coiller.

coin miller. Person who operated machinery in a mint, putting the milled edge on silver coins in order to stop debasing by rubbing fragments of silver off the edges.

coiner/coin minter. Maker of coins.

coir dealer. Dealer in coconut fibre.

coir mat manufacturer. Maker of rough doormat type rugs from coconut fibre.

cois(t)ell(er). A knight's private groom.

coistril. An under groom.

coke drawer. Kiln worker making coke from coal.

cold presser. Cloth process worker.

col(l)let(t). Anciently a servant of the church of inferior rank.

collar maker. Maker of animal (usually horse) collars. Also a clothing industry worker making shirt (etc) collars.

collector. Collector of money for the poor following suppression of the monasteries in 1547. In Victorian times a self employed scavenger who would collect (or steal) items for resale.

collegatary. Someone who jointly shared an inheritance.

collier. Originally a charcoal burner/seller, later a coal miner, coalman or sailor serving on a coal carrying ship.

colly-molly-puff. An 18th century colloquial name for a street seller of pastries. Also known as a pastryman. It was also used at that time to indicate an effeminate man and was probably the origin of the modern term 'puff'.

colo(u)rator. Same as colo(u)rman.

colo(u)rman. Dye/paint industry worker. Also housepainter's assistant.

colonellus. Colonel.

colonus. Farmer.

colporteur. Travelling book seller.

Columbian. Celtic monk or nun (prior to the conquest in 1066). Their convents/abbeys are thought to have consisted of individual huts, rather than one large building. The best known sites of these religious houses are Iona, Whitby and Tintagel. Also an early British term to describe a resident of the American continent (North or South).

comandronas. Country midwife and healer using plant medicines.

comb maker. Industrial (textile) or hairdresser's comb maker.

comb setter. Textile worker who set and straightened the pins used for wool combing.

comber. Comber of cloth yarn etc in the textile industry.

comedian(us). Originally an actor.

come-outer. A political radical.

comes, comitis. Earl.

commanditaire. Stock investor in a joint venture whose

potential loss is guaranteed to be limited to his investment amount.

commendatary. A caretaker clergyman who is holding office until another is found.

commissary. Provisions officer (usually in the army).

commission agent. Anyone who acts as a middleman, buying or selling on a commission basis.

commissionaire. Originally a messenger.

common cook. In an abbey, in spite of the name this was not a lowly position. He was in charge of all cooking arrangements and staff.

common cursitor. A vagabond or vagrant (as opposed to a cursitor - see also under that entry).

common informer. An expression used in Tudor times when the system of law allowed any citizen to inform on anyone else who had broken a law. If found guilty, that person paid a fine which was given to the common informer. The system wasn't formally abolished until 1951.

common mariner. A mariner involved in the coastal trade who only navigates within sight of land and other ships (ie someone who is skilled but not highly skilled at their trade). See also proper mariner.

common stage operator. A carrier who operated a regular stage service for goods using a heavy wagon and a team of six or eight horses.

common ware potter. A self employed potter who made inexpensive basic household items.

commoner. A term given to an ordinary student of a British university, as opposed to a 'gentleman commoner' from a very wealthy family. Commoners were also known as servitors or sizars.

compact moulder. Same as sinterer.

compeer. Someone from the same group or of equal social standing.

complotter. A cohort. Also someone who plotted with others.

composer. Printing industry type setter.

compositor. In the printing trade, one who sets (makes up pages of) type.

comptista. Accountant.

con man. Originally same as conder. Later a term for a confidence trickster.

concher. In the confectionery trade, one who smooths chocolate.

concubine. Though the term means a secondary wife (in societies where multiple wives are permitted), it was often used to indicate a mistress.

conder. One who gives nautical directions.

conductor. Collector of fares on trains, buses and trams (see also bus conductor). Also someone who leads an orchestra.

conduit maker. Maker of clay pipes for drainage and carrying water. In early days never called a pipemaker.

coney. For coney read 'rabbit' (e.g. coney catcher - a common rabbit catcher).

confectionarius. Same as confectioner.

confectioner. Originally someone who made medicines palatable by the addition of honey or sugar syrup. Later a sweet manufacturer.

confratern. Title given to any group which was considered, or known, as a 'brotherhood'.

congreve (match) maker. Maker of matches (for lighting fires etc).

conjurator. A magician. Also one of a number of people bound together by a common oath.

conner. Same as conder.

conservator. A constable. The term conservator is a shortened version of the full title of the post 'Conservator of the Peace at Common Law'. He had varying tasks ranging from police officer to collecting tolls, impounding loose farm animals, stopping public games on the Sabbath and preventing vagrants from entering a parish. Also any guardian or protector.

The duties of the early constabularius (see left in the picture) later evolved into those of the village constable.

consilarius. Councillor.

consociate. A partner or associate (particularly in business).

consort. Title given to anyone accompanying anyone else in a legal or official capacity, ranging from a husband, partner or companion to an ambassador or queen.

constable. A kind of cross between town inspector and policeman with many official duties. Also an early (1200s) name for a ship's master.

constabul(arius). Local constable. (See illustration.)

contrapuntist. Maker or embroiderer of bed coverings.

contravallator. A soldier employed in building defences for their own army under the walls of another army whose castle was under seige.

contriver. Inventor.

conventer. Member of a 'conventicle' (a group of 13 monks or nuns needed to start a new monastery). The words 'convent', 'convert' and 'coven' all derive from the word conventicle.

conventicler. Official delegate at a meeting. Also anyone who attended any meeting.

conversus. Adult convert to monastic life. In a Cistercian abbey, a lay brother or outside worker.

conveyor. General carrier of goods. Also a juggler.

convive. Companion.

cook of the convent. Same as coquinarius.

cook shop owner. Cafe proprietor.

cooper. Barrel maker/repairer. (See also couper.)

co-ordinate. Military term used for people of the same rank.

coparcener. Joint heir.

copeman. General dealer (later became synonymous with a dealer in stolen goods).

coper. Horse dealer.

cophin/ius/iarius. Maker of basketware.

copier. Transcriber of documents (particularly in law or in a monastery). Also known as a copyist. Also an imitator or impressionist.

copper. Colloquial term for a policeman.

copper beater. Copper worker.

copper boiler. One who hired out a large copper boiling vessel for the boiling of meat, lobsters etc.

copper bottomer. Copper worker who specialised in constructing the bottoms of containers.

copper van driver. Driver of a tram.

copperbeter. Same as copper beater.

coppersmith. Metal worker specialising in working with copper.

coppice man. Man who works in a wood where the trees are cut back to ground level each year so as to provide a plentiful supply of poles. Also called a copse man.

copra dealer. Same as coco(a) meat dealer.

copse man. Same as coppice man.

copy turner. Operator of a specialised lathe that copies items put upon it.

copyholder. Prior to 1922, a holder of manorial land by title during a person's own lifetime. On the copyholder's death, the land was returned to the lord of the manor who usually made the deceased's heir the new copyholder. In 1922 all copyhold land was declared freehold.

coquarius. Cook.

coquiller. Glass blower.

coquinarius. A civil cook at an abbey. Not to be confused with cellerarius coquinae, he was in charge of other sub-cooks such as the infirmary cook and the common cook.

coquus. Cook.

coracle maker. Maker of small, one or two man, round, river fishing vessels (particularly in Wales).

coralius. Leather worker who treated the raw skins.

corbio. Basket maker.

Cord wood cutter. Cord wood was rough wood complete with its bark. The cord wood cutter's job was to saw this up into pieces which could be used as rough posts for fences etc.

cord wood cutter. Sawyer who cuts rough wood into fixed lengths. See illustration.

cord(age) spinner. Someone who spun 'cordage' (a string or twine made from mixed materials such as hemp and manilla).

cordebanarius. An early form of cordwainer (shoemaker).

cordelier. Franciscan friar. So called from a knotted cord around his waist.

corder. A kind of weights and measures inspector engaged in the sale of wood.

cordiner. Same as cordwainer.

cordonnier. An early name for a cordwainer.

corduanerious. Same as cordebanarius.

cordwainer. Shoemaker (not a boot maker). Originally using Cordovan Spanish leather. In practice, cordwainers also made many other objects from leather (e.g. leather bottles).

core maker. Metal casting worker.

corerius. A courier or message carrier.

corf (basket) filler. Mine worker who filled baskets known as corfs with minerals.

coriarius. Courier.

coriator. Leather tanner.

cork cutter. Someone who cut bottle corks (and other items) from sheets of cork.

corker. Bottle cork or general cork object maker.

corn chandler. Corn merchant.

corn cutter. Either an agricultural worker or a foot-care specialist.

corn factor. Corn dealer.

corn meter. Corn weights and measures man.

corn striker. Medieval measurer of corn into fixed sized drums to check quantity before pouring into sacks.

cornerer. Any tradesman who created his own market by hoarding supplies.

cornist. Musician (who played a cornet).

cornopean player. Musician who plays the cornet.

cornutarius. Craftsman who made objects from animal horns.

coronar(ius). Coroner.

coroner. Originally an elected royal official whose duty was to hold investigations into crimes.

corporator. Strictly, a member of a city corporation but generally applied to any member of any body, club, etc. (i.e. a 'member'). Also known as a coterist.

corralius. Leather tanner.

correctarius. General broker.

corretier. Dealer in or hirer of horses.

corrigiarius. Leather belt maker.

corrodist. A pensioner or someone receiving benefits of money, food or clothing, generally from the monks of an abbey.

corsair. Pirate.

cortinarius. Maker of curtains and drapery.

corveer. Title given to a tenant or resident who had certain obligations to the Lord of the Manor (e.g. to keep a certain road in good repair).

corver. A 'corve' (basket) maker, used in the coal industry.

corversarius. A shoemaker. Also a basketmaker.

corveysor. Same as cordwainer.

corviner. Same as cordwainer.

corvisarius. Shoemaker. Also used for small basket makers.

corviser/corvisor. Same as cordwainer.

corypheus. Head chorister in a choir.

coshar/cosher meat seller. Seller of meat killed in the kosher Jewish fashion (as opposed to 'Tryfer' meat killed in the Christian fashion).

cosier. Unskilled labourer. The term was also used colloquially for a careless worker. Also called a coser.

cosmograher. Map maker.

costeaner. Tin miner or prospector.

coster boy/girl. A young costermonger.

costermonger. Street salesman or pedlar (generally of fruit and vegetables - originally an apple seller).

coteler. Same as cutler.

coterist. Member of a group or club. (See also corporator.)

cottager. Smallholder or small farmer living in a 'tied' cottage which came with the job. (See illustration.)

cottarius. Cottager/smallholder with obligations to work for his lord at certain times.

cotter/cottar. Same as cottager.

cottier. Same as cottager.

cotton feeder. Cotton industry factory worker.

cotton master. Labour organiser for the cotton industry.

cotton stone worker. Asbestos worker.

cotyler. Same as cutler.

This Victorian engraving shows a cottager and his family. In the background can be seen a pair of beehives.

coucher. Paper industry worker who in the days of hand-made paper was responsible for stacking alternate sheets of wet paper and felt before the pressing process.

counter. An early form of solicitor. Also someone who counts anything as part of their work duties.

countercaster. Any merchant.

count palatine. See under palsgrave.

countour. Rate collector.

couper. Cattle/horse dealer (see also cooper). Sometimes used in connection with the selling of other merchandise. However, this is normally clarified in the title (e.g. 'fish couper').

couple beggar. Travelling priest who performed 'instant' weddings up to 1754. Also known as a 'hedge priest'.

coupler. Walking stick/shepherd's crook manufacturer. Also a coal miner in charge of the coal trucks.

courage bater. Someone who castrates cattle, and other animals. (See also master bater.)

couranteer. Journalist/publisher.

courier. A person who personally delivers messages or goods on behalf of another (often internationally).

courser. A hunter (usually of rabbits or hares).

court driver/manufacturer. Driver or maker of a special horse-drawn cart called a court.

court roller. Ancient court record keeper.

court tooler/maker. See court driver/manufacturer.

courtier. Originally anyone who attended the Royal Court. Also a horse and ('court') cart driver.

cousin. In early records, this indicated any relation. To avoid confusion, a real cousin (i.e. first cousin), was often described as a 'cousin german'.

cousin german. See under cousin.

Cousin Jack. Colloquial term for a Cornish tin miner when working abroad.

covenantor. A political supporter of the Scottish National Covenant of 1638.

Coventry weaver. Weaver of ribbons (usually made of silk).

cow leech. Ancient vet.

cowherd. Cow keeper.

cowkeeper. Same as cowman.

cowl carrier. Either of two men who carried water (or other liquids) in a vessel called a cowl. This was suspended between the two men on a pole.

cowman. Person in charge of or who bred cows.

cowper. Maker of wooden items.

cox. Same as coxswain.

coxcomb. A jester. In medieval times the word was used colloquially to mean anyone who made a fool of himself (e.g. an habitual drunk or foolish member of the aristocracy).

coxswain. Person who steers a boat (pronounced coxun).

crab boiler. Worker associated with the sea fishing industry who boiled crabs and lobsters either for himself or others before selling them on to the public.

Coxcomb.

crab pot maker. Maker of traps in which fishermen catch crabs and/or lobsters. Though modern ones are made of weighted wood and a net stretched over a framework, originally crabs were caught in traps made of pottery (hence the name).

cracker boy. Same as cracker jack.

cracker lad. Same as cracker jack.

cracker jack. Quarry or mining worker (usually a boy) who sorts impurities from coal/stone crushed by the 'cracker' machine.

craet-wyrhta. The term is Anglo Saxon and means crate-maker. However, it was used to describe a manufacturer of carts.

craftiman. Same as craftsman. Anyone with specialist knowledge.

craftman. A craftsman of any kind.

cramer. Travelling salesman, especially of books.

crane ganger. Member of a team in a stone quarry operating or assisting with the operation of a large crane.

crapper. Slate quarry worker.

crate man. Originally a pot seller but later anyone who sold items door to door often from a wooden crate (and on credit).

crease(s) girl. Same as crease(s) seller.

crease(s) seller. Street or market seller of watercress.

creche attendant. A kind of funfair attendant. Originally (circa 1910) creches were designed as 'parking places for children' and consisted of a kind of fairground with children's rides etc where children of all ages could go to play. Often their parents would also use the rides and amusements.

credente. A believer in the Albigensian belief system in the Middle Ages who promised to undergo initiation prior to death, and so become a 'Perfect'. Credentes were part of the Outer Order or Third Order and professed to live by The Third Way, the objective of the One World Religionists.

creditman. Same as crate man.

creditrix. Female creditor.

creel maker. Maker of lobster or crab pots.

creep tester. Metal industry worker who tested metals for stress and elasticity.

crepe roller. Rubber industry worker who rolled sheet rubber through heavy rollers in order to give it a corrugated surface.

crier. Either a town crier or one of many street salesmen and women who would shout out what they had to sell in their own distinctive ways.

crimp. Press gang man. Also one who recruits staff, especially for ships.

crimper. Someone who puts decorative edging on a product (many industries).

crimpet seller. Same as crumpet seller.

crinculturalist. Person who made a living from his or her claim to be able to make hair grow on bald heads.

crispin. Shoemaker.

crocker. Potter. (See also croker.)

crofter. Smallholder (especially in Scotland) who often has another occupation such as bleacher or cloth dyer. Hence the occasional use of the term 'crofter' for a bleacher or dyer who was not a smallholder.

croker. Saffron crocus grower. Also a crockery maker/salesman. (See also crocker.)

crook maker. Maker of walking sticks and shepherd's crooks.

cropper. Agricultural worker. Also someone who cut woollen cloth with shears until shearing machines were introduced in the early 1800s.

crossing sweeper. Someone who would buy a brush and sweep road crossings, in front of shops etc (without being asked) in the hope of tips from passers by. Some attracted extra payment by acting as a kind of pavement artist, making designs in the dust and mud with their brushes. It was considered a lowly but honest job and most crossing sweepers were regarded as law abiding individuals who were a necessary part of keeping the city streets clean. (See also fake sweeper.)

crowd shoveler. Construction or quarry worker who operates a large earthmoving shovel.

crowner. Coroner.

crusher. Colloquial name for a Victorian policeman (at least in London).

cryptographer. A person who was employed to encode or decode messages.

cryptozoologist. Someone who studies the possibility of unknown lifeforms.

crystallomancer. Professional fortune teller who used crystals or transparent stones for divination purposes.

C.S. Clerk to the Signet. (See under that entry)

cu. A cook in monastic times.

cuinage officer. Official with the duty of stamping gold ingots.

cuhreur. Same as currier and curryer.

cuirassier. Soldier on horseback. So called because the defensive armour he wore on his chest was called a 'cuirass'.

culler. Someone who castrates cattle and other animals. Also, someone who slaughters animals. Also, someone who measured timber stacks. (See scaler).

culter. Small farmer.

cultivator. Farmer.

cunctator. Person who delays something (e.g. someone who monitors machinery and slows it down as necessary in a manufacturing process).

cunnere. Ale tester.

cunreur. A leather worker in medieval times, generally meaning a currier.

cuper. Alternative spelling for cooper.

cupper. Usually unofficial doctor who 'drew' blood using suction cups.

curandero. Medical healer who used plants and other natural medicines.

curate. A clergyman with special duties to assist a rector or other vicar. (See also perpetual curate.)

curd miller. Cheese worker who cut up the curds into small particles.

cure. A curate.

curer. One who preserves something, generally by smoking (e.g. ham, tobacco, fish).

curioso. A term added to a title to indicate someone notable for any reason (e.g. physician curioso, actor curioso).

curistor. Same as cursitor.

curmudgeon. Originally used in business, etc, to describe a competitor or other person jealous of the achievements or possessions of others. Now used to describe a surly or miserly person.

currier. Horse groom. Also same as curryer.

curryer. Leather trade finisher who greases the dry leather to make it flexible.

cursitor. Chancery Court clerk dealing with writs, wills etc. A common cursitor was a rogue or vagabond.

curtal friar/monk. Though no one is certain, the title is assumed to refer to a monk in charge of a pack of guard dogs (or hunting hounds) owned by a monastery (e.g. as in Friar Tuck the 'curtal friar').

custos. The word means 'keeper of'.

custos fabricae. Keeper of the works, a medieval clerk of the works in charge of major building operations.

custos pacis. 'Keeper of the peace'.

custos rotulortum. 'Keeper of the records', a position usually held by the Lord Lieutenant of the County.

custumus. Medieval official similar to a modern customs officer.

cut and draw worker. Embroiderer.

cutler. Maker/repairer/dealer in knives and other cutlery.

cuttelar(ius). Knife maker/cutler.

cutter. In the coal mining industry, one who loads coal onto the conveyer belt. Also a cloth cutter.

cutting shop owner. Owner of a shop selling goods at discount prices.

cuvin collector. Gatherer of cuvins (periwinkle or 'winkle' shellfish) from the sea-shore. Collecting of cuvins was sometimes a full time occupation involving the boiling of the shellfish before selling them on to a retailer for food use. In coastal areas it was often used to supplement income from other jobs, or was used as a means of earning pocket-money by school children. Many bucketsfull were collected until stocks diminished in the mid 1960s. (See also winkler.)

cycgelman. Manufacturer of wooden clubs to be used as weapons in Anglo-Saxon times. The word cycgel means 'cudgel' and not 'sickle' as is often supposed.

D

dab(ster). An accomplished person or expert in any trade (hence, the modern expression to be 'dab hand' at any task).

daguerreotype artist, daguerreotypist. Early photographer.

daia. Dairy maid.

dairyman. Farmer who specialises in milk products. Also one who deals in cheese, milk etc.

Dalriad. Member of an Irish tribe who settled in Scotland.

damaskeen worker. Someone whose job was to inlay iron, brass or steel with designs.

dame. School mistress. (Also used to describe old unmarried women.)

damoiselle de comptoir. A Victorian office worker who supplemented her income as a part time or occasional prostitute. She was considered a little higher class than the dolly-mop.

damster. Dam builder, particularly in the timber trade.

dandy loom weaver. Hand loom weaver.

danseuse. Professional female dancer.

danter. Silk mill overseer.

dapifer. Personal steward.

dapstone. Foreman in a stone quarry.

dareman/woman. Dairy worker.

darg man/worker. Worker paid by the day (usually a manual worker).

daring. A man who traps larks for a living, using a net and a mirror. Also called a doring man.

darner. A woman who would mend holes in socks etc by weaving new wool over the hole with a large 'darning needle'.

dataller, dateller. Casual worker (various industries).

daunsel. Male servant of a gentleman.

day cabman. Literally a cab driver that would not operate at night. In Victorian London (and elsewhere) few respectable cab owners would operate at night. The distinction between 'day' and 'night' cabmen was also one which hinted at status and respectability.

day labourer. A common casual labourer employed on a daily basis only. Same as dataller.

day tale man, day teller. Same as dataller.

daya. Dairy worker (man or woman).

days man. A umpire, judge or official arbitrator who fixed a day upon which a hearing would take place to make a judgement.

deacon. Originally the term meant a person empowered to care for the poor and to collect and distribute alms.

deaconess. An ancient order of nurses which was organised to take on the nursing of the sick, a task once part of the work of church deacons. It was abolished in AD 533 but revived briefly at various times during the monastic period.

dean. He presided over the members of a church chapter. (See also chapter member.)

death hunter. Colloquial term for a Victorian street seller of copies of speeches made by people on the scaffold, death bed confessions and similar morbid literary subjects.

debitor. Debtor.

decanus. Church deacon.

decenarius. Local constable.

decimer. A court leet representative who was elected by householders as a kind of ombudsman to deal with domestic decisions and crises.

decker. Carpenter specialising in making the decks of ships.

deckhand. General ship's labourer who assists where needed on deck. Once common on wooden sailing ships.

decorticator. Someone in any trade who stripped off the bark or husk from something.

decoy man. Assistant to a shooting party when hunting.

decreer. Same as decreetist.

decreetist. Legal officer.

dedimusee. Official who was empowered to act in the place of a judge.

deemer. Judge.

deemster. Isle of Man judge.

defender. A member of an Irish Roman Catholic organisation set up to oppose the Orangemen.

defensor. Legal defendant in medieval times.

dei minister. The term means 'Minister of God'. It usually indicates a non-conformist minister of religion.

deia. Dairyman.

delain(e) maker. A maker of muslin, originally made of wool but later, of mixed fabrics.

delator. An informer, usually as an official part of his job.

delinquent. A term used during Cromwellian times (1600s) to describe a royalist or a non-conformist.

delver. Digger (as in grave delver).

demephitizer. Someone employed to disinfect or sanitize a room or building or to rid it of foul air.

dempster, demster. Judge.

dennet driver. Driver of a light two-wheeled carriage pulled by an animal.

denunciator. Prosecution lawyer. Also someone who informed the authorities of someone else's wrong doing.

departer. A refiner of metals by separation.

deplumer. Feather worker who stripped off or plucked the feathers.

depositary. Trustee (holding something on behalf of others).

depositer. Biscuit baker who receives a 'peel' of biscuits from the chucker and arranges them in the oven. (Also called an oven man.)

depredator. Pirate, plunderer or robber.

depurator. A cleaner (in any sense).

deputy. Assistant in some capacity. Also in mining a safety officer.

derrickman. One who maintains/erects framework for drilling, particularly oil.

deshabile maker. Maker of underclothing. Also, maker of a kind of loose morning dress or dressing gown.

detailer. An inspector or examiner. Also same as dataller.

devil. Boy assistant or junior worker who learns his trade by assisting (e.g. a printer's devil or a barrister's devil).

devil operator. Rag making machine worker.

devilkin. Strictly, a mythical imp or little devil, but used to describe a boy assistant.

deviller. Same as devil operator.

deviser. Inventor or originator of a technique.

devisor. A kind of clerk of works but with no technical training.

dexter. Dyer.

dey wife. Woman who milked the cattle that the husbandman attended. Often working as a team.

diagraphic artist. An artist who specialised in perspective drawing.

dialist. Maker of machine dials.

diamond mounter. Maker of platignum mounts in the jewellery trade.

diaphane weaver. Weaver of silk cloth containing transparent or translucent figures or patterns.

dibbler. Gardener or agricultural worker employed to use a 'dibble' for making the holes in which he put seeds or plants.

dicast. Ancient term for a juror.

dichord musician. Musician, player of a two stringed lyre.

dicker. Counter in a factory (usually of animal hides, but also other objects).

dickeyman. A carrier or other man using a donkey in his trade. Also a coachman who did not control the horses (i.e. he sat on the spare 'dickey seat' at the front or back of a coach).

die maker. Maker of metal shape punches (e.g. to punch out coins from metal).

dieter. Originally someone who prescribed a diet for someone (i.e. not someone on a diet). Also called a dietetist.

digester. Writer or a compiler of other people's written works.

digger. Someone who digs. Also a coal or quarry labourer.

dignitary. Originally a member of the clergy who held a 'dignity' or 'preferment' over a priest or canon.

dikeman. Hedge and ditch maker.

diker. Ditch or trench digger.

dilly driver. Driver of a 'dilly' type of stage coach.

dimissory. An officer or official who granted leave of transfers.

dimity weaver. Loom weaver of a heavy cotton cloth, which was often used for hanging around a four poster bed.

diplomat. Originally the term was used for any person granted a royal diploma granting special privileges.

dipper. Glazer of pots in a pottery.

dirigible pilot/crewman. Person who flew a balloon shaped airship.

discifer. Steward.

disgerbigator. Farm worker engaged in haymaking.

dish thrower, dish turner, disher. Potter.

dishorner. A worker engaged to de-horn cattle, deer, etc.

disme collector. Collector of tithe duties (a 'disme' being one tenth of anything).

dispensarius. Same as dispensator.

dispensator. Private steward.

dispenser. Same as dispensator.

displatter. Used in a number of trades to describe a worker who unplaits rope, wool, twine or threads.

dispreader. Old name for a publisher.

dissecting manager. An accountant.

dissenter. A non-conformist (usually in the religious sense to mean someone who did not follow the rule of the Church of England).

distaff maker. Carver or turner of distaffs (part of a spinning machine).

distemperer. Wall painter using whiting, often tinted with a colour.

distillator, distiller. Someone who distilled alcoholic drinks/ perfumes etc.

distributor. Originally an officer attached to a poorhouse.

ditcher. Ditch digger.

dive proprietor. Owner of a low class, cheap eating house often situated in the cellar kitchen of a house.

diviner. Same as dowser.

dna. Abbreviation for domina.

dns. Abbreviation for dominus.

dobber. Loom machine worker in cloth industry.

dobber in. (Many trades.) Someone who dipped something in a solution (e.g. candlemaker's assistant).

dobby (loom) worker. Same as dobber.

docimater. Metallurgist.

docker. Dock worker carrying out a number of different tasks.

doctor. Originally a term used to describe a teacher and not a doctor of medicine or an academic.

doctor plaster face. See under plaster face.

doctress. Female physician.

dodderer. Person employed to lop off the horns of farm animals.

dodger. Victorian name for a criminal who 'dodged' from the police.

doffer. Spinning factory worker who would take off the full bobbins from the mules or spinning frames.

dog breaker. Dog trainer.

dog cart maker. Manufacturer of small carts intended to be pulled by dogs. See illustration.

dog cart man. Operator of a small cart for transport of small items or a single person.

dog catcher, dog killer. A kind of parish dog warden with powers to destroy dangerous dogs.

dog leech. Veterinarian.

dog/cat meat seller. Buyer and seller of low quality meat for the consumption of animals.

dog turnspit maker. Manufacturer of a wheeled device (similar to those used in hamster cages today) which was designed so that a dog would walk around inside and turn a spit over a fire for roasting meat. (See also turnspit maker.)

dog whipper. Person in control of a set of hunting hounds.

doggerman. Sailor on a Dutch fishing boat.

doliar(ius). Barrel maker.

A coracle dog cart being used as a children's coach. Dog cart makers manufactured a number of different kinds of small carts or coaches, all designed to be pulled by domestic dogs. Some of these were used for transporting goods, others for carrying children or small adults. The above picture shows a typical dog cart to be used as a plaything by children. Often this type of conveyance had a willow basket for the seat.

dolls eye maker. Though they originally made glass eyes for dolls, they later manufactured false eyes for humans also.

dolly bluer. Laundry worker who added the blue dye used to make clothes appear white.

dolly-mop. A Victorian servant or shop girl who supplemented her income as a part time or occasional prostitute. This is the origin of the modern expression dolly girl. (See also damoiselle de comptoir.)

dolly shop owner. A dolly shop was a low grade shop where goods that would not be accepted by a pawnbroker were taken to sell. Often the dolly shop sold such items as second hand goods, rags, marine goods, etc.

domesman. A judge. Also an umpire. Also known as a doom(s)man.

domett weaver. Weaver of a cross-woven and cotton material called domett.

domifex. Carpenter.

domina. Head woman or lady.

dominie. School master or employee.

domino boy. Victorian boys (usually of immigrant fathers) who made and sold poor quality dominoes complete with container.

dominus. Lord or master. Before 1600 it could refer to a clergyman.

donkey man/boy. Engine operator. Also someone in charge of donkeys or donkey.

donkey stoner. Someone paid to whiten steps using a special white 'donkey stone' sold for the purpose.

doorman/keeper. A guard or attendant at a doorway.

doper. Varnisher (various trades).

dorcas. Clothing worker or seamstress.

dorfer. Same as doffer.

doring man. A man who made a living trapping larks using a mirror and a net. Also called a daring.

dornick weaver. Weaver of a type of linen. Also known as a dornock weaver.

dosel maker. Manufacturer of rich draperies used for churches, castles, etc. Also known as a dosser.

Dorset button maker. Maker of a special kind of button made from thread wrapped around a miniature wire frame.

double plush weaver. Weaver of a plush piled fabric.

doubler. Usually a cloth industry worker but the term is used in other industries.

doupheal(le) maker. Gauze knitter.

dowager. A widow who received a legal proportional share of her husband's land on his death.

dowlas weaver. Weaver of a coarse type of linen known as dowlas.

downstairs maid. A low grade maid who worked 'below stairs' in the cellar and not upstairs in the living quarters.

dowser. Water finder using dowsing rods.

dozener. A court leet representative elected by householders.

Dr. Abbreviation for doctor (not always medical). Graduate clergymen often used this abbreviation before their name.

drab weaver. Weaver of a coarse woollen cloth which was thick and colourless.

drag server. Someone serving a fixed prison sentence of three months (known as a 'drag').

dragman. Sea fisherman who uses a drag net.

drago(man). Ancient interpreter (originally between the Greek and Hebrew languages). Also called a turgeman and a meturgeman.

dragons blood dealer. Dealer in resin and gums.

dragoon(er). Originally any soldier but later one on horseback. The name came from the dragon's head on the carbine (short gun) he carried.

dragsman. Horse carriage driver.

drainer. Drain cleaner. Also drain and drainpipe maker.

drap man. Same as draper.

F

faber. The word means manufacturer or smith but is often used on its own for a metal smith.

faber aererium. Copper smith or general brazier.

faber chartae. Paper maker.

faber clavarum. Locksmith.

faber clavi, faber clavorum. Nailmaker.

faber cupri. Copper smith.

faber ferrarius. Blacksmith (general iron smith).

faber horologicum. Clockmaker. See illustration.

The faber horologicum was an early clock maker. The scene above shows the typical open type of shop which was in existence in most areas of Britain up until the 17th century. At night, the open windows would be sealed with large shutters.

faber lignarium, faber lignarius. Carpenter or general wood-worker.

faber rhedarum. Coach builder.

faber rotarius. Wheelwright.

fabler. Author.

fabri. Metal smith.

fabricant. A manufacturer (of anything).

fabricus sericarius. Locksmith.

fabrifer. Blacksmith specialising in wrought ironwork.

fabulist. Inventor. Also a fiction writer.

factor. Originally an agent in a foreign country who acted as a middle man for British businesses. Later a middleman of any sort. Also a steward. In Scotland he was an estate manager/rent collector for the steward.

factotum. A person employed to do a number of different jobs in one place of work.

fag. An English university colloquial term for a student who acts as menial servant (usually under pressure) for an older student. In the U.S.A. the term has come to mean a homosexual.

fag ender. Cloth factory worker employed to trim off loose bits of cloth or thread known as fags.

fagg. A baker.

faggot seller. Firewood seller.

faggoter. Same as faggot seller.

faience potter. Ancient term for someone who produced glazed earthenware.

fairer. Specialised shipwright who lays down the keel.

fairey. Originally an ancient term for a blonde person (who was in some cultures thought to have mystical powers).

fake, faker. In the early days of photography, someone who painted over a photograph to make it look like an oil painting.

fake sweeper. Another name for crossing sweeper (see under that entry). Fake was a slang name for a crossing.

fakement-dodger. Criminal specialising in faking letters and written documents.

false worker. Specialist joiner who constructed wooden arches to support bricks or stones used in arches.

familiarus. Ancient name for a family (or general) servant.

famulist. A servant (particularly in a university).

famulum. Servant.

famulus. Male servant.

fancy man. Victorian cab driver who lived off the earnings of prostitutes, often using the cab in the plying of their trade.

fancy pearl worker. Mother of pearl craftsman.

fane guardian. Caretaker of a fane (i.e. a church, temple or other building signifying a fixed belief).

fanmaker. Makers of fans were once common in Britain. Indeed a Worshipful Company of Fanmakers was set up to cater for their interests.

fanner. Farm worker who sorts wheat from chaff.

fannier. Fan maker/seller.

fantoccini. Street entertainer in Victorian times.

farandams maker. Maker of a mixed wool and silk fabric.

farandman. Travelling merchant selling farm animal skins.

farcing maker. Manufacturer of sausage meat.

fardeller. A factory worker who packaged goods into bundles.

farl seller. Street salesman selling hot thin and crisp oatcakes.

farmer. Apart from the agricultural farmer, the term was also used for a private tax collector or customs officer who had a licence or commission to carry out the work on behalf of authorities.

farrier. Blacksmith who specialises in horse-shoeing.

farthingale manufacturer. Maker of a roll of stuffed cloth used as an undergarment around the waist in the 17th century to force out a top skirt so that it fell in a circle around the legs.

fascinator. Stage hypnotist. Also a supposed witch.

fast harpooner. A newly appointed, qualified harpooner on a whale fishery vessel. (See also specksioneer and lose harpooner.)

fat collector. Collector of waste fat from hotels and restaurants which was sold on, for the making of soap.

father of the chapel. Term fastly disappearing for a leader of a trade union or a group of workers in a place of work.

faulkner. Someone who breeds and trains falcons.

faunist. Professional naturalist.

fearnought worker. Weaver of a thick woollen long lasting cloth called 'fearnought'.

feather beater. Same as feather dresser.

feather dresser. Cleaner of feathers.

feather worker. Someone (generally a woman) who prepares ordinary large feathers for decorative work and use in clothing using a variety of processes including ironing, dyeing, curling etc. Feathers were divided into 'white', 'half white' and 'grey', white being the best quality. They were sold by weight and often had fine sand added to make them appear to weigh more.

featherer. Stoneworker who drills holes in stone before splitting.

fell monger. Dealer in dead cattle/ hides.

feller. Tree cutter or woodsman.

fellow. Originally an independent governor of a university or society.

fellow commoner. See under gentleman commoner.

felon. Class of criminal who had committed a serious crime (ranging from murder to theft). Before the 19th century a felon could be sentenced to death and before 1870 could have their property forfeited.

felter. Someone who works with felt in the clothing trade, particularly with hats. Also a shipyard worker who places strips of tarred material in place ready for the caulkers.

feltmaker. Maker of felt material in the woollen trade.

femina. Housewife.

fence(r). Someone who knowingly buys or deals in stolen goods.

fencible. A defender (e.g. of a coastline).

fenerator. Moneylender; also someone who hired out machinery, etc.

Fenian. Member of an Irish, originally secret, society which spread to the U.S.A. In the late 1800s, a number of acts of violence brought it to public notice. An offshoot of the Fenians was the 'Invincibles'.

feodar(ius). Tenant.

fermillet maker. Manufacturer of buckles and clasps which were jointly known as fermillets.

feroner. An ironmonger.

ferrarius. Blacksmith.

ferrator. Metal smith.

ferreter. Silk dealer. Also someone who uses ferrets to catch rabbits.

ferrier. Iron smith or iron worker.

ferrifaber. Blacksmith.

ferruminator. A welder of metals.

ferryman. Someone who operates a river ferry.

ferur. Same as ferrarius.

fettler. A manual worker in many trades (especially in the heavy steel manufacturing industry). Also someone in the light metal casting industry who cleans off the rough edges from castings before they are sent to be machined.

feud holder. Someone who held a piece of land in exchange for being under an obligation to carry out military service.

fewster. Carpenter who made wooden stands.

fiar. Owner of property 'in fee simple'.

fictor. A clay modeller.

fief holder. Same as feud holder.

field master. Same as field reeve.

field nurse. An army nurse usually on active service in a field hospital.

field reeve. An officer of the manor with jurisdiction over the fields.

field worker. Usually a woman or child who worked in the field alongside the farm labourer, carrying out less heavy tasks.

A photograph of a rope operated ferry taken at an unknown river location in 1920.

fieldman. General agricultural temporary worker. Also same as field reeve.

fifer. Musician who played a fife.

fifteen(er). Member of a church select vestry. These were not elected by the congregation and were often drawn from the town dignitaries and gentry.

figulus. Potter.

figurant(e). Dancer in an opera.

figure caster. Astrologer.

figurist. Mathematician.

filaturist. Silk worker who reeled silk from cocoons.

filecutter. Maker of files and rasps for woodworking/metal working etc.

filler. Victorian dustman who filled the high sided wooden cart with refuse. Also a silk industry worker.

filler in. Someone who shovelled refuse into the sieves of sifters. (See under sifter.)

fillibeg maker. Manufacturer of kilts worn by Scottish high-landers.

financier. The term was originally used for a public revenue officer (i.e. tax man).

finder. In Victorian times a scavenger who collected and sold anything.

fine drawer. A mender of garments in the tailoring trade.

finestiller. Distiller (usually of perfumes).

fingrom comber. Producer of fingrom, a combed woollen cloth.

finisher. Factory worker in a number of trades (e.g. railway works finisher).

Finmar furniture maker. Maker of tables, chairs etc, from moulded plywood. A process popular in the 1930s.

fire curtain artist. A title often adopted by background artists (see under that title).

fire curtain manufacturer. Maker of large fire resistant curtains for music halls and theatres.

fire guard. See under fire watcher.

fire man/fireman. Someone who puts out fires with a fire engine. Also someone who stokes fires or boilers (e.g. on a steam train or ship). See illustration.

fire-ward. An official whose job was to direct the fighting of house fires in a town or city.

fire warden. See under warden.

fire watcher. Second World War officer whose duty was to watch for fires breaking out. Later called the Fire Guard. They were organised in 'street parties' (to guard one street).

firebeater. Boiler worker in a mill.

firer. Person who lit the boilers in a factory etc.

firmar. Farmer.

firmar(ius). In an abbey, same as infirmarius. Other than in a monastic setting, a farmer.

first hand. A machine weaver.

fiscal. Official treasurer of public money.

fisherman. Apart from the literal meaning, the term was used in the Knights Templar for a knight who had the specific job of obtaining new recruits to the order.

Fireman·1822

Fireman· 1892

An illustration showing the change in firemen's costume in the 70 years between 1822 and 1892. As can be seen, firemen of 1822 acted and dressed more as business men than emergency personnel. Many entrepreneurs saw the opportunity of starting 'fire clubs', where individuals clubbed together to pay for the privilege of having the use of a fire engine or water pump. This movement led to the Fire Insurance companies. Those who were not insured would find a fully equipped, hand-operated fire engine standing idly by their burning home until a subscription was paid by the occupant. Later 'badges' were issued by insurance companies in the form of large decorative lead symbols. These were fixed to the outside of houses to show that the occupants were insured by a particular fire company. A number of such badges on one house was a sure sign of wealth.

fish fag(ger). Fish seller.

fish girl. Woman (not necessarily a girl) who gutted or packed fish (particularly in the herring fishing days of the 1950s).

fisher. Same as fyshdriver.

fishwife. Wife of a fisherman who gutted fish and baited lines.

fistic. Bare knuckled boxer.

fistuca operator. Operator of a primitive pile driver using a system of pulleys and heavy weights.

fitch brush maker. Manufacturer of artist's brushes from a fitch (pole cat) and animals with similar hairs.

fistulator. Piper (this can mean a musical pipe player or a water pipe maker).

fitter. Used in many trades, e.g. gas fitter, machine fitter etc. A skilled assembler.

fitter-out. A person who fits out the interior of a basic shell (e.g. canal boat fitter-out, caravan fitter-out, etc).

flabberator. A person who folds cloth or paper products in the shape of a fan or in a backwards and forwards manner.

flackie (maker). Manufacturer of flackies. These were shaped trusses used to protect a horse from injury caused by the load on its back.

flailer. See under thresher.

flang maker. A blacksmith in a mining area who forged double pointed miners' picks known as flangs.

flashe operator. Someone who operated a sluice on navigable rivers to raise and lower water levels.

flasher. Fitter of lead 'flashing' to waterproof gaps in building work. Also a glass worker.

flat bar machine operator. Someone employed in the knitting machine industry.

flat driver. Same as drayman.

flat ironer. See sad ironer.

flatman. Same as flatterman.

flatter(er). House painter.

flatter(man). Operator of a flat bottomed boat used for cargo.

flaun(t)er. Maker of sweetmeats.

flax dresser. Cotton worker employed in the early stages of preparing the flax.

flax retter. Same as flax steeper, an agricultural worker who takes the harvested flax and soaks it in water to obtain the stringy fibres later used for making cloth.

flayer. A worker who stripped skin or hair off animal hide. Also used colloquially for someone who whipped someone for punishment.

fleake maker. A hurdle maker. (One was recorded in Flore, Northants, in the 1891 census.)

fleaker. Thatcher of houses using reeds in place of straw.

Fleet parson. Any parson in Fleet Street debtors prison, London. They were allowed to perform marriages and charge a fee in order to pay off their debt.

flenser. A man in the whaling industry who would obtain blubber from the whales' carcasses.

flesh ewer, flesher. Butcher.

fletcharius. Same as fletcher.

fletcher. Bows and arrow maker or dealer, also a butcher (flesher) in some areas.

flexarius. Same as fletcher.

flint knapper. Shaper of flint stone (for flint-lock guns etc).

flither picker. Fisherman's wife or daughter who had the job of collecting 'flithers' (limpets) for bait.

flitter. Rag merchant.

float builder. Maker of floats for machinery such as sea-planes.

float driver. Driver of a special cart designed to carry certain items. (See cattle float driver.)

float maker/manufacturer. Maker of floats for fishing lines.

floater. Colloquial name for a vagrant.

floor cloth maker. Maker of flooring material made from linseed oil thickly coated on hessian etc.

floor walker. Undercover store detective, also sometimes a supervisor of a factory etc.

florist. Originally only a person that grew flowers (not a seller).

flory (boat) man. Operator of a ferry between a steamer and the shore.

flugel man. Soldier who was picked out as having special qualities and positioned in the lead or at the edge of a group of infantrymen as an example for the other soldiers to follow. Also known as a fugelman.

flunk(e)y. A servant who dressed in uniform or livery, later used for any servant whether uniformed or not. Also a snob. The term comes from an old word meaning to flaunt and referred to the impressive uniform or livery worn by such servants as opposed to the plain dowdy dress of others.

Flint knappers at work in Brandon, Norfolk. Flint knapping is perhaps the oldest trade in existence. It dates back to the Stone Age when arrow-heads were chipped from pieces of flint. Later flints were produced for flint-lock pistols. In the above picture taken in 1928, three Brandon flint knappers can be seen carrying on the trade as their ancestors had done for centuries.

flusher(man). Drain cleaner.

flute hirer. Person who hired out a long thin boat known as a flute.

fluvialist. Geologist who studied the effects of streams and rivers.

fly maker. Manufacturer of fishing fly lures for freshwater fisherman.

fly man. Scenery worker in a theatre who worked in the scenery loft or 'flies', above the stage.

fly poster (man). A man who for a fee would find empty spaces to paste up advertising posters.

flying. Used to describe any mobile trader (e.g. flying blacksmith).

flying ambulance officer. Army ambulanceman of Napoleonic times.

flying boat pilot. Pilot of an aircraft designed to land on the sea.

flying stationer. See under running patterer.

flyman. Small passenger coach driver.

fobber. Bottle filler (usually in a factory).

fodder maker. Saxon worker who made waterproof covers, particularly for haystacks.

fogger. A pedlar. Also a farm manager. Also a groom or general servant. Also a hardware salesman. Also used colloquially to describe a low class lawyer.

foil stone maker. Manufacturer of artificial gemstones for the jewellery industry.

foister(er). Carpenter.

fool. See under jester.

foot guard. A soldier on foot (i.e. not mounted on horseback).

footman/boy/maid. General servant who wore uniform. His duty was to take care of small unskilled tasks for his master or mistress. The job was seen as the first step towards being a butler or steward. The head footman was usually also the under-butler.

footpad. Common thief who robbed people in the street.

footpost. Letter carrier.

foot stall maker. Manufacturer of a kind of horserider's stirrup made for women's use.

forager. Farmer or animal handler who took his animals on to another's land to eat (with or without permission).

forel coverer. Ancient bookbinder who covered books with forel, a kind of parchment.

foreman of the field. An officer of the manor with jurisdiction over the fields.

forestaller. A businessman who buys commodities cheap, to sell on at a dearer price.

forger. Apart from criminal forging, the term generally refers to a metal worker or blacksmith.

forlorn hoper. Old military term for a soldier appointed to lead an assault on the enemy, or similar dangerous task.

formulus. Attorney or law maker.

forest glass maker. Itinerant glassmaker who made green glass as he moved round from place to place. (See also waldglas manufacturer.)

forester. A huntsman (see huntsman). In an abbey this was a uniformed position, not just a job. He would live outside the abbey with his own family and would have a range of staff under him. By law, foresters and huntsmen were the only persons allowed to carry bows and arrows in the King's forests in medieval times.

forrestar(ius). Forest worker or forest manager.

Forty-Niner. Colloquial term for a gold digger. A term derived from the goldrush in California in 1849.

fossator. Ditch digger.

fosset maker. Tap maker (particularly beer barrels).

fossicker. Usually a miner of gemstones or prospector but also applied to anyone who 'grubs', digs or hunts for anything (including a hunter for information of any kind).

fossilist. Fossil seller or dealer.

foster(er). A child's nurse, sometimes used for a general nurse. Also known as a foster dam.

fother maker. Same as fodder maker.

foulard dealer. A seller of foulard, a kind of silk material used for ladies' dresses.

founder. Caster of brass and pewter objects. Also an iron worker.

foundling. An abandoned or 'found' baby.

fourth rate captain. Captain of a vessel known as a fourth rater which carried between 50 and 70 guns.

fowerer. Street sweeper.

fowler. Hunter of wild birds (to sell for food).

frail maker. Basket or other weaver who used reeds rather than willow or other wood.

frame spinner. A weaver.

framework knitter. Knitter of fabrics using a machine.

franc tireur. Mercenary sharpshooter. The term is borrowed from free sharpshooters who were utilised as guerilla fighters in France during the war of 1870.

Franciscan. Friar or nun belonging to an order founded by Saint Francis of Assisi.

franklin. Originally an English landowner who held his lands from the crown. Later, an English freehold landowner. Also known as frank tenant.

frater pontifice. A monk specialising in building bridges. They originated in Italy but spread throughout Europe.

freasman. Same as fresher.

freedman. A slave or tied worker given his freedom.

free companion. Same as free lance.

free house publican. A publican who is not tied to selling only one brewery's products.

free lance. Originally a 15th century mercenary soldier with no master except the one who paid him at any particular time.

free peasant. Same as freeman.

free trader. A euphemism for a smuggler.

freeman. A free tenant who paid rent to the lord for his holding and had the right to have his disputes heard in court. Also a free citizen of a city.

freeman of London. Colloquial expression in 18th century London, and possibly in other cities, for a street seller of copper pots and pans.

freezer. Early name for a trader in frozen foods.

freighter. Labourer who loaded and unloaded ships.

French tavern owner. Owner of a high class and expensive type of tavern which became popular during Stuart times.

frere man. Worker in a friary.

frerer. Religious friar.

freser. Same as friezer.

fresher. An old English term for a student in their first term at university. The term is associated with the American university system. (See also freshman.)

freshman. Someone new at a job etc (See also fresher.)

fretworker. Someone who produces decorations on wood or metal objects using a fret-saw to create a design from the holes cut into the object.

friar. A type of monk who generally worked within the community (rather than separated from it in a monastery).

Friend. A member of the Society of Friends, better known as Quakers.

friezer. Specialist plasterer who made decorative friezes.

frieze manufacturer. Maker of a coarse woollen cloth or material with a raised nap on one side.

fringemaker. Furniture trade worker.

fringer. Cloth worker who would take shawls etc home at night to twist tassels on the edges for extra pay.

fripper. Second hand clothing dealer.

frizzer. Hairdresser.

frizzler. Curler of wigs and hair pieces.

frobisher. Armour polisher and finisher.

frog maker. Manufacturer of fastenings used on cloaks known as frogs.

froise seller. Street food seller of a kind of bacon pancake know as a froise.

fructuary. Anyone who anciently had right to pick fruit on his lord's land. The right sometimes extended to other produce.

frumentar(ius). Corn dealer.

frunes. Leather tanner.

frunio. Same as frunes.

fueller. Supplier of wood, coal or other fuel.

fugator. Animal drover.

fugger. An early merchant who also acted as a banker.

fugleman. See flugle man.

fuller. Cloth finishing worker.

fume cupboard worker. Early nuclear power industry worker.

fumifugist. Someone employed to rid a building or other place of offensive smells, by fumigation.

funambulist. Performer on a tightrope (as in a circus).

funer(ius). Rope/twine maker.

funicular railway operator. Someone who operates a railcar up and down a steep cliff side. Once popular in seaside holiday resorts.

fur former. Worker employed in the first stage of making a hat from rabbit skin.

fur(ius). Thief.

furber, furbisher. The person who carries out the finishing processes of making armour (polishing etc).

furnarius, furner. Baker.

furrier. Manufacturer of fur clothing.

furze dealer. Same as a gorse dealer.

fustian cutter. Cloth worker who trims corded fustian cloth.

fustian manufacturer. Maker of a coarse, thick twilled cotton cloth called fustian.

fustian weaver. Weaver of corded cloth.

F.W.K. Commonly used abbreviation in textile working areas for a framework knitter.

fyrd man. Anglo-Saxon member of the local militia.

fyshdriver. Victualler, licensee or provider of food to travellers.

fysher. Same as fyshdriver.

G

gabbarage maker. Manufacturer of a coarse cloth of this name, once used for packing material.

gabelier. Medieval tax collector.

gaderian. Gatherer, usually of taxes, tolls, etc. particularly in Anglo-Saxon times.

gaff shop owner. Owner of a 'penny gaff', a shop turned into a basic temporary theatre to which entrance cost one penny.

gaffer. Same as gaffman. Also a supervisor or head worker.

gaffle fitter. Someone who fitted gaffles (artificial spurs) to birds in cock-fighting pits.

gaffman. Bailiff or water bailiff.

galerius. Cap, bonnet or wig maker.

galleyman. Ship's cook.

galloon maker. Weaver of silk or worsted fabric called galloon. Also a maker of fine, close-knitted lace with the same name.

galligaskin maker. Manufacturer of wide open hose-type stockings known as galligaskins. Also called a gaskin.

gallows maker. Manufacturer of braces or suspenders for holding up a man's trousers.

galpin. A 13th century messenger. Also the boy who turned the spit in a large household kitchen.

galvaniser. Metal worker who coats iron with zinc.

gambadol(e) maker. Manufacturer of leather leggings called gamba-does.

gambron maker. Maker of a twilled linen cloth used for lining clothing.

game dealer. Seller of the meat of wild animals and birds such as rabbit, pheasant, grouse, deer etc.

game keeper. Someone employed by a large estate to take care of the wild animals and birds (often later to be shot for food).

gamester. Professional gambler, also a colloquial term for a prostitute.

gang(man). An ordinary seaman who was chosen to lead other ordinary seamen in a particular task.

gang labourer. One of a team of labourers working on a particular job.

gang sweeper. A member of a road 'gang' of street cleaners who would descend on a particular part of a town or city and sweep it clean of rubbish and horse droppings. (See also beat sweeper.)

ganger. Foreman, especially a foreman platelayer on the railways.

gangrel. One of a band of roving beggars.

ganister (getter). Person who removed ordinary ganister rock from coal in a mine.

ganter(ius). Glove maker or seller.

garbler. Worker on a waste disposal site who sifted the refuse for items that could be re-used or recycled.

garcifer, garcio. Servant boy.

gardian(us). Church (or other) warden.

gardinarius. General gardener.

gardy loo man. Colloquial name for a refuse collector or nightman. The term was once common in Edinburgh and elsewhere and is derived from the French practice of calling 'Gardez l'eau' before throwing water (and urine) from their windows on to the streets below.

garibaldi maker. Maker of hats (or jackets) of a type worn by followers of Garibaldi.

garlekmonger. Seller of wild onions.

garreteer. Strictly, someone who lived in the roof space of a house (in a garret). Usually the term was used for servants, apprentices or anyone of a lowly position.

garthman. Herdsman or yard worker. Rarely a fish keeper.

gasilier maker. Manufacturer of a special kind of gas chandlier used in the early days of the gas industry.

gaskin. Manufacturer of wide open hose type stockings known as galligaskins. Also called a galligaskin maker.

gasogene drink supplier. Maker or seller of fizzy drinks.

gasser. Someone in the lace-making industry whose job was to singe lace netting to remove hairy filaments.

gate warden, gater. Night watchman.

gatherer. Glass worker. Also someone who clears stones from fields.

gatherer's man/lad/boy. Assistant to a gatherer in the glass trade.

gatling operator. Soldier who operated a repeat firing Gatling gun, named after its inventor.

gatward. Goat herder/keeper.

gauffeur. A plaiter of straw, paper or other materials.

gauger. Excise officer with powers to assess and collect duty.

gaunter. Gauntlet seller/maker.

gaveler. Auctioneer. Also a female agricultural worker. Also a granter of licences to work a mine.

gavelman. Someone who owns only a very small amount of land. It derives from the gavel system used in Wales (and elsewhere) whereby inherited land was continually divided equally between heirs.

gawn man. Operator of a small tub shaped water vessel known as a gawn.

gazetteer. A journalist or writer who contributed to a publication (hence the word 'gazette').

gear cutter. Maker of cog wheels for industrial machines, from wood or metal.

gebur. An Old English peasant higher in status than a cottar but less than a geneat.

geburus. General term for a villager.

gelder. Same as castrator.

gemmarius. Jeweller.

genappe worker. Textile worker who manufactured genappe, a smooth worsted yarn used in making fringes, etc.

geneat. An Old English peasant higher than a gebur and liable for military service.

generos(a)(us). Lady; gentleman.

genesiologist. Early genetic scientist.

geneva distiller. Gin maker.

gent(leman/woman). Anyone who had inherited or achieved wealth/status within their community so that they did not have to work. High ranking 'workers' such as judges, doctors etc were also given the title of gentleman. Originally signified male ranked above a yeoman.

gentleman at arms. A member of the royal bodyguard.

Gentleman commoner. A term once given to rich British university students. They were also known as fellow commoners.

gentleman usher. An usher to royalty who attended at state balls and functions.

Gentleman Usher of the Black Rod. Originally the guard of the King's/Queen's Council chamber. He was the chief Royal Usher. He is now attached to the House of Lords.

geogonist. Scientist specialising in the study of the Earth. Also called a geonomist.

geomancer. Fortune teller who used figures or features of the Earth for divining purposes.

geometer. Mathematician specialising in geometry.

geonomist. Scientist specialising in the study of the Earth. Also called a geogonist.

geoponist. Agricultural scientist.

gesith. Part of the King's household. Some were considered aristocracy though others were not.

gewgaw salesman. Seller of trinkets and cheap baubles (pronounced 'jew jaw' or 'jew gaw').

giant crane operator. Operator of a particularly large tower crane often known as a 'Hammerhead'.

gibeonite. Menial worker of the lowest grade.

gift buyer. Someone who knowingly bought stolen goods. Also known as a fence(r).

Gilbertine. Member of the only purely English foundation of monks in Britain. Nuns of this order followed either Benedictine or Cistercian rules whilst monks followed that of the Augustinian canons.

gilder. Someone who decorates objects with gold leaf.

gill seller. Seller of malt liquor medicated with gill (ground ivy).

gillie, gilly. Water bailiff or game keeper.

gimcrack seller. Seller of cheap and trivial mechanical toys known as gimcracks.

gimler, gimp maker. Manufacturer of a kind of twisted silk used to edge clothing, etc.

gimper. Car making machine operator.

gin operator. Worker using one of the many different kinds of factory machines called engines. (E.g. pile driving gin and spinning gin).

gin pit miner. Open cast miner who worked in a very small area known as a gin pit, where all of the miners were often from one family (including women and children).

gin trapper. Hunter of small animals using wire loop 'gin traps'.

gineer, giner. Engineer.

ginger. Someone who lined a pit shaft with supports. (the Gs in ginger being sounded like the G in goat).

gingle driver. Driver of a two-wheeled covered cart, particularly in Ireland.

girandole maker. Maker or assembler of chandeliers.

girdler. Belt making leather worker. Also specialist woodman who killed trees by cutting circles around the bark at the base of the tree.

girth weaver. Specialist weaver.

girthoxter. Same as girth weaver.

glairer. Varnisher using glair (the white of eggs) as a varnish. Also glarer.

glass coachman. Driver of a glass sided horse-drawn coach (used for funerals or ceremonial occasions).

glass drawer. Someone who makes fibre-glass threads in a glass factory.

glass dust seller. An 18th century street salesman who broke up and ground down bottles, selling the resulting glass dust for using in the making of glass-paper, etc.

glass grinder. Someone who decorated individual glass items using a grinding wheel.

glass maker. Anyone making glass, but particularly someone who was versed in the craft of making different colours of glass for decorative work. Originally (because of the great heat involved) it was only a winter occupation.

glass polisher. Finisher of individual glass items to bring them to a highly polished finish.

glass setter. Same as a glazier.

glass worker. A craftsman using glass decoratively (e.g. in stained glass windows).

glassman. Same as a glazier.

glasswright. Glass maker.

glazed goat tanner. Leather worker.

glazer. Factory worker who smoothed calico cloth. Also a potter's assistant who put the glaze on pottery.

glazier. Glass maker/workman.

gleaner. Member of a poor family who farmers would allow to follow the sheafmakers at harvest time, picking up stray pieces of wheat etc which he or she was allowed to keep without payment.

glebae adscriptitii. An ancient class of tenant whose holdings were permanent in exchange for services.

gleeman. Anglo-Saxon travelling street entertainer (of any kind) who travelled in groups (also called a jongleur).

gleve. Spear carrying soldier or private guard (also spelt gleave).

glim maker. Maker of candles or lights from reeds, etc.

glist worker. Worker involved in the mineral industry, glist being the mineral mica.

globbard collector. Someone who collected and sold globbards, (glow-worms).

glossarist. Strictly, a compiler of glossaries but also used for someone who wrote commentaries.

glosser. A polisher. Also an instructional or technical writer who wrote glosses (glossaries).

glossologist. Inventor of new technical terms or one who coined words and phrases for inclusion in glossaries (see also glosser).

glottologist. Philospher studying the differences and the comparisons of different languages.

glyphographer. Engraver who produced etched engravings which left the design in relief.

glyptic sculptor. A sculptor who carved rather than moulded figures. (See also plastic sculptor.)

glyptographer. Someone who engraved on precious stones.

G-man. Member of the secret service of the USA.

gnomenologist. Scientist who studied the measurement of time.

goaf closer. Mine worker with the job of shutting off part of a mine (known as a goaf or gob) that was worked out.

goafer. Person who collected waste coal from the goaf (waste heap) of a mine, either as a job or for their own use.

goat carriage driver. Driver of a small horse-drawn carriage.

gob closer. Same as goaf closer.

gobber. General part-time worker (probably a common misspelling of jobber. (See also gob man).

gobha. Gaelic title for a smith (i.e. blacksmith, etc.). It was pronounced similar to gower. (See gower and gowan.)

gob man. Stone quarry worker who takes the waste stone, known as gob, to the surface or top of the quarry.

godman. Anglo-Saxon title used loosely for headman or anyone in charge of anything.

godsmith. Maker of religious figures.

goffer. Cutlery trade worker.

goffering sewer. Frill sewer on garments, etc. (the fluting at the top of the frill being called the goffering).

goitre stroker. Medical healer who used plants and other natural medicines to cure goitres and other ailments.

gold beater. Manufacturer of decorative gold leaf, beaten from thin rolled sheets of melted gold. Fifty square inches of gold leaf weighed one grain and a cubic inch of the metal contained almost 5,000 grains.

gold stick. Title once given to British Life Guard Colonels and to Captains of Gentlemen at Arms. The name derives from a gilt rod carried on state occasions when attending the sovereign.

gold tooler. Craftsman who engraved leather and created designs using gold leaf.

Goliath operator. Controller of a giant mobile crane known as a 'Goliath'.

goloe-shoe maker. Maker of waterproof over-shoes which were worn over ordinary shoes. The name goloe-shoes was later used for Wellington boots but by then was spelt galoshes.

gomelin worker. A factory worker who produced gomelin, a starch used by weavers.

gomer. Person who greased car wheels (gome was a black grease).

gommer maker. Maker of a preparation used in soups, called gommer, which was made from black amel-wheat.

goose herd, gooserd. Keeper of geese.

gorse dealer/seller. Collector and seller of gorse and broom branches for use in brooms/brushes etc.

gorzeman. Same as gorse seller/dealer.

gossip. A god-father, god-mother or other 'sponsor' of a child that was to be baptised in a church.

governante. Governess. Either looking after children or acting as a chaperone to young ladies.

governess. A child minder and teacher combined.

governor. Anyone in charge of others, but especially one who carries out the wishes of a higher body such as a king or a government department. Originally it meant someone who was put in place to direct the actions of others. It derives from the Latin 'gubernare' meaning 'steering'.

gowan, gower. A smith. See also gobha.

gozzard. Goose keeper.

grab operator. Operator of a crane fitted with a grabbing device for lifting or carrying materials.

graffer. A scribe or notary.

grafter. A general labourer.

Grandimont monk. Member of an alien order with allegiance to Grandimont (also known as Grosmont) in France. (See also Alien monk.)

Grandmont monk. Same as Grandimont monk.

granger. Bailiff or officer in charge of a lord's farm.

granny woman. Country midwife (and healer using natural plant medicines).

grass dresser. Tin mine surface worker who worked on the 'grass' (above the mine).

graticulator. An artist or draughtsman who enlarged or reduced drawings using a system of drawn squares, scaled in size.

graver. An engraver (usually of metal). Also someone who works on ships' hulls in a dry dock.

grazier. Cattle or sheep farmer.

great coat maker. Manufacturer of heavy overcoats.

Great Enoch (man). Colloquial term given to both a giant hammer, and the person using it to smash machines in the woollen industry in a protest at the loss of jobs done by manual workers.

great(er) dustman. Owner of a fleet of refuse collection carts who employed drivers.

greave. Foreman or bailiff.

grechel. Grocer. Also grecher.

green brick maker/stacker. Worker who makes or stacks bricks before they are fired in the kiln.

green grocer. Fruit and vegetable seller.

greensmith. Copper worker/craftsman.

grefi. Early Norman-English meaning count, earl or other position of high order (also spelt gri(f)).

greg(g). Shepherd. Also gregard.

gregarius. Herdsman (all animals).

grenadier. Originally a soldier equipped with grenades, later a member of the First Batallion of Foot.

grenwich barber. Sand seller.

Grey Friar. A friar monk belonging to the Franciscan order. (See also under Fransciscan.)

greyve. Steward, bailiff or supervisor c11th century.

grice rearer. Someonewho reared grice (small pigs).

grieve. Foreman or bailiff.

grinder. Used in many trades, mainly metal, stone or glass.

grissette weaver. Manufacturer of a cheap rough woollen cloth used by those considered lower class.

grist miller. Miller of grain.

groat miller. Someone who was employed to take the husks off grain.

grocer. Originally this meant a large scale general wholesaler.

grocer/us/ius. Dealer in foodstuffs.

grogger. Rum seller.

groggery owner. Strictly, a rum seller, but used generally for a publican.

grogram maker. Maker of a cloth material made from silk and mohair. Also spelled grogran.

groom. Person in charge of the horses. The term was also used as a shortened version of 'Groom of the Chamber'.

Groom of the Chamber. In small households he was head of staffing, in larger ones he was directly under the instruction of the House Steward.

Groom of the Stole. Royal official in charge of the King's clothing.

Grosmont monk. Same as Grandimont monk.

grossier. A wholesaler (generally of groceries). See also under pepperer.

groundsel collector/seller. Gatherer and streetseller of groundsel weed (for feeding cage birds).

groveller. Someone who crawls as the main element of his job (e.g. in a mine).

grub-streeter. A poor or jobbing writer. (Grub Street was a thoroughfare in Moorfields, London, where such people once lived.)

grubber. Someone who weeds a garden or field by hand.

grunter man. Pig keeper. The name was used in areas where it was said to be unlucky to say the word 'pig'.

guard lacer. Someone who laces up ladies' bicycles to prevent dresses getting caught in the mechanism.

Guardian. Administered the running of workhouses between 1834 and 1929.

guardianus. Local guardian (e.g. churchwarden).

guildsman. Trader or professional who was a member of one of the many trade guilds or livery companies.

guillevater. Distiller and/or brewer.

guinea pig. Colloquial term for an odd job man who quoted a guinea (£1 1s 0d) fee for any odd job.

guipure maker. Manufacturer of an imitation antique lace.

guiser. An actor taking part in a play where fancy dress is involved. Also a mummer (see under that entry). Also applied to anyone in disguise.

gummer. Repairer of old wood cutting saws.

gunfounder. Maker of gun barrels and the metal part of gun stocks.

gunny manufacturer. Maker of sack cloth from jute which was more tightly woven than hessian.

gunnyman. Dealer in sacks and sacking.

Making gutters by hand in an old factory. In the above illustration, gutter pourers can be seen pouring molten metal from ladles into sand filled moulds. The picture was taken around 1930 before the onset of mass production and the later innovation of producing gutters made from hard plastics.

gunsmith. Maker/repairer or dealer in guns and weapons.

gutta percha man/worker. Dealer or worker in raw rubber latex.

gutter pourer. Metal worker in a factory producing moulded guttering from molten metal. See illustration.

gynour. Same as gineer.

gyp(py). Colloquial term for a college/university servant, particularly at Cambridge and Durham Universities.

gypsoplaster. Caster of plaster of Paris figures.

gypsum hauler. Driver of a small engine that hauled the mineral gypsum. Also called an 'oil engine hauler'.

gyromancer. Fortune teller who walked in circles whilst making predictions.

gyve smith. A person who fitted manacles or leg irons to prisoners.

H

haberdasher. Dealer/salesman of cloth etc.

hack weaver. Saxon worker who would weave open gratings and frames for various agricultural and general uses.

hacker. Agricultural hand tool maker.

hackler. 18th century flax worker who drew the flax through wires.

hackner. Same as hacker.

hackney (carriage) proprietor. Horse-drawn taxi-cab proprietor. Later a motorised taxi proprietor.

haft turner. Maker of wooden handles for long brushes, rakes, hoes and other tools.

haggard. A hawk or falcon trainer.

haggler. Someone who haggles. (See under higgler.)

hair dealer. Specialist dealer in all sorts of hair for use in household products. This included human hair, pig bristles, horse hair, 'ox-hair' (the hair from inside the ears of cattle but never the exterior hair), etc.

hair man, hair weaver. Someone who weaves using human or animal hair.

hairdresser. Originally, hairdressers were also wig manufacturers as well as carrying out shaving of beards etc.

half knight. Person who held land jointly with another and who jointly paid the knights fee. Also used in a derogatory sense to belittle a true knight.

half-timer. A child who spent half his time at school and half at work (especially in woollen mill areas).

hallier. Wild bird catcher who caught birds alive (i.e. not a hunter).

hallier maker. Manufacturer of a special kind of net for catching wild birds.

hamberghmaker. Manufacturer of horses' collars and bridles.

hamberow. Same as hamberghmaker.

hame maker. Leather worker who specialised in making collars for draught horses.

hammerhead operator. Same as giant crane operator.

hanaper (maker). Basket weaver specialising in making fortified carrying baskets for valuables (hence the word hamper). Originally a hanaper was a small container for carrying drinking vessels.

hand barrower. One of two men who carried a barrow (without a wheel) suspended between them on poles.

hand block printer. Printer of designs (generally on cloth) using wooden blocks which are pressed upon the material by hand.

hand finisher. Woman in the weaving industry who hand-finished garments and cloth products.

hand moulder. Potter who shapes items by hand (as opposed to using moulds).

hand pack miller. Tinplate factory worker.

hand-stuffer. An old term to describe the finishing treatment of leather using grease or oils.

hand tamper. Worker who flattens and levels concrete etc, during a construction process, usually using a piece of flat wood.

hand woman, handywoman. A cleaner. Also a midwife. Also a colloquial term for a 'loose woman'.

Hanseatic merchant. Member of a powerful trading group of merchants similar to the Staplers and the Merchant Adventurers.

harbinger. Originally one who provided food and lodgings for travellers. Later, one sent ahead to make arrangements for the accommodation of travellers. Later, a messenger sent ahead to announce someone's arrival or transmit a proclamation.

hardener. Steel industry metal worker.

hards (collector). Someone who dealt with hards, the refuse from wool and flax manufacture. (See also hurdsman.)

hardware seller. Ironmonger and seller of hard household requisites such as nails, locks, ropes etc.

harler. Worker in flax or hemp treatment/manufacture.

harlot. Originally a common woman servant, later a woman tramp, then a prostitute.

harmonist. Composer of music.

harnesser. Person who fits horses with their harness each day whilst in the employment of a stable or other establishment with many horses.

harper. Harpist (player of the harp).

harping ironer. Harpoonist on a whaling ship.

harpooner. Operator of harpoon on whaling or similar ship.

harrower. Agricultural worker.

harvest bottle maker. A woodworker who specialised in making large hollowed out wooden containers for holding liquids.

hat blocker. Person responsible for shaping of hats in a hat-making factory.

hat maker. Traditionally the hat maker used the skins of beaver, rabbit and goat (known as 'camel hair' due to supplies of this being conveyed by camel).

hatcheler. Flax carder.

haulier. Originally someone who used heavy horses to pull heavy loads. Later a deliverer of heavy goods (particularly over long distances).

hautboy player. Musician who played a reed instrument called a hautboy.

hawker. Travelling salesman or pedlar. In 1888 hawkers were legally distinguished from pedlars by the ruling that pedlars travelled on foot, hawkers by horse or beast of burden. Also one who bred and trained hawks.

hawser layer. Rope worker manufacturing rope consisting of three twisted strands.

haymonger. Hay dealer.

haytimer. Seasonal farm worker engaged to assist with haymaking.

hayward. An official who supervised fences and enclosures. Later a fence maker.

hazzarder. A businessman who took risks. The equivalent of the modern entrepreneur.

head footman. See footman.

head spinner. A workman involved in the pin making industry who used a kind of spinning wheel to produce the pin's head. (See also pin maker.)

headborough. A chieftain or leader of ten families. Also a deputy constable.

header. Factory worker who puts heads on pins or nails.

headsman. An old name for an executioner.

heather seller. Seller of moorland heather for thatching and fuel.

heaver. Dock worker involved in loading and unloading.

hebdomadary brother. Clergy in an abbey who were attached to an abbey but did not live in it. They took turns to officiate at various weekly services.

Hebrew dealer. Any Jewish trader.

heck maker. Manufacturer of a kind of lattice-work which was used for catching fish, penning-in cattle, etc.

heckler. Dresser of hemp fibres before spinning.

heddler. Weaver.

hedge… Term usually followed by a trade, indicating someone who is not formally skilled in that trade. See entries below.

hedge carpenter. Unskilled carpenter or joiner.

hedge layer. Someone who planted hedges and came back to 'lay them' by half breaking the branches and interweaving them so as to form a dense barrier. See illustration.

hedge-looker. Same as a hayward.

hedge priest. Same as couple beggar.

hedge schoolmaster. A teacher at a school for poor children (often untrained).

Hedge layer. Hedge layers, though still part of the country scene are becoming exceedingly rare. The skill of knowing how to weave half-broken branches in such a way that they will continue to grow into a strong natural fence was once guarded keenly, only being passed down to a single person at a time. Conversely, now that hedge laying is becoming a 'dying trade', training courses are springing up throughout the country in an effort to teach as many people as possible.

heidersceoil. Found in Gaelic records and meaning an interpreter.

heird. Literally, 'herd'. Usually found in Anglo-Saxon times after the name of an animal or bird he was attending (e.g. gos hierde meaning goose-herd).

heirat. Any clergyman.

heirophant. Mystic religious teacher.

heiwardus. Same as hayward.

heliograph operator. Signalman using a system of flashing mirrors.

helliar. Same as hillier.

helm(sman). In Anglo-Saxon times a person in control of a plough or a rudder. Later, a person who steers a ship either at the wheel or rudder.

helper-up. Pit boy in a coal mine.

helve maker. Maker of wooden handles for tools such as hammers and axes.

hemp smoker. Someone who fumigated hemp rope to rid it of insect pests.

henchman. Originally a servant or page.

heptarch. Any one of the seven ancient Saxon rulers of Britain when it was divided into seven kingdoms.

herbarian. Herbalist.

herbege. Medieval name for a lodging house keeper.

herbergiator. Innkeeper.

herbist. Herbalist.

heredis. Heiress.

heres. Heir.

hermetic. Alternative name for an alchemist.

hermit. Religious monk or friar who often (but not always) lives a solitary existence.

herring curer. Someone who smokes herring fish to make kippers, or other types of fish to make what were once known as 'red herrings' to distinguish them from true herrings. Kippers are split in two, unlike bloaters which are smoked whole. (See also bloater seller.)

herring lass. One of a group of women fish gutters and barrellers (usually Scottish) who followed the fishing fleet from town to town following the herring shoals.

herser. Anciently, one of four or more estate holders under the direction of an earl at a fee of 20 marks in exchange for also keeping 20 warrior on call ready to serve the king.

hessian dealer. Dealer in hessian, sacks and sackcloth.

hethe dealer. Same as heather seller.

hethelder. Provider of fuel for domestic fires, particularly dry heather.

hewer. Digger or miner. Also an axeman or tree feller.

higger, higgler. Pedlar, usually with a horse and cart. (Also called a haggler. The word haggler, that is someone who bargains, comes from this name).

High Constable. Similar to a Chief Constable in modern times, though constable duties differed then. (See also seneschal.)

highwayman. Originally an officer in charge of the King's Highway. Later used as a term for a highway robber.

hill man/woman. In the Victorian refuse trade, a person who contracts to employ sifters etc to sort refuse. The contract usually lasted all year. The 'hill' referred to the pile of refuse. (See also sifter.)

hillier. Roofer and tiler.

hind. Farm labourer.

hinker. Reaper of grass, etc.

hinny dealer. Person who bred or sold animals, particularly the offspring of a male horse crossed with a female ass. Also once a common name for an animal doctor or vet.

hippopath. Once a common name for a horse doctor but often used to describe a vet.

hireling. A mercenary soldier or someone employed for a limited time to carry out any duty.

historiographer. An official or royal historian.

histrionist. Actor or actress.

hiver. Beekeeper or dealer in bees and hives.

hoarder. Person who put up hoardings, (i.e. someone who boarded up windows or fenced off areas with large boards). See also horder.

hoar stoner. Person employed to mark out boundaries with 'hoar stones' (landmarks made of white stones).

hob(bler). Shoe mender. Also a canal worker. Also a soldier on horseback. Also a clown who took his name from a mythical being in the shape of a fairy or dwarf.

hobit man. Soldier who operated a mortar or a short gun.

hod carrier/man. Builder's assistant who carried bricks or mortar in a hod, which consisted of an open half box, carried over the shoulder and held by a wooden pole.

hoe press operator. Printing/newspaper industry worker, operating a large 'Hoe Double Octuple' fully automated press.

hog-man, hoggard, hoggarth. Pig keeper/drover.

hoggerel, seller. Sheep dealer specialising in sheep that have reached their second year.

hoggers seller. Seller of stockings specially made for miners to wear whilst at work in the mine.

hogget seller. Same as hoggerel seller but also used for sellers of one year old colts.

hogherd. Pig-keeper.

hog-reeve. A kind of warden who dealt with straying pigs, especially used in the British colonies during the days of the British Empire.

hogringer. A court leet officer with responsibility to impound and ring stray pigs.

hoistman. A term used in many occupations but particularly for the person operating a hoist in a mine which brings ore, coal etc to the surface.

hokey pokey man. Colloquial term for an Italian ice cream seller with his barrow. See illustration.

hold(en). Northumbrian term of Scandinavian origin meaning a nobleman.

holder. General term for any tenant of a house or land.

holder-on. Part of a two man team who rivet large steel girders together. The other team member being the 'hammer riveter'.

holer. Same as eyer.

holland manufacturer. Maker of a fine linen, once only obtained from Holland.

Hollands seller. Seller of Dutch gin.

hollow-ware man. Pewter craftsman using 'light' pewter. (See also sadware man and pewter beater.)

holloware turner. Pottery worker.

holster. Groom or horse-handler.

holt. A woodman or forest worker.

homager. A person who held land in exchange for providing a service to or for another.

homilist. A preacher.

A rare surviving picture of customers at a hokey pokey barrow in London around the turn of last century. The hokey pokey man was a common part of the scene in the days before World War One, selling ice cream in parks and on street corners. The brightly coloured hand carts from which ice cream was sold, were generally fitted with an equally gaily painted canvas cover to protect the salesman from sun and rain. Hokey pokey men were generally, but not always, of Italian origin, and often sold fruit flavoured water-ice rather than the traditional ice cream we are used to today. As their wealth grew, many of them bought horses and carts with which to ply their trade. These were still to be seen as late as the 1970s in some towns, though the term 'hokey pokey man' had by this time been long forgotten.

homographer. A signalman who used white handkerchiefs or cloths to pass messages over long distances.

hood and apron maker. Worker who assembles pram hoods together with the piece of material (the apron) which covered the top and was designed to hinge up and clip onto the hood to provide protection from wind and rain.

hood maker. Name used in a variety of trades for someone who makes rain-proof coverings e.g. for prams, motor vehicles, covered carts etc.

hooker. Reaper.

hooper. Cooper's assistant who put the wooden or metal hoops round casks and barrels.

hop ale man. Itinerant seller of bottles of beer.

hopper boy. Boy who raked grain in a grain store.

hoppet keeper. Gaoler/attendant of a small town lock-up gaol which was generally used for short term imprisonment, such as someone recovering from being drunk and disorderly. The term hoppet was derived from likening the barred window to a small basket called a hoppet.

hoppet maker. Maker of small baskets.

hoppler. Someone who made fetters fitted to grazing animals' legs to stop them from wandering very far.

horder. A gypsy or member of any itinerant group of people. See also hoarder.

horilogiographer. Watch or clock maker.

horn blower. A kind of watchman or guard with a horn which he blew to sound the alarm.

horner. Maker of drinking vessels, musical instruments etc out of animal horns.

horolog(i)arius. Clock maker.

horologic(us). Clock maker.

horologi fabricator. Clock maker.

horse couper. Horse dealer.

horse courser. Racing jockey.

horse holder. Someone paid to look after a horse temporarily.

horse-knacker. Purchaser of old, worn out or dead horses to be used in the manufacture of glues, manures and other products.

horse-leech. Blacksmith who specialised in shoeing horses and treating them when sick (i.e. unqualified vet).

horse whimmer. Man who operated a horse-drawn lift in a mineshaft, etc.

horseless carriage builder. Early motor car manufacturer.

horses' milliner. Specialist saddler or leather worker who produced ornamental leatherwork and decorations such as roses to be fitted to saddles and bridles.

hortar(ius), hortulan(ius). Gardener.

hose braider. Factory worker responsible for covering rubber hose with a layer of continuous cotton braid using a machine for the purpose.

hose maker. Same as hosier. Also a maker of tubes of any kind.

hosier. Stocking manufacturer/salesman.

hospes. Tenant (often farmer).

hospital master. See under master of the hospital.

Hospitaller. A member of the Knights Hospitallers set up to take care of the sick and injured during the pilgrimages to the Holy Land in medieval times. Some were soldier monks. They developed into the Knights of St. John, and the modern St. John Ambulance Brigade. (See also hostler.)

hospitator. Drinking house keeper.

host. Tavern keeper.

host house keeper. Innkeeper.

hostellar(ius), hosteller. Innkeeper (with accommodation).

hostillar(ius). Innkeeper with stables.

hostler. In monastery terms he was also known as the hospitaller. He had staff who dealt with visitors and their horses. In general terms same as ostler.

hot potato man. Street vendor selling hot potatoes from a barrow. Also called a hot tater man or hot taytie man.

hot presser. Operator of a pressing machine (various trades).

house detective. A plain clothes security man employed by a hotel or store.

house master. A teacher, tutor or manager in charge of a group of people (e.g. in a university, institution etc).

house steward. Male head servant in a household who acted as a manager, hiring and firing servants and keeping accounts etc in many cases. He dealt mainly with the master of the house. (See also housekeeper.)

housekeeper. Originally this meant the owner of a house (male or female). The term later came to mean female head servant who was answerable to the lady of the household and dealt with bedding, cleaning and the staff involved. She was a female version of the house steward.

housemaid. A maid servant.

hoverer. Term applied both to smugglers and to customs men (both would 'hover', waiting an opportunity to act).

hoyer. Various trades. Someone who throws something (e.g. stone hoyer).

hoyman. Water boatman using a single masted sloop known as a 'hoy'.

huckster. Travelling salesman in small items, also a woman street seller of ale who was often also a prostitute.

Hudson Bay man. Member of the Hudson's Bay Company set up as a chartered trading organisation. Its members had exclusive rights of colonization and trade in the Hudson Bay area of Canada.

Huguenot. French Protestant, many of whom escaped to England.

huke maker. Manufacturer of a garment first worn over fighting armour. This later developed into a general garment worn by civilians (1600s).

huller. Someone who once separated seed or grain from its husk using a device like a large pestle and mortar. (See also muller.)

humhum dealer. Seller of humhum, a kind of coarse Indian cloth made from cotton.

hundred constable. In charge of all constables in one area. (See High Constable.)

hunfrid. Saxon guard or boyguard.

hunger house proprietor. This was usually a butcher who also owned a slaughter house. Animals were kept in the hunger house so as to ensure that the slaughtered animal's stomach was empty when killed. A fee would be charged for other butchers' animals to be kept there.

A hurdle maker at work. Hurdle making was a respected country craft because in country areas where nails were not available, the hurdle maker's skill at weaving fences from whatever materials were available made him a useful member of the community. These fences or hurdles would be used for penning in cattle, fencing off areas of land and even providing the basis for wattle and daub houses. When used for building purposes, the man making them was often called a wattle hurdle maker, though in effect the methods of making hurdles was the same in both cases.

hunta. Hunter.

hunter, huntsman. In ancient times the only people in a forest allowed to carry bows and arrows. Also in abbey terms, the head huntsman in charge of the 'foresters' who were also known as huntsmen with additional responsibility for guarding the deer. (See also under forester.)

hurd(sman). Dealer or worker in the flax/wool industry, dealing with the refuse and leftovers from the normal manufacturing industry. Also called a hards collector. See under that entry.

hurdle maker. Temporary fence builder. See illustration.

hurdy gurdy man. Street musician who plays a hand operated musical instrument called a hurdy gurdy which looks like a violin but is played with a revolving handle rather than a bow.

hurrier. Young girl who worked in a mine.

hurst (keeper). Woodman or forester who looked after a small wood or grove.

husband. In shipping terms a man who personally managed his own ship. See also dey wife.

husbandman, husbandus. Farmer who worked with animals. Also a general name for a farmer in the 1700s.

hush house/shop keeper. Keeper of an illegal drinking house.

hydraulic pressman. Someone who fits wheels to vehicles using an hydraulic press. Also someone who uses an hydraulic press in other trades.

hydrographer. A person who draws up marine charts.

hydromancer. Fortune teller who used water as his/her divinatory means.

hyetographer. Someone who scientifically studied rainfall and its effects.

hylicist. A materialistic philosopher.

hypothecator. Someone who pledged land or goods as security for a loan.

I

ianius. Butcher.

ice cream man. Itinerant seller of ice cream by bicycle or horse and cart, often with a sign saying 'Stop me and buy one'.

iceman. Ice seller.

icicle maker. Craftsman (usually in tin) who would make hanging baubles, fancy goods and decorations such as (but not only) those for hanging on Christmas trees.

iconoclast. Originally someone who attacked churches in the 16th century, destroying idols or religious images. Later used as a term for an innovator or inventor.

I.D.B. Euphemism used to describe someone who was a dealer in cheap diamonds. The term stands for illicit diamond buyer.

illuminator. Pretentious self-given title used by lamp-lighters in the days of gas-powered street lighting.

imbricator. Moulder of curved roofing tiles.

imp. Term given to an extra worker assigned to a job (various industries).

impaster. Someone whose job entailed making paste or dough.

impleacher. A cloth weaver.

impostor. Old term for a tax collector.

improver. An apprentice whose normal term of apprenticeship has had to be extended so that he can improve his work before becoming qualified for his trade.

in law. A term which before 1900 often meant simply 'by law' (e.g. a son in law, could be an adopted son).

in service. A servant.

inceptor. General term used in any trade to indicate someone who was still learning.

incorrigible rogue. The title given to any one convicted of more than one offence of being a rogue or vagabond, the penalty for which was one year's imprisonment.

incumbent. Chairman of the parish vestry committee and (sort of) parish clerk. Church minister such as a rector or vicar.

incunabula dealer. Antiquarian book seller of books printed prior to the 1500s.

incusser. A term used in many trades for someone involved in the stamping of something (e.g. patterns into leather).

india rubber worker. Rubber industry worker who extrudes rubber (like toothpaste from a tube) before it is manufactured into goods by cutting to shape.

india worker. Rubber worker.

inewardus. General warden or watchman.

ineyer. Strictly, one who inoculates, but used in other than medical jobs, e.g. a specialist gardener or nurseryman.

infermarer. Same as infirmarius.

infirmarian. Nurse or worker in an infirmary. See also marian.

infirmarius. In a monastery he was in charge of the staff who looked after the sick and aged. He had his own cook in a separate kitchen from the abbey's. He acted as doctor (and head gardener, tending medicinal plants).

infirmary cook. In an abbey, special cook for those who were sick or old.

informator. Tutor.

infumator. Person in charge of a beacon, bonfire or furnace.

ingein. Frequently used in place of engine, e.g. ingein driver.

ingenuus. Freeman or yeoman.

inkle maker. Manufacturer of a broad linen tape known as inkle.

inlayer. Marquetry craftsman.

innger. Harvest worker who gathered in the grain.

innholder. Inn keeper.

insnarer. Poacher or professional hunter using snares.

intaglio printer. Same as photogravure printer.

intelligencer. Newspaper reporter.

intendant. Supervisor.

interagent. Agent in a business transaction.

internuncio. Person whose job entailed passing messages between two armies or opposing sides.

interpolator. Interrogation officer.

interpreter. In the days of silent cinema, a commentator. See under benshi.

interrex. A governor or regent.

intruder. Puritan minister who was installed following the expulsion of a priest or minister during the British Civil War and Commonwealth.

inuster. Person who worked with a branding iron.

Inverness supplier. Clothing supplier of a heavy, rainproof garment, often with matching cape.

Invincible. See under Fenian.

iron founder. Iron worker in a foundry.

iron master. Early craftsman ironworker generally with his own foundry.

iron puddler. Wrought iron worker.

iron smith. Blacksmith or general maker of iron objects.

ironist. Writer, particularly of satirical works.

ironmonger. Hardware dealer.

issuer. Someone who searches out capital for businesses.

Italian iron maker. Manufacturer of a specialist smoothing iron used for fluting etc. It consisted of a round tube attached to a handle and heated by the insertion of a hot metal bolt.

Italian warehouseman. Owner of a food emporium, originally selling Italian foods and goods, but later any shop or store selling unusual or high class groceries, etc.

ivory worker. Maker of ivory objects from raw ivory.

J

jack. General term for a male worker (e.g. lumber jack).

jack framer (tenter). Cotton industry worker.

Jack Ketch. A hangman. The name derives from an actual hangman of that name.

jack maker. Maker of stout leather jackets, often reinforced with steel plates. Also a maker of black leather drinking tankards known as black-jacks. Also a manufacturer of a variety of jacks or specialist tools meant to hold or act as a guide for a piece of metal, wood or other material to be worked upon.

jack smith. Maker of machinery for lifting etc. Often self employed.

jack straw maker. Manufacturer of straw dolls, scarecrows and straw woven products. This was generally a job of low esteem and the term 'Jack Straw' gradually came to mean a person of low income and worth.

Jack tar. Ordinary sailor, used in later years (but not exclusively) to describe a Royal Navy seaman.

jackadandy. Another name for a 'dandy' (i.e. a man who dresses flamboyantly).

jaconet maker. Manufacturer of jaconet, a soft muslin cloth used for dresses, etc.

jaegar. Hunter of game.

jagger. Fish pedlar. Later a name for a general worker in a number of jobs. Also a mine worker in charge of the carriages which hauled the coal or other rocks that were known as jags.

jagger maker. Manufacturer of cog wheels.

jagging iron maker. Maker of a tool with a toothed wheel used for marking and cutting pastry.

jake(s) farmer. Cess pit digger/emptier.

jalousie maker. Manufacturer of a type of blind similar in design to venetian blinds.

jam stitcher. Maker of child's frocks worn by both sexes and known as jams.

jambee maker. Maker of a particular kind of fashionable walking cane.

jangler. Term used for street traders who called their trade but was applied to any noisy, troublesome or drunken man.

janitor. The term was once only applied to a door-keeper (i.e. it was not a general caretaking or domestic position).

japanner. Person who made 'japanned' objects using the Japanese lacquer technique.

jarman. Qualified tradesman (a journeyman). Also, jorman.

jarv(e)y. Colloquial 19th century name for a horse-drawn cab or coach driver. Also known as a jehu.

jasey maker. Manufacturer of jaseys, a worsted wool wig.

J.C.R. See under S.C.R.

jeames. General servant or attendant (often a boy).

jehu. See under jarv(e)y.

jenny operator. Operator of a spinning machine known as a 'spinning jenny'.

jerk butcher. Seller of pieces of meat cut into thin strips and dried for the use of military expeditions or for ships' rations.

jerker. Same as jerquer. Custom and excise officer. The act of searching a ship by customs officials was known as jerquing. Also someone who dries meat.

jerkin manufacturer. Maker of a short windproof or weather-proof jacket, often made of leather.

jerquer. Same as jerker.

jersey comber. Raw wool comber.

jess maker. Manufacturer of small leather straps used for securing the legs of hawks when used in sport. See also jesse maker with which the title can be confused.

jesse maker. Manufacturer of large or ornamental candlesticks such as used in churches. See also jess maker.

jester. A court comedian who was often someone simple (hence his other title, 'fool').

jet merchant. Someone owning a jet works or jet shop and usually employing jet workers.

jet turner. A jet ornament/jewellery maker.

jet worker. Someone employed in the 'jet' (a semi-precious stone) jewellery trade.

jig maker. Engineering worker who designs or manufactures specialised machines or tools for carrying out a specified new task in the process of manufacturing items.

jigger. Owner of a still (usually illegal) who made alcoholic spirits. Also a miner who cleaned and sorted ore in a wire or wooden sieve. Also a potter. Also a dancer.

Jim Crow. Type of street clown who dressed in a standard fashion (probably 'blacked up').

jippo maker. Maker of stays for women's undergarments. Also manufacturer of a kind of very tight uncomfortable waist-coat used to shape the figure of a man or a woman. This was often painful to wear, leading to the expression 'jip' or 'jippo' for pain, e.g. 'This bad tooth is giving me jip.'

job coacher, job master. Driver/hirer of coaches for special occasions.

jobber, jobler, jobling worker. A buyer/seller (of anything in small lots) or a casual worker.

joculator. Medieval street entertainer.

Johnny (cake) seller. Street seller of cakes made from cornmeal.

jongleur. Same as gleeman.

Joseph manufacturer. Maker of women's riding coats consisting of a jacket or habit which was buttoned all the way down to the skirt. Also manufacturer of a special kind of thin, unsized paper.

journeyman. Fully qualified tradesman who had served as an apprentice of any trade. Originally he was employed and paid by the day as opposed to a 'master' who would have his own business where he could set his own rates and employ others.

journalist. Originally a record keeper.

jouster. Travelling female fish seller.

jowler keeper. Person who made his money using hunting dogs called jowlers.

joy loader. Coal miner who operated a machine which sent coal to a shuttle car.

joyner. Joiner/carpenter.

J.P. Magistrate (i.e. Justice of the Peace). The term is an ancient one. Ancient 'Justices' also acted as policemen.

judas maker. Manufacture of dummy candles for churches, particularly the middle candle used in the seven branched candlestick once used widely at Easter.

judex, judex ordinarius. An ordinary judge in medieval times.

juffer maker. Sawyer or carpenter who manufactured juffers (small squares of wood approximately six inches square) used for road-making, tiling floors, etc.

jump(er) maker. Manufacturer of a kind of light jacket.

jupe maker. Manufacturer of petticoats. Also used to describe a maker of a kind of jacket made from flannel material.

jurat. An official with different powers in different localities, ranging from those of a magistrate to acting as a bailiffs assistant. In some areas, the equivalent of an alderman.

jurisconsult(us). A person well versed in the matters of law in various capacities ranging from judge to personal advisor. Also called a jurisprudent, or juris.

jurisperitus, jurista. Lawyer.

juster. Person who took part in or judged trials by jousting. Probably the origin of the word 'justice'.

justice. A magistrate or judge.

justice in eyre. One of a group of itinerant judges who would travel to courts in various English counties.

justicier. Judge or law officer. Also called a justiciary.

justifier. Defending lawyer or advisor.

jute batcher. A worker who softened jute by soaking it in an emulsion of whale oil and water.

jute dealer. Dealer in jute, but also hessian, sacking etc.

K

kalsominer. House painter who used water based emulsion paints known as kalsomine or kal.

kaolin miner. Miner of sedimentary china clay used in the pottery industry. In England this is found only in Cornwall.

kapok cleaner. Production worker who cleaned kapok (a flossy seed material) before stuffing into pillows etc.

kayle maker. Manufacturer of kayles, or skittles used for recreational games.

kedger. Fisherman.

keeker. Coal mine weighing officer.

keelboat operator. Fisherman.

keeler, keelman. Bargeman.

keep gest, keeper. Inn keeper. Also a warden of some kind.

Keeper of the Privy Purse. A royal position, originally the person who carried all of the King's/Queen's money, paid for expenses and received monies payable to the sovereign.

keeve maker. Manufacturer of large vessels for holding liquid known as keeves, used by breweries to ferment liquors.

keir (boiler) man. Cloth worker who boiled or bleached cloth.

kelp burner. Maker of fertiliser, etc., by burning kelp seaweed.

kellog(g). Animal slaughterer.

kelt weaver. Scottish manufacturer of rough cloth made from the wool of the native black sheep.

kemper. Cloth or wool worker.

kennel digger. Ditch (or canal) digger.

kerfer. Sawyer (the kerf being the channel cut by a saw).

kermes dealer. Dealer in dyes obtained from a female insect (possibly cochineal). Also known as a scarlet grain dealer.

kersey maker. Manufacturer of a coarse cloth made from wool.

kerseymere weaver. Weaver of a cloth made from rough wool cross woven with fine wool or silk.

kettle-pin maker. Maker of skittles.

keu. Medieval name for an ordinary cook.

khan keeper. Ancient keeper of a plot of land where people could camp for the night. The khans were eventually enclosed with walls and later had a lodging house built upon the land. Khan later developed into the word 'inn'.

kibble man/lifter. Mine worker who lifted materials up a mine shaft using an iron bucket and lifting tackle or a rope.

kidcatcher. A school truancy inspector. See illustration.

kidder, kiddier. Dealer in goats/goat skins.

Kidderminster weaver. Carpet weaver (originally in the town of Kidderminister).

kilner. Any kiln operator but usually lime kilns.

kin. See under kith.

kine keeper. Cow keeper.

King's cooper. A cooper who was attached to a customs and excise office. Every custom-house employed one.

King's waiter. A customs official.

kingsman seller. In Victorian times a street seller of large fancy embroidered handkerchiefs known as 'kingsmen'.

kinsman. Indicates a relative, but can also indicate one who lives in the same region or even country. (See kith.)

A 'kidcatcher' (school truancy inspector) of 1870 being assisted by a 'bobby' (police constable). The kidcatcher was a product of the 1870 Education Act. This gave local school boards the power to force children to attend school. Though financed by the state, board schools originally charged a small entrance fee. This however was soon dropped and free schooling for all became the order of the day. The kidcatcher constantly patrolled the streets looking for children, forcibly returning them to the school they should have been attending. The system began to die out in the early 1960s when children (and parents) were finally free of the fear of the dreaded truancy officer's knock at the door.

kipeman. Maker or user of basketwork nets for catching fish.

kiper. Fisherman who caught fish using a kind of net basket.

kipper house proprietor. Someone who smokes herring and other fish – sometimes meat. (See herring curer.)

kipper trapper. Salmon poacher (spawned salmon being once commonly referred to as kippers).

kipskin maker/curer. Manufacturer of a medium grade leather, heavier than calf-skin but lighter than cowhide.

kirkmaster, kirkwarden. Churchwarden or vestryman.

kirtle maker. Maker of tunics.

kisser. Polisher (of armour etc).

kitchen cellarer. Powerful position in an abbey just below cellarer. He was master of the abbey's non-religious staff.

kitchen stuff collector. A kind of rag and bone man who specialised in collecting old used oil, wax and fat.

kitchener. In an abbey, same as coquinarius.

kite maker. Though kites as toys are an ancient idea, kite makers were military in origin and designed warfare kites that would carry incendiary devices or even men over walls when castles were under siege.

kith. A close or adopted relation that is not a blood relative (e.g. a wife would be kith as would her family and her mother and father's family), as opposed to 'kin' which were blood relatives (e.g. sons and uncles on the father's side). The terms kith and kin have become confused in modern times as is evidenced by the fact that a wife can be next of kin.

kiver. Brewery worker.

knacker(er). Dealer in old/dead horses.

knackerman. Sometimes used for a dealer in horse tackle.

knapper. Same as flint knapper.

kneller, knoller. Bell ringer. Also a chimney sweep.

knife-grinder. Sharpener of knives, scissors, shears etc using a grinding wheel (usually itinerant). See illustration.

knight. Originally someone who had learned horsemanship (see radknight). It was a title of honour, not always conferred by Royalty. Also a member of a religious order (see under Templar and Hospitaller).

knight bachelor. See under banneret.

knight errant. A knight who travelled, earning his living by hiring himself to fight (either as a mercenary or as a tournament 'champion').

Knight Hospitaller. See under Hospitaller.

Knight Templar. See under Templar.

A knife-grinder at work in 1900. Knife grinders were a regular part of the scene in most towns and cities. Though some would travel around from town to town, many had a particular 'round' or street position. Traders and householders would expect them on certain days and would have their knives and scissors ready at a set time. The screech of metal on sandstone was a familiar one before the Second World War, but from about 1950 onwards, few knife grinders continued to ply their trade. With the coming of cheaper replaceable knives and scissors, and innovations such as cheap stainless steel blades, this once respected trade virtually ceased to exist. The machine shown above is operated by a treadle which in turn operated a large wheel. This turned the grindstone upon which implements were sharpened.

knight of the shire. Once any member of the British parliament.

knittle-stringer. Someone who threaded lace, string or rope through garments, hammocks, purses, etc.

knock nobbler. Churchwarden with the job of turning unruly dogs out of church.

knocker-up. Person employed to wake up workers on shifts, particularly in factory areas (sometimes self-employed).

knockout station worker. Man in a car assembly plant who would extract mouldings from their moulds.

knubs winder. Person in a silk factory who would wind silk onto cards ready to be spun.

knuller. Same as kneller. Also a door to door tradesman.

knur maker. Maker of parts for the game 'knur and spell'. Usually a potter.

kobil fisherman. Sea fisherman who used a small clinker-built open boat.

kobold(er). A miner. The name derives from an elf-like spirit, the kobold, that was supposed to haunt mines (and some houses).

kolinsky furrier. Dealer in rat skin furs.

kramer. Same as cramer.

krang hauler. Person who worked on the flesh of whales (the krang) after the blubber had been taken away.

krooman. Common alternative spelling of the word 'crewman', meaning a sailor.

kruller man. Street seller of a kind of crispy fried cake.

kuklos man. A member of the secret society Ku Klux Klan. Though associated with the U.S.A. membership was known in other countries including the U.K. The word 'kuklos' is Greek for 'circle'.

kurkee weaver. Blanket weaver using coarse wool.

L

laborar(ius). General labourer.

laborator. Labourer.

labour exchange clerk. Clerical worker at a benefit office for the unemployed (first opened in 1909).

labourer. Apart from its modern meaning as a general manual worker, a labourer was a specific name given to a bricklayer's assistant. His job was to mix mortar and to carry it and the bricks to the bricklayer.

lace drawer. Child assistant in the lace industry.

lace laker. Someone in the dyeing trade.

lace maker. Though lace was later made in factories, it was originally a solitary pursuit by homeworkers.

lace master/mistress. An employer of lace workers (sometimes in their own home).

lace runner. Lace embroiderer.

lace seller. Itinerant shoe-lace seller. Sometimes also used for a laceman.

laceman. Seller/dealer/manufacturer of lace products.

lacer. Various trades. Someone who puts laces on a product. See also guard lacer.

lackey. A boy servant who attended his master. Later used to describe anyone who always accompanied another.

lackland. A person with no land holdings whatsoever.

lader. Labourer who loaded ships, carts etc. Also any person who worked on a canal, waterway or water-course.

lady in waiting. High ranking lady's (or queen's) maid.

lady's maid. Female equivalent of the valet.

laet. Anglo-Saxon semi-free peasant with obligations to his lord.

laggard. A sailor (particularly a lazy one).

lagger. Common sailor.

lagreat man. A kind of police constable.

laic. Layman (learned non-cleric).

laird. Generally a lord (Scotland) but also a large landowner.

lairstaller. Person who prepared a grave inside a church, the grave being known as a lairstall.

lamenter. Specialist singer (e.g. in a choir or at funerals).

lametta worker. Person who worked with gold and silver, making thin wire, foils or goldleaf.

lamia. A supposed witch or sorceress.

lamp lighter. Man employed to switch street lights on and off in the days of oil, gas and early electricity.

lanarius. Wool dealer, weaver or merchant.

lanary worker. General labourer in a wool store.

Lancaster school master. Same as monitorial school master.

land reeve. Assistant to a landowner's steward.

land waiter. Customs man in charge of landed cargo.

landau proprietor. Owner of open top horse carriages for hire.

lander. Mine worker who 'landed' buckets of ore at the top of a shaft.

landing officer. Customs officer.

landlady. Keeper of house which lets rooms to visitors, often at seaside resorts.

landsman. Sailors' term for someone on their first sea voyage.

langrage man. Collector of old metal such as rusty nails, old bolts, screws and various industrial small waste iron. This was sold on to shipowners to be bound together and shot from cannons during warfare. Also known as a langrel man.

laniator. Butcher.

lanius. Butcher.

lapboard maker. Person who manufactures boards used by basket-makers to rest their work upon.

lapidarius. Stone carver/mason.

lapidary. Someone who works with precious or semi-precious stones making jewellery items.

lapper. Textile industry worker. Also someone who wraps up goods or materials as part of their job.

lappior. Mine worker who salvages good ore from that discarded as waste previously.

larderer. Keeper of the larder in an abbey or large household.

lardner. Food warehouse man.

largeman. Medieval juror or burgess.

larruper. Person appointed to whip or lash a prisoner. Also called a lasher.

lascar. Title given by Europeans to any non-European sailor or seaman (19th century).

lasher. Person appointed to whip or lash a prisoner. Also called a larruper.

last maker. Originally a person who made a mould of another's foot in order that a shoemaker could make shoes from the cast. Later, the maker of metal cobblers' lasts used for mending shoes.

latchet seller. Street seller of shoelaces (considered a beggar).

laster. Shoemaker/mender.

laterarius. Brick and/or tile maker.

latex worker. Worker in the rubber industry who dealt with the raw, milky liquid used in making hard rubber.

lath bridge builder. Specialist bridge builder over shallow swampy areas. Two lines of posts were driven into the mud from shore to shore. The post lines would then be separately interwoven with thin 'laths' of wood or twigs and filled in with earth and stones, to form a causeway or footbridge.

lath render. Also called a cleaver. A machine cutter of wooden laths (strips of wood used in plastering of walls). The work was carried out generally in a sawmill or carpenter's joiner's workshop. The term is not to be confused with a lath renderer who actually plastered walls.

lath renderer. Plasterer of interior walls, plasterer's assistant.

latouner. Same as latten worker.

latten worker. Metal worker in latten (similar to brass).

launderer. Someone who works in a laundry.

laundress. Woman who washes other people's dirty washing.

laundry maid. Servant who ironed and dealt with the laundry (but did not always actually do the washing).

laundry woman. Woman who worked in a commercial laundry washing clothes (as opposed to a washerwoman who did the same job in her own home). The terms are sometimes interchangeable.

laura priest. Priest who lived in a hermitage.

lavender. Launderer or washerwoman.

law officer. Though historically used to describe any officer of the law, the title strictly applies to only the Attorney-General and the Solicitor-General which are both political appointments made by the Prime Minister.

law rightman. Constable/law-keeper.

lawman. Same as law rightman.

lawn weaver. Weaver of fine fabrics.

lay. An outsider not holding an official church position but acting the part (e.g. lay brethren, lay preacher etc).

layer out. Same as streaker.

layer worker. Paper industry worker.

laylander. Farmer who never ploughs his fields (e.g. keeper of animals, etc.).

lead baker. Person who baked graphite rods in a pencil making factory.

leader. A delivery man (usually of coal or timber). Also a legal expression for a Q.C. who conducts a case in court himself, giving the junior barrister two thirds of his fee.

lead(s)man. Person in a boat or ship taking water depth measurements using a line and a lead weight.

lea(h)man. Person with the task of keeping a clearing free of re-growth in a wood or forest in medieval times.

leam maker. Craftsman leather worker who made dog leams (leads), small straps for hawks, etc.

learner. Someone who once formally learned a skilled trade but without any legal apprenticeship agreement.

leaser. Member of a poor family who was allowed by the farmer to freely pick up loose grain which fell on the ground at harvest time. Also called a gleaner.

leather cloth worker/dealer. Artificial leather worker/dealer.

leather cutter. Cutter of leather in the manufacture of shoes in medieval times. Generally worked in the same building as shoemakers.

leave looker. Inspector (often of food in a market).

lector. Someone who stands at a lectern to give religious or political speeches. Also a lecturer.

lecuarius. Sheep or cattle (milk producing) farmer.

lederer. Leather worker.

leech. Physician/vet.

leet. Same as laet.

legate. Originally someone who represented another (in any capacity). Later, an ambassador or a Pope's representative.

legger. Canal boat worker, particularly someone specialising in manually 'legging' canal boats through tunnels using only their legs whilst they lay on their backs.

legist. Anyone who was skilled in matters of law and sold their expertise.

leighton(ward). Gardener.

lend leaser. A tradesman who sold items on a similar system to hire-purchase but where (strictly) the goods never belonged to the purchaser.

leno salesman. Seller of net curtains (leno being a kind of gauze used for making them).

leper. It is now recognised that many people described as suffering from leprosy during early periods (particularly at the time of the Crusades) were probably suffering from chronic skin diseases relating to malnutrition and the living conditions of the time. It is possible that this was known at the time and the word leprosy was used in a more liberal sense than today to describe such people.

letter carrier. Early form of postman.

letter caster. A specialist type founder (see under that entry) who is involved with the actual pouring of the metal into moulds.

letter cutter. A kind of engraver who cuts the moulds used by a type founder.

letter founder. A specialist type founder (see under that entry) who is involved with the actual making of the metal moulds.

Leveller. Member of an Irish Protestant secret society who levelled the fences enclosing common land. They were also known as Whiteboys (because of the white smocks they wore), Rightboys and Peep of the Day Boys. Also a 17th century English radical.

lewis (operator). Person in a stone quarry who operated or assisted with the lewis contraption, used for dragging a block of stone from its original position to the quarry floor. The word lewis is said to be an English translation of the French term Louis, used in French stone quarries and said to be named after King Louis XIV. The contraption consisted of two short iron wedges with broad feet into which was driven the 'bolt', which pierced the stone and allowed it to be lifted or dragged using a chain.

libellant. Originally a person who brought a known libellous utterance to the notice of a church congregation. Later, a court officer who brought libel actions.

libeller. Though strictly a person who libelled, the term was once used to describe a cartoonist.

liber baro(n). Free lord.

liber rusticus. Free countryman.

libertine. Originally a worker who was freed from obligations to serve a lord or master. Later, a person with non-conventional religious beliefs. Later still, a person, male or female, with loose morals.

librarius. Librarian.

lidster. Dyer.

liege. A feudal lord.

liegeman. Same as vassal.

lieutenant. Originally the term meant 'deputy' and was used in trades as well as military situations.

lighter. Same as lamplighter.

lighterman. Operator of a small cargo vessel (i.e. a water boatman). Sometimes used to describe a lamp lighter.

lignarium(us). Carpenter.

limator. Tradesmen involved in smoothing or polishing something.

lime burner. Operator of a kiln for the treatment and production of lime.

limitary. Guard or watchman.

limner. Woodworker or general craftsman/artist. Also a specialist water colourist.

line baiter. Someone (usually a woman) who baited multiple hooks on a professional fisherman's fishing lines. (See also long-line man.)

liner. Flax worker.

liner off. Shipyard worker who identifies by marks work that others must do.

linesman. Electric telegraph maintenance engineer. (See illustration.)

linhay shed man. Man in charge of the storage shed in a china clay quarry.

link boy. Same as linker boy.

linker boy/man. Licensed guide for hire (carrying a lantern or torch)

A flat-capped telephone linesman stretches out to repair a line, circa 1940.

through unlit city streets. Less often used colloquially as a term for a general servant.

linkletter. A kind of postman who delivers letters between two points or stages in the full course of its journey to its final destination.

linoleum cement mixer. Process worker who mixed the basic 'cement' which was made into linoleum floor coverings.

linotype operator. Keyboard machine operator in the newspaper trade.

lintearius. Linen dealer.

linter. Cloth finishing worker in textile industry.

liripoopist. A clergyman. Also a man who made a particular type of hood worn by clergyman known as a liripoop.

lister. Dyer. Also an ancient scribe.

literatus. A term meaning anyone who could read Latin (i.e. the equivalent of the modern word 'literate').

lithochromatic printer. Printer who specialised in printing in colour (rather than black and white) using the litho process.

lithographer. Printing trade worker who reproduces pictures for printing on metal plates (originally on stone).

lithoglyphographer. Person who engraved on jewellery and precious stones.

lithologist. Geologist.

lithotinter. Litho printer who produced tinted pictures (e.g. black and white prints with a single colour added).

litium procurator. Solicitor.

litster. Same as lister.

litte(n) man. Churchyard worker. Also litter(n) man. Also litton man.

litterateur. A writer, learned man, or literary teacher.

litterman. Stable worker.

liveryman. A member of a trade guild who is entitled to wear its livery (uniform).

loafer. Originally a street salesman of bread loaves who stood or sat at a street corner. Because everyone required bread, customers came to him and he had no need to wander to find new trade. The name came to indicate a lazy worker.

loblolly lad. Errand boy/unskilled assistant (especially to a ship's surgeon).

lobster pot maker. See crab pot maker.

lock keeper. Canal lock attendant.

lockram weaver. Weaver of a coarse linen cloth.

locumtenens. Lieutenant.

lockist. Philosopher.

lockeer. Medieval locksmith.

lock-up attendant. Someone employed to feed and see to the needs of prisoners in a town's small lock-up gaol.

locky(er). Same as lockeer.

lodesman. The person on the rudder of a boat or ship.

loftsman. Shipyard worker.

Schoolchildren crossing the road in the 1930s. The term lollipop man/woman is derived from the round stop sign which they hold to stop traffic whilst the children cross. As can be seen from this picture, the original sign was a square one.

loggats maker. Manufacturer of skittles.

logotypist. Print worker who cast illustrations in the same way as metal type was made.

logwood worker. Maker of textile dyes from log wood chips.

Lollaer. Member of an old heretical movement. The term is loosely translated as 'one who mumbles'.

Lollard. Same as Lollaer.

lollipop lady/man. Schoolchildren's road-crossing patrol man or woman who carries a large 'Stop' sign in the shape of a large lollipop, hence the colloquial term. Though the position is now an official one that carries payment, it was once carried out by volunteers. See illustration.

long day man. A cab driver who worked during daylight hours but extended work into the night-time (as opposed to a long night man who worked throughout the night and continued into daylight and the short night man who worked only in the dark).

long line man. A professional fisherman who uses a very long line fitted with multiple hooks which were suspended between two marker buoys.

long night man. See long day man.

long song man/woman. Roaming sheet music seller who would sometimes sing the songs on the music he/she wrote or sold.

longshoreman. Dock worker.

loom maker. Builder of knitting/weaving looms.

lopper. Cheese maker.

Lord Chamberlain(e). Royal official, originally in charge of the King's bedchamber and wardrobe. He also took charge of all personal service staff including personal grooms and lords in waiting. Other duties included organizing ceremonies (including religious ones) and theatre visits. (See also under Lord Steward.)

lord in waiting. A male personal servant of the King.

Lord Lieutenant. A Crown official in charge of the local militia. (See also custos rotulorum.) In modern terms he is the equivalent of the old officer called a 'sheriff'.

Long song woman.

Lord Steward. One of the three chief dignitaries of the Royal Household in England, the others being Lord Chamberlain(e) and Master of the Horse. The Lord Steward's original job was to take personal charge of domestic staff, kitchens, servants and household accounts.

lordling. Someone who had aspirations or ambition to be a lord.

lorgnette supplier. Spectacle manufacturer/supplier of a pair of glasses held on a long handle.

loricater(or). Ship worker or armourer who reinforced constructions with leather or metal plating.

lorimer. Spur manufacturer/horse tackle manufacturer/saddler.

loriner. Same as lorimer.

lormer. Same as lorimer.

lorry driver. Driver of a large heavy truck designed for carrying goods or animals which was more generally referred to as a 'lurry' in the days of horse-drawn vehicles.

lose harpooner. Trainee harpooner on a whale fishery ship. (See also specksioneer and fast harpooner).

lotseller. Street salesman.

loy maker. Manufacturer or long narrow spades called loys.

lucabrater. Any worker who worked by candle light.

lucifer seller. Itinerant seller of 'lucifers', the fore-runner of the common household match for lighting fires etc. The lucifer seller often also manufactured the items he sold.

Luddite. Originally one of a group of factory workers loosely joined in a movement to smash factory machinery which was taking away the jobs of manual workers. Later the term was applied to anyone who refused to take on new ideas or working methods.

ludimagister. School master (literally games master).

luffing crane operator. Crane driver operating a crane often fitted with a grabbing device for unloading ships.

lum(b) cleaner. Chimney sweep.

lum(b) swooper. Chimney sweep.

lumber man. Timber worker or unloader.

lumper man. Same as lumber man. Also, a man who unloaded fish from fishing trawlers or other goods from cargo ships.

lunt maker. Manufacturer of match cord once used for firing canons.

lurry driver. Same as lorry driver.

lush seller. Drug dealer who sold laudanum.

lutanist. Musician who played a lute.

luter. Person in charge of keeping tidal berths in order.

lyam maker. Leather worker who specialised in dog leads and similar items.

lye (letch) maker. Maker of a cheap soap substitute using ashes of various kinds.

lyner. Flax worker.

lyricist. Originally a person who composed poems that could be sung to the accompaniment of a lyre. (See lyrist.) Sometimes used also for lyre player.

lyrist. Musician who played a lyre. Also called a lyricist.

M

macadam layer. Road gang worker who seals road with tarmac(adam).

macaroni seller. Victorian street seller of a kind of savoury scone made from a mixture of flour cheese and water. Often confused with the term macaroon seller (see below).

macaroon seller. Victorian street salesman of sweet cakes made from almonds. Often confused with with the term macaroni seller (see above).

macellarius, macerarius. Someone providing food and refreshments.

macer. Scottish court officer.

machine binder. Book binder. The term was used to distinguish the trade from the craftsman who bound by hand.

machine breaker. Also known as a Swing rioter.

machine minder. A worker in a number of trades whose job is simply to watch a machine to ensure it keeps working. Though he/she sometimes also acts as mechanic, the job is generally unskilled.

macine tamper. Operator of a machine used for flattening and levelling a road surface during construction.

macon. Stonemason.

macun. Mason or builder.

madam. See under Mrs.

madderer. Same as maderer.

maderer. Collector of wild plants for food.

magister. Often used to indicate a person with a college degree (abbreviated as Mr.). From this comes our term Mister (Mr.) which was originally a title of respect for gentry and clergy.

magister artium. Master of Arts with a university degree.

magister operis. Abbey officer. Also known as master of work and master builder. A high position in charge of all building operations and repairs.

A magnet worker feeling very attached to his work. The above picture shows a light hearted moment in a factory in 1933. The magnet operator is suspended from the electro-magnet he normally operates, held only by the metal studs on his working boots.

magnet operator. Operator of a large electro-magnet in the scrap metal and similar trades. See illustration.

mail (coach) driver. Driver of a horse-drawn vehicle carrying letters, parcels and other mail.

mail maker. Maker of chain mail for armour and security bags.

major(is). Mayor.

major domo. Master of a house, head of servants or a steward.

maker-up. Someone who made up prescriptions in a pharmacy. Also someone who assembled garments etc in a number of industries.

making room operative, maker. Shoe maker in a factory who attached the bottoms to the uppers.

malapert. A term used to describe someone who is impudent or 'saucy'.

male manufacturer. Same as mail maker.

malefactor. A criminal or wrongdoer in the eyes of the state.

malender. Farmer.

malkin. A female kitchen worker in Shakesperean times.

man-mercer. Seller of small items of menswear such as gloves, ties, hosiery and handkerchiefs.

mammet(ier). Puppeteer or a clown dressed like a puppet.

man mercer. Gentleman's outfitter.

maltster. Brewer.

Manchester man. Seller of towels and cloth products.

manchon maker. Same as muff(e) maker.

manciple. A steward.

manequin. Originally someone paid to act as an artist's model.

mangler. Woman laundry worker who rolled wet washing between two rollers to press out the water using a 'mangle' operated by a handle or wheel.

mansionarius. Sexton or grave digger.

mansioner. Same as mansionarius.

mantelet manufacturer. Maker of small cloaks for women.

man-trap maker. Specialist blacksmith who made man-traps. (See under man-trap setter.)

man-trap setter. An early gamekeeper. The name comes from his task of setting large versions of animal traps to catch human poachers on his master's lands.

mantua maker. Strictly a veil-maker but more generally a dealer in women's wear. Mantua makers were known for producing dresses from paper patterns. Those with French sounding names were considered more fashionable.

marbler. Specialised painter who simulated marble.

marc dealer. Trader who bought marc, the residue of seeds and fruit after the oil had been extracted. Marc was often sold for manure or animal feed.

Marconi apparatus operator. Electric telegrapher.

marescallus. A military marshal.

margaric worker. Worker in the pearl industry.

marinarius. Mariner.

marine policeman. Set up in 1798 to police the Thames. A marine policeman could either be a 'water policeman' or a watchman.

marinellus. Mariner.

mariner. Anyone whose work entailed them going to sea. (See master mariner, proper mariner and common mariner.)

marker. A biscuit baker who took the shaped biscuits from the moulder and marked and stamped them in pairs before passing them on to the splitter.

marker-off. Shipyard worker.

marker-up. Person in a stock-brokers' department who chalked up prices of stocks and shares as they were received by telephone.

market carrier. Driver of a vehicle carrying goods to or from market.

market clerk. Same as market superintendent. In an abbey this was a uniformed position, not just a job. He would live outside the abbey with his own family and would have a range of staff under him.

market inspector. Person who checks that goods sold in a market are up to standard with regards to weight, strength, quality etc. (Often also in charge of letting stalls and collecting dues.)

market superintendent. Person responsible for a market, issuing licences, collecting fees etc.

Marian. Same as Maryan.

marmorial mason. Stone mason or craftsman who specialised in working with marble.

marplot. Title given to secret government or military agents in the 18th century.

marriage house keeper. Keeper of a 'chapel' for marriages before the laws of marriage were regularised. The person conducting the marriage was often a publican or other non-minister of religion and collected a fee for the ceremony. The establishment's sign showed a pair of clasped hands.

marriage shop owner. Same as marriage house keeper.

marsh man. A game warden/land agent in marshy lands.

marshal. Someone who gathers together and organises men, horses, soldiers etc.

Marshal of the Diplomatic Corps. A position of the British Royal Household who attended to the reception of ambassadors and foreign officials.

martia. Housewife.

Maryan. In the Middle Ages, a follower of the cult of St. Mary. It was a sub division of the monastic movement. (Also called a Marian.) Also a nurse in infirmaries often run by the Knights Templar or religious groups. (See also under infirmarian.)

mash maker. Brewery worker.

maskell. Originally a blacksmith who specialised in shoeing horses (i.e. a farrier) but later the title was used to describe an official or a marshall of military forces.

mason. Builder.

master. Male person in charge (e.g. ship's master or school master), also a person who has served his time in a trade (e.g. master capper). Up to the 16th century the term was used to signify social standing and was abbreviated as Mr. (See also magister and journeyman.)

master bater. In the 16th/17th century one who attended to the artificial insemination of cattle and other animals. (See also courage bater.)

master builder. In monastic terms same as magister operis.

master dustman. Someone who dealt in refuse and scrap. He would often deal with greater dustmen (see under greater dustman) or would also be one himself.

master mariner. A seaman who had passed his examination to become ship's master and so be in charge of a ship.

master of novices. In a monastery the person who trained and looked after the novices who lived separately.

master of the altar. A position in larger abbeys. He looked after the altar of the abbey's patron saint and sometimes side chapels (e.g. a Maryan - see under that entry).

master of the horse. Originally in charge of the Royal stables and kennels. In modern times also in charge of motor transport and parades. (See also under Lord Steward.)

master of the hospital. In medieval times and earlier, the person in charge of a hospital (in the modern sense), a hostel for the infirm, a school, or a wayside inn, a charitable institution or sometimes with a mixed purpose.

master of the household. A Royal official in charge of all Royal staff at the King's/Queen's place of residence.

master of the parish. A member of the church select vestry.

master of work. Same as magister operis.

matchbox maker. Mid to late 19th century home worker who made boxes for the growing phosphorus and later safety match industry. Whole families were engaged in making matchboxes before the industry was mechanised.

matchmaker. Manufacturer of strips of wood dipped in melted brimstone for lighting fires, candles, pipes etc.

math gatherer/raker. Agricultural worker who assisted with the harvest or the mowing of grass.

matron. Woman in charge of the welfare of adults or children in a welfare home, school etc. In a hospital the woman in charge of all the wards. The first recorded use of the term in a nursing sense is in 1557.

maud (weaver). Weaver (usually at home) of a basic undyed brown or grey wool once used by Scottish shepherds.

mayer. Chemist or physician.

mayor. Originally civic head of a city and in the 1200s of boroughs also.

mayor's brethren. An alderman or councillor under a mayor.

Maypole manager. Confusing term which indicates the manager of a dairy retailer who had branches throughout the country called 'Maypole'. The shops were known for their tiled interiors and sawdust covered floors.

mead(er). Same as meadower.

mead man. Agricultural worker, from mead being 'meadow'.

meadower. Agricultural worker who mows fields for hay.

meal seller. Seller of animal feeds.

medal(l)ist. Maker or engraver of medals.

medicaster. Derogatory name for anyone considered an inferior or 'quack' doctor.

medicus(inus). Medical doctor/physician.

melanger. In the confectionery trade, one who grinds cocoa beans with sugar.

melder. Metal worker. Also a miller.

mell man. Honey gatherer.

member of the royal household. Originally any member of the King's or Queen's close associates but now anyone of either a high or low office who is involved with the Royal Family.

mender. A skilled job in the textile industry mending flawed finished fabrics.

mendicant. Originally a type of travelling religious friar who did no work and owned nothing, hence he begged for a living. Later another name for a beggar.

menestrallus. Craftsman (any trade).

menticulturalist. Pretentious title assumed by educators and lecturers indicating their job was to improve the mind.

mercator. Merchant.

mercator pecoris. Cattle dealer.

mercator pecu. Cattle worker paid by the job and not permanently employed.

mercearius, mercer, mercerius. Originally a general merchant but soon came to mean someone who deals in silk and satin.

merchant. General term for a buyer or seller of anything, though generally he was an educated man with a good business sense and often (if a travelling merchant) a knowledge of other languages.

Merchant Adventurer. A member of a traders' company formed in the 13th century to promote the cloth trade.

merchant banker. Originally a merchant who used his wealth in banking activities.

Merchant of the Staple. One of a 14th, 15th and 16th century group of wealthy wool exporters.

Merchant Stapler. Same as Merchant of the Staple.

merchant taylor. Armour maker/dealer, also dealing in military camp equipment and clothing.

merciarius, mercinarius. Same as mercer.

meresman. Parish officer in charge of boundaries, fences, bridges etc.

meretrix. Common prostitute.

merkin maker. A manufacturer of merkins, a term to describe both a kind of false hairpiece and a mop used for cleaning of gun barrels.

mesial manager. A 19th century middle manager in a large firm or organisation.

mesne. A lord or landlord who was a tenant but sub-let to another (Norman-English).

messager. Another term for a messenger.

messenger (boy). A man or boy who takes messages, either from office to office, or across towns and cities. Also sometimes called a courier.

messor. An officer of the manor with jurisdiction over the fields.

metage clerk. Clerk employed at a weighbridge or on a dock where goods were weighed on loading or unloading. Also called a meter.

metal blower. Glass blower.

metal mixer. Steel works production worker.

metal washer. Metal worker who specialised in covering a variety of objects with a thin coating of metal.

metaphrast. Person employed to translate literally, word for word, documents or speeches in a foreign language.

metayer. Caretaker landholder who looked after someone else's land for a share of profits or produce (generally a half).

meter. (See under metage clerk).

meturgeman. Ancient interpreter (originally between the Greek and Hebrew languages. Also called a turgeman and a drago(man).

mezzotint engraver. An engraver who used a technique which involved first digging hundreds of tiny pits into the printing plate using a tool called a 'mezzotint rocker'.

miles, miletes. A general term for a soldier. The word was also used as a sign of respect at the start of writing letters. (In modern letters the term 'Dear Sir' has replaced this.)

militia man. Generally a soldier who was not a regular infantryman (e.g. bound by service or a volunteer).

militis. Soldier.

militum praefectus. Army officer.

milk collector. Man who drove from farm to farm collecting quantities of milk in churns (later by tanker).

milk finisher. Factory worker involved in the pasteurization of milk.

milk maid. Either a farm girl who milked cows or a woman who sold milk on the streets.

milk seller. Apart from selling milk from the churn or bucket, milk sellers in London in the 1800s would obtain licences to set up in St. James's Park selling milk directly from the cow which they took with them. Often the milk was drawn into a cup or container which contained wine, sugar or spices, providing an 'instant warm drink'.

milk woman. A street vendor who would sell milk from pails, usually with a characteristic personal cry to advertise her wares.

mill furnisher. Specialist hardware dealer who supplied goods to textile mills.

Milkmaid.

mill grinder. Paint industry worker.

miller. In an abbey it was a position, not a job (i.e he was in charge of all abbey mills and their staff).

milliner. Woman's hatmaker/seller.

miniature artist/painter. Artist who specialised in painting miniature works of art (usually portraits) on such things as brooches and other kinds of jewellery.

minikin manufacturer. Maker of a particularly small type of pin known as a minikin.

minister. A widely used term for minor and medium rank officials. Also a clergyman or lay preacher. In ancient times, the title meant simply, servant.

ministrant. Clergyman.

ministress. Literally, a female who ministers, often used to describe a nurse but used in other senses also.

minnesinger. Travelling singer of love songs (originally from Germany).

minorite. Alternative name for a member of the Franciscan (Grey Friars) religious order.

minstrel. The word originally meant 'servant' but is generally regarded as implying a professional musician (usually a traveller).

minter. Used to describe someone who manufactured coins in a mint. Also used to describe an inventor.

mintmaker. Confectioner. Also a mintmaster.

mintmaster. Keeper of a small local mint issuing coins/tokens.

miscellanarian. A writer employed to compile miscellaneous facts for encyclopaedias, etc.

Misericord sister. A nun of the Misericordia order who specialised in nursing during the monastic period.

mis(s). Rarely found in early records, but up to the mid 1800s was only used to indicate unmarried women of some social standing.

miskin player. Musician who played a minature bagpipe called a miskin.

missioner. Someone (often a clergyman) in charge of a hostel, seaman's mission, or similar establishment.

mistress. Abbreviated as Mrs. This indicated social standing (not that the woman was married). In fact many women with this title were single. Children also used this courtesy title.

Mistress of the Robes. A Queen's personal dresser who also looked after her wardrobe. She was always a titled lady and in charge of all of the ladies in waiting.

mocado worker. Cloth worker.

modeller. A sculptor. Also someone producing miniature models of larger objects.

modist(e). Late 19th, early 20th century title for anyone who sold high fashion clothing. Also used to describe anyone who dressed at the height of fashion.

moiderer. A 19th century term for a labourer.

molandar(ius). Miller.

molarius. Miller.

mole catcher. Someone who hires himself out to rid fields or gardens of moles.

mole drainer. Operator of a machine driven by caterpillar wheels, which drains land by digging trenches.

mole-mason. Stonemason who specialised in building sea and naval defences, forts etc.

molend(in)arius, molendinator, molinar(ius). Miller.

molitor. Author or originator of something. Someone who puts something in motion. Also a mill builder.

monachus. Monk.

money changer. A kind of banker who would exchange coins for gold or silver.

moneyer. Someone who worked for one of the regional mints, making coinage.

monger. Seller (of anything e.g. iron monger).

monialis. Nun.

monitor. Originally an assistant teacher in a 'monitorial school'. Later just a pupil given special status by doing jobs in the school (e.g. ink monitor who filled ink wells).

monitor operator. The person who washes down the china clay in a quarry.

monitorial school master. The only teacher in a monitorial school where older children, known as 'monitors', carried out all other teaching duties under the master's control. These were also known as Lancaster schools after their Quaker founder, Joseph Lancaster (and Dr. Andrew Bell, an Anglican vicar). See also monitor.

monitress. A female teacher, often a teacher-pupil. Also used to describe a governess or female warden.

monk. Someone who conforms to a religious order (but not always dresses as a monk - see private monk).

monkey. A boy on a ship e.g. 'powder monkey', 'rigging monkey' etc.

monkey boat man. Narrow boat operator on a canal.

monocle manufacturer. A maker of a single eye spectacle, sometimes to correct bad eyesight but often for show only.

monotype operator. Type machine operator in the newspaper trade.

mop hirer. Person engaged by a landowner to hire servants at country fairs or the annual hirings. Mop being another name for a country hiring fair.

mopper. A cleaner with a mop and bucket (often colloquially called 'Mrs Mop').

moppet man. Puppeteer, also known as a mopsey man.

Moravian. Member of a religious movement that had descended from the earlier Bohemian Brotherhood (founded 1457). The Moravians were founded in the mid 18th century and by missionary work, had spread throughout the world in the mid 19th century.

mordant seller. Someone who worked closely with traders in the dye industry, supplying fixants for the dyes.

morning man. A cab driver who worked from 7am-6pm (as opposed to a long day man - see under that entry).

Morocco worker. Specialist leather worker.

moss reeve. Official with specific duties regarding swamps and boggy areas.

mould loft worker. Person who works on developing plans for the building of a large ship using chalk outlines of the various parts on the floor in a large room specially constructed for the purpose and known as a mould loft.

moulder. A general term used in a number of moulding industries but often indicates an iron worker. Also a biscuit baker.

moulder's runner. Boy who acts as a general help in a pottery.

mouldiwarp catcher. Mole catcher.

moulinet man. Person who attended a kind of 19th century turnstile, often collecting entrance fees.

mountebank. Street entertainer in Victorian times.

mousseline weaver. Weaver of muslin cloth.

movement controller. Used in various trades but usually refers to someone directing planes, trains, etc (especially in wartime).

movement maker. A maker of clock or watch movement wheels. These were sent to the tooth cutter before being returned to the movement maker for finishing.

moviola operator. Person who cut and edited moving film using a 'Moviola editor'.

mower. Originally someone who cut grass, straw etc with a scythe or sickle.

Mr. The modern abbreviation for Mister was at the time of the Norman conquest, and after, used to indicate a Frenchman (Monsieur). Later, it was used as an abbreviation for 'Master', signifying someone of high social status.

Mrs. Often used in early times to signify status (i.e. Mistress). Many marriage registers showing the bride's name preceded by the abbreviation Mrs. are wrongly assumed to indicate she was a widow when in fact she was a single woman of high social status. Female children of high status families also used this abbreviated title. The title Madam has at various early times been used to replace the word Mistress.

Mrs. Mop. Colloquial term for a cleaner of offices etc.

mudlark. Usually a boy who would steal coal, ropes and other items from barges laid up on the mud, under the cover of darkness, when the tide receded at night. (See also coalwhipper.)

mueman. Maker of small cages for pet animals and birds.

muff(e) maker. Generally a fur worker who made warming 'muffs' for hands and feet from scraps or whole pieces of fur. Muffs were also made of other fabrics, lined with fur. Muffs also acted as a kind of handbag and often had compartments inside in which to keep small objects. French women were known to carry small dogs in this way.

muffin man. Street seller of muffins (hot toasted bread cakes).

mule spinner. Cotton machine operator.

muleskinner. Carrier of goods by mule or donkey. Member of a team in the U.S.A.

muleteer. A mule driver.

mull carver. Craftsman who made snuff boxes, called mulls, from the pointed ends of animal horns.

muller. Someone who once ground corn or other seeds using a quern or round stone ball. (See also huller.)

multigraph operator. Office worker who operated a multigraph, an early type of multiple copying machine.

multurer. A miller of corn or other grain.

mumm maker. Manufacturer of masks for carnivals etc.

mummer. A variety of street performer, particularly on public holidays or religious festivals who would act out plays etc.

munitions worker. Worker in an ammunition factory.

munuc. Though the word means monk; it was used widely to describe anyone who worked at, or for, a monastery.

murderer. Animal slaughterer who may have had his own small slaughterhouse, or may have travelled from farm to farm.

murenger. Officer in charge of city walls.

musicus. Musician.

mussel ska(i)ner. Usually a woman who takes mussels from their shells to be used as fishing bait.

mustard man. Maker or specialist seller of mustard.

mustarder. Grower, grinder and/or seller of mustard.

myrmidonian. A low rather that high official. Most often used in law to describe bailiffs, sheriff's officers, policemen, etc.

myl(en)weard. Anglo-Saxon miller (usually in someone else's mill).

mysgatherer. Tax collector.

myslayer. Tax assessor.

N

nab. Found sometimes in Gaelic records as a tile for an abbot.

nai(c)k. Term used by the British in colonial India to describe a native soldier in the British army.

nail master. Supplier of raw materials to the nail-making trade. The nail master would then re-buy the finished products using goods or tokens. These tokens could only be used in the shops owned by the nail master, known as 'Tommy shops'.

nailer. Same as card nailer. Rarely one who uses nails for construction.

nailor. Nail maker.

nailsmith. Same as nailor.

naked priest. A clergyman who for a fee would unlawfully allow a naked burial, ie. the burial of a corpse without the woollen shroud as once prescribed by the Woollen Acts, thus saving on both a certificate and a shroud.

nan(ny). Midwife (sometimes herbalist or 'wise woman'). In Victorian times, a child minder.

napier. Servant in charge of linen. Also someone who manufactures table linen.

narrator. An early form of barrister.

narrow weaver. Weaver of tape, ribbons and cloth belts.

nativus. Villein (manual worker).

naupegus. Ship builder.

nauta. Common sailor.

navarchus. Ship's captain.

nave maker. Specialist worker in a large wheelwright factory who only made the nave or central hub of the wheels.

navigator. Originally a boatman. In more modern times a general labourer digging ditches, building canals and later railways (navvy).

navis praefectus. Master mariner.

N.C.S. officer. Member of the Naval Control Service who planned the movement of ships across the seas during World War 2. All were medically unfit for sea service and were drawn from the Royal Naval Reserve and the Merchant Navy.

neatherd(er). Official appointed to stop cattle straying, later a cowherd.

necessary man/woman. Someone who emptied chamber-pots or dry toilets.

necker. Cardboard box factory worker.

necklace girl. Usually a young beggar girl who would sell home-made necklaces made from red berries, nuts etc strung on rough string, often put on dolls or children.

necrologist. Person once engaged after battles or disasters to supervise the counting and recording of the dead. Also a writer of obituary notices.

necrotomist. A 19th century pathologist or other person who dissected dead bodies.

nedder. Needle/pin maker.

needle felt worker. Process worker in the production of 'needle-felt' which is felt made from fibres other than wool.

needlemaker. Though found throughout Britain, the centre of the needle making industry in the 17th, 18th and 19th centuries was in the English Midlands. Needles as we know them were first made in this country by an Indian immigrant in 1545. However, on his death, the process was lost for a short while before being re-discovered by Christopher Greening.

needlewoman. A woman who sews for a living.

negotiator. When in Latin it indicates an agent.

neif. Same as a villein.

neogagmist. A newly married person.

nethinim. Ancient term for a servant who had specific duties of gathering wood and drawing water.

nettle woman. Collector of wild nettle plants for the making of nettle beer.

newing maker. Maker and seller of yeast or barm.

news seller. Same as news vendor.

news vendor. Seller of newspapers in the street, each with their own distinct cry.

newsagent. Originally someone who passed on news. Later a newspaper seller.

nib piercer. Worker in a factory making writing pens.

nib separator. Process worker in the chocolate industry who separates the 'nibs' from the 'germ' and 'husks' of the cocoa bean.

News vendor.

niello craftsman. A jewellery maker using a special technique of melting precious metals or alloys into an engraved design.

night cabman. See under day cabman.

night walker. Prostitute.

night watchman. See under watchman.

Nightingale nurse. A nurse under Florence Nightingale's scheme to make nursing 'a respectable profession' rather than its former status on a level with servants. The Nightingale School for Nurses was set up in 1860.

nightman. Watchman. Also a nightsoil man.

nightsoil man. Town or city worker who emptied dry toilets in the days before modern plumbing.

nipper. Delivery boy assistant on a horse-drawn wagon.

nipperkin maker. Often misinterpreted as a napkin maker. However, a nipperkin was a kind of small cup.

nippy. Coloquial title given to a waitress in a Lyons' Corner House café.

nit nurse. A nurse who visited schools to inspect the children's health by looking at their nails, tongue, and searching through the child's hair for the eggs of head lice, known as 'nits'.

Nitty Norah. One of many colloquial terms for a nit nurse.

noble. Person once hired to act as a guard for strike breakers in any industry.

noctograph salesman. Salesman who sold noctographs, specialised writing frames for the blind, popular at the turn of the 19th century.

nogging builder. Builder of wooden partitions or walls, often filled with brick or rubble.

noiler/noily. Dealer in noils, new scrap wool offcuts.

noon tender. A daytime version of a night watchman.

norris(cus). Nurse (male only, when the term was in use).

norroy. One of the English kings-of-arms whose jurisdiction lay north of the river Trent. The term comes from nor-roy, meaning northern king.

nosologist. Scientist or medical work involved in the classification of diseases.

notar(ius). Notary or lawyer.

notary. Someone with legal power to sign or witness the signature of legal documents.

notcher. Someone in a tree-planting gang who makes notches with a mattock to indicate where the young trees are to be planted.

novice monk/nun. Entrants to monasteries had to pay a fee in either cash or land to train as a monk. Novices were on probation for a year and could not join a monastery under the age of 18.

noweller. Worker in a foundary who worked with moulds made of loam.

nuisances; Inspector of. Usually appointed by the Rural Sanitary Authority, they were given the often hazardous task of enforcing the numerous Public Health Acts arising from the Poor Law of 1834 e.g. Common Lodging Houses, Bath and Wash-houses, and others.

numacius. Toll collector.

nummularius. Banker.

nunchin house owner. 18th century victualler who specialised in supplying mid-day snacks, then known as nunchins.

nuncio. One of the Pope's collectors of taxes against the clergy in the Middle Ages. These were generally Italian and caused great controversy in England leading after many years to the King, rather than the Pope, receiving the taxes.

nuncius. Originally this meant something akin to 'sergeant' but later came to mean beadle (see under beadle).

nung baler. Packer of goods into bales, particularly in the spice trade.

nuntius. Messenger.

nutrix. A general nurse or wetnurse.

nyctalops. Strictly, a medical term for someone who could not see in daylight but had excellent night vision. The term was also used in a military sense for someone with the condition who was employed to use their night vision for military purposes.

nymph. Colloquial name in factories for a young unskilled woman. Derived from a class of inferior young women divinities who guarded places where water flowed in mythology.

O

oakum… E.g. oakum spinner, oakum packer etc. Shipyard worker or someone who works on a ship assisting to make ships water-tight. Oakum was the fibre obtained by unpicking old ropes.

oarsman. A waterman who operated a boat rowed only by a single man (himself) as opposed to a sculler operator who operated a boat rowed by two men.

obeisant. General title for anyone who was in a position where they must bow or show other acts of respect to a master of mistress.

oblate. Usually the child of a wealthy person who was put into a monastery to be brought up there. The system was changed by the Cistercians who would not allow anyone under 16 years of age to enter their order. Cistercian converts also had to spend one year on 'probation'. This system turned the recruitment of monks from a conscription basis to a voluntary system and was rapidly followed by other orders.

observer. Used in many industries to describe a supervisor or security officer. Also a fortune teller who used cloud formations for divination purposes. Such fortune tellers were also called observers of the times.

obstetrix. Midwife.

odalisk. Female foreign slave (also spelt odalisque).

oddfellow. Same as oddman. The Society of Oddfellows was possibly a tradesman's lodge for those whose occupations did not entitle them to join other specific trade guilds.

oddman. A person with no specific task (or multiple tasks) within a workforce.

oeconomus. Churchwarden.

oenopola. Wine maker/merchant.

off-sider. Assistant in any trade, (orginally to a cart or coach driver).

offal collector. Employed or self employed man with a horse and cart who collected stable manure from farms etc for use as manure.

offal separator. The word offal, originally meant literally 'that which falls off' but came to mean 'waste' or 'left- overs' . The term was used in many industries including the production of flour. The term is now almost exclusively used in the meat trade.

officiator. Officer or other person in charge.

officer of the refuge. Same as refuge officer.

oil cake miller. He worked in a factory producing cattle feed. Oil-producing edible seeds were crushed before compacting the seeds together.

oil engine hauler. Driver of a small 'oil engine' locomotive that hauled the mineral gypsum along railway lines. Also called a gypsum hauler. See illustration.

Oil engine hauling gypsum. An oil engine hauler (also known as an oil engine driver) operated a small one-seater locomotive which travelled on rails. Its purpose was to haul heavy loads. In the picture shown above, it was involved in pulling large quantities of gypsum, somewhere near Nottingham in 1929.

oil sand moulder. Moulder of motor car parts in a car or other machinery production plant.

oilman. Oil seller.

oiltank driver. Driver of a vehicle fitted with a tank(s) for oil.

olator. Olive (and other) oil merchant (or mixer, for perfumery).

old clothes man. The old clothes man was a walking version of the rag and bone man. He would walk from door to door, swapping old clothes for worthless trinkets or small change. He could be identified by the sack he carried on his back and his 'trade mark' of wearing more than one hat on his head.

ole clothesman. Same as old clothes man.

Ole clothesman.

olitor. Vegetable gardener.

omnibus driver. The original name for a bus driver.

one string fiddler. A street musician who was more akin to a beggar.

open (cast) miner. Someone who mines from the surface rather than in tunnels underground.

operar(ius). Craftsman or skilled worker.

operative. General worker in any industry or trade who may or may not have specific skills.

operator. See telephonist.

ophiologist. Scientist or naturalist who studied snakes.

opifex. Craftsman or skilled worker.

opifex ephipporum. Leather craftsman (e.g. saddler/harness-maker).

opilio. Shepherd.

oppo. Colloquial term for a workmate of equal status. (Derived from 'my opposite' driver/worker).

optime disputasti. Though used as a self styled title, it was really an expression of how well someone had done in a University examination and meant 'very well you have argued'.

orange peel dredger operator. Operator of a dredger using a large automated grabbing device.

Orangeman. Member of an Irish Protestant society which in 1795 became an offshoot of the Orange Lodge of Free-masonry in Belfast. It spread elsewhere, particularly to the U.S.A.

orarius. Clockmaker.

orderly. Originally a soldier who was attached to a civil official either as a servant or advisor.

ordinary keeper. Innkeeper with fixed prices for drinks and meals.

ordinary seaman. A rating of seaman, below that of able seaman but above that of landsman.

organ grinder. Street musician who plays an organ (often with a pet monkey that may or may not perform tricks). Regarded as a street entertainer, rather than a beggar.

orgue maker. Maker of rough pointed posts (sometimes planks) covered in iron.

orismologist. Natural history scientist.

ormolu worker. Craftsman who specialised in coating objects or furniture in brass or imitation gilt in order to imitate gold.

orographer. Scientist who studied mountains. Also called an orologist.

orrery manufacturer. Astrolabe maker.

orrice weaver. Silk cloth weaver.

orris worker. Jeweller or craftsman who specialised in creating gold or silver lacework.

orter/ortman. Refuse collector. Sometimes a rag and bone man or collector of other types of individual household waste.

osier peeler. Basket industry worker who stripped the willow ready for soaking.

osier weaver. Basket maker.

osman. Someone whose work involved bones (e.g. rag and bone man, worker in a charnel houses, etc.), 18th century.

osnard. Horse or cattle herder.

ostelier. Inn keeper or an officer in charge of seeing to the hospitality of guests in monasteries and castles.

osteologer. Surgeon specialising in bone disorders.

ostiarius. Usher or door keeper.

ostiar(y). Door keeper of an abbey.

ostler. Someone who takes care of horses.

out-wanderer. Someone who travels to another area or country to work.

outfitter. Person who fitted out the empty hulk of a ship after it was built.

outlaw. Someone who through committing a crime was declared outside the protection of the law. Up to the 14th century an outlaw's possessions were forfeited to the Crown and anyone might kill him without penalty. The penalty of outlawry was decided by a Shire court and was not abolished totally until 1879.

outlier. Any worker or offical who did not reside in the area where he or she worked.

outworker. Various trades. Someone who works at home for a manufacturer, weaver, etc.

oven man. Same as depositer.

over modeller. Sculptor's assistant who produces the basic shape upon which the sculptor will work.

overhead wagon driver. Someone who drove a cart or wagon fitted with a tower, ladder etc to attend to high objects such as tramway wires.

overlooker. Same as overseer.

overman. Same as overseer.

overseer. A low grade supervisor. Also an official (such as Overseer of the Poor).

Overseer of the Poor. Civic position with jurisdiction over poor laws.

oversman. A 19th century overseer or umpire. In Scotland a person called upon to decide an issue on which two other judges or arbiters failed to agree.

ovium pastor. Shepherd (sometimes used in a religious context for a clergyman).

owler. Smuggler who worked at night and contacted his companions on shore by the use of owl hoots.

owser. Worker in a tannery who was responsible for a large vat or pit of bark and water.

oxbow manufacturer. Maker of yokes for oxen.

oxymel maker. Manufacturer of oxymel, a mixture of vinegar and honey.

oyster woman/man. Seller of oysters, often carrying them into the countryside on the back of a donkey or horse together with other seafoods for sale.

oysterman/dredger. Oyster fisher.

Oyster seller.

P

pack thread spinner. Maker of thread.

packman. Travelling salesman or carrier, usually with a donkey or horse, but often only with a pack on his back.

padar miller. Miller who specialised in producing coarse meal or flour.

padelle maker. Manufacturer of a kind of basic lamp which consisted of a shallow vessel containing grease which was burned using a wick.

padmaker. Maker of tiny baskets (often used as measures).

paedogog(us). School teacher (male).

page. General servant with specific duties such as Page of the Hall, Page of the Stable, etc. They were dressed in livery or uniform (even in abbeys).

pagen. Sometimes spelt pagan, a land tenant who owed military service to his lord.

painter/paintress. Usually a house painter, rarely an artist (until modern times). Also a painter of crockery.

pail maker. Maker of wooden buckets and other small liquid containers.

pailing maker. Maker of wooden fence posts.

paladin. A knight attached to a palace or royal court, who often acted as champion in combat.

palatot maker. Originally a manufacturer of a special kind of coat worn by religious pilgrims but later a manufacturer of loose overcoats for ordinary men or women.

palfrey hirer. Person who hired palfreys (small horses for the use of ladies).

paling man. Fish seller.

palis(man). Maker of fencing posts. Also someone who erects fences.

palister. Park keeper or warden.

palmer. A pilgrim who has returned from the Holy Land.

A couple of packmen attempting to sell goods to a passing gentleman. Packmen is a general term for a whole range of travellers who carried goods in packs. Some used a donkey, whilst others had a pack upon their backs. Many packman tracks are still to be found throughout the country consisting of stone slab roads about two or three feet wide, often stretching for miles across fields or wild countryside. These tracks were the foot-roads of their day. Packmen would travel these roads, selling goods, carrying items from one area to another, or simply hiring themselves out, for the transport of goods to and from market. Those tracks that have survived serve as modern day footpaths through woods and country places.

palsgrave. A count who superintended the palace of a king or queen. Also called a count palantine.

palsgravine. The female consort of a palsgrave (see above).

palterer. Originally a dealer in old clothing but later used to describe any insincere or untrustworthy trader or person. The word *paltry* is derived from the term.

pamphleteer. A writer (not distributor) of pamphlets prior to the 1900s.

pan man. Breadmaker.

pancratist. 19th century gymnast.

pane worker. Title given to a variety of workers in different industries using panels (e.g. of wood) or squares (e.g. of cloth or tiles). Also a person employed to do a certain part or division of a job of work.

panegyrist. Person who was paid to write or deliver a eulogy.

panel beater. Metal trade worker.

panicius. Baker.

pannage warden. Warden responsible for the ancient right of pannage, the right of people to allow their pigs to eat beech nuts, acorns, etc, in a landowner's wood or forest, either free by right or for a fee.

pannarius. Cloth salesman (often a traveller).

pannel maker. Manufacturer of a kind of rough saddle known as a pannel.

pan(n)eler. Someone who fits panels into a framework (e.g. in the motor-trade). Also a saddler, particularly one who embossed or decorated the leather.

pannier maker. Manufactuer of wicker baskets used for bread and later slung in pairs over horses (hence the modern meaning of a pannier bag).

pannier man. Traveller/salesman /carrier with horse or donkey carrying either his own or other people's goods.

pannifex. Textile worker.

pannitonsor. Cloth cutter.

panopticon guard. Inspector, guard or supervisor who, unseen, would watch prisoners or workers without their knowledge.

pansmith. Maker/repairer of industrial pans (e.g. used in the salt trade for evaporation of salt water).

pantalet maker. Maker of loose undergarments for women. Not to be confused with pantaloon maker.

pantaloon maker. Prior to mid 1800s, only used to describe a maker of the type of mens 'long johns', being stockings and under-breeches all in one. See also pantalet maker.

pantile maker. Manufacturer of curved tiles designed for use in guttering but later used for house roofing.

pantler. Officer in a large establishment who was in charge of bread ordering and distribution.

pantochronometer maker. Manufacturer of a scientific instrument that combined the compass, sundial and time-dial.

pantographer. Person who works in a draughtmen's office or similar establishment and used a pantograph device to enlarge or reduce drawings and plans.

panurgist. Person who could be employed to carry out all kinds of tasks and would be termed today as a 'Jack-of-all-trades'.

paper hanger. Decorator using wall paper.

paper man/seller. Man who sold newspapers from a fixed position on a town's streets. Each had his own distinctive (often unintelligible) cry.

paper worker. Apart from the normal sense of someone who works in the paper industry, the term was also used for newspaper (and other literature) sellers on city streets.

paperer. Decorator using wallpaper. Also someone in the needle industry who placed needles into packets for sale.

papiropalus. Maker of paper especially from papyrus leaves.

papyri fabricator. Paper manufacturer.

paraclete. Nurse or companion employed to look after the chronically sick or dying. Also a general term for anyone who comforted anyone else.

parbuckler. Old naval term for someone employed to raise goods using a heavy parbuck rope, either on a dock or on board ship.

parcheminer. Manufacturer of parchment from animal skins.

pardon seller, pardoner. Someone in medieval times who sold 'pardons' supposedly given by the Pope against sinners. These were often sold wholesale to traders by abbeys and quite often were forged by the sellers themselves. The term 'to beg your pardon' comes from someone wanting to make amends for their sins but not having the money to pay for a pardon from a pardon seller.

pargetter. Ornamental plasterer.

parish clerk. Keeper of parish records, also often with other parish duties. This was often a life long position.

paritor. A town or church officer, otherwise known as a beadle.

parker. A gamekeeper on land termed 'imparked'.

parlaw. Lawyer. (Also spelt parlour.)

parmentar(ius). Tailor.

parochius. Parish priest.

parquetrist. Craftsman who designed and laid wooden mosaics in flooring.

parsnip seller. A street seller who would bring parsnips from the country and sell them in the city. The 'street criers' had their own distinctive call advertising their wares.

parson. Originally a Church of England minister from a poor family who had neither the education or standing to progress further than the position of curate.

parterreist. Specialist craftsman gardener who designed and laid out flower beds with intervening walkways.

partlet maker. Manfacturer of collars, ruffs, bands, etc.

pasquilant. Satirist or theatrical lampooner.

passage man/keeper. Person who keeps a passageway clean.

passarius. Ferry operator.

passiagiarius. Same as passarius.

pastor. Apart from the use in the sense of a clergyman, the term was used for a conventional shepherd.

pastoralist. A poet or sometimes a painter who specialised in portraying idyllic countryside scenes.

pastryman. Street seller of pastries. Known colloquially in the 18th century as a colly-molly-puff.

patcher. A home worker who made a modest living patching other people's clothing. Also a term given to someone who carried out a job badly. Also called a piecer.

pater familias. 'Head of the household'. Appointer of the clergy at a given church (usually the founder or benefactor of the church/monastery).

patibular. Hangman.

patrician. Roman nobleman or respected head of a party, religion or organisation.

patten maker. Clog maker (pattens were rough wooden clogs with high heels, or heel attachments). Also someone who constructs the mould assembly in a metal works.

patterer. General term for a street salesman who called out to his customers whilst advertising his wares.

pattern maker. Clogworker or mould maker in a factory.

patty man. Maker and/or seller of small pies.

pauper. A poor person but not necessarily a beggar.

pavement artist. An artist (often talented) who draws in coloured chalk on pavements in the hope of payment from passers by.

pavement stenciller. A kind of sign writer who uses stencils.

paver, pavior. Originally an official position for upkeeping paths. Also a paving workman.

pavyler. Erecter of tents.

pawnbroker. Person who gives money against items lodged with him for security.

payniser. Specialist woodworker who hardened wood for special purposes.

pea seller. Itinerant salesman with a barrow from which he sold 'mushy peas'.

peace keeper. Minor church official with the task of taking dogs, noisy children, etc., outside whilst a service was in progress.

pearl button maker. Manufacturer of clothing buttons from mother of pearl, which is obtained from the inside of various sea mollusc shells.

peat collector/seller. Someone who gathers and sells moorland peat for fuel.

peat cutter. Rural dweller who cuts large squares of moorland peat for drying and selling as fuel or thatch.

pecker. Metal worker who picked out designs using a pointed instrument.

pecuar(ius). Animal grazier.

ped maker. Manufacturer of small pack saddles used as leather hampers.

pedasculea. School teacher.

peddar. Same as a pedlar.

One of the first 'peelers'. The above interesting picture shows an early 'peeler' in full uniform, enforcing the outdated punishment of putting a miscreant in the stocks. The name 'peeler' is derived from the name of Robert Peel who was home secretary when the new police force came into being, replacing the old 'charlies' or night watchmen.

peder. Same as a cottar.

pedlar. Itinerant seller of goods (on foot). The name literally means 'ped (basket) carrier'.

peeler. Colloquial name for a British policeman. Named after Robert Peel, the Home Secretary who introduced the modern police force. See illustration.

Victorian children visiting the peepshow man. Pleasures were simple in Victorian times and many children would gladly spend a farthing of their pocket money to visit the travelling peepshow man. Children would delight in paying their farthing and peeping through a hole into a box filled with some sort of scenery, or unusual items. Part of the thrill of the peepshow was that the scene or objects would be different each time the peepshow man came around. One week the contents might show a circus ring complete with cut out performing animals, another might exhibit a tropical forest complete with a whole array of animals which would never be found together in the wild. The popularity of the peepshow man lasted well into the 1920s when inflation had brought the price of a 'peep' to one penny.

peeling machinist. Wood industry worker employed in peeling veneers from wooden logs for use in plywood or decorative work.

Peep of the Day Boy. Same as Leveller.

peepshow man. Street trader who would make a charge (generally a penny) for children to look at scenes contained in a box fitted with a peephole. See illustration.

peever. Pepper dealer/seller.

peg top maker. Either a tailor specialising in trousers known as peg-tops or a maker of small wooden spinning tops to be used as toys.

peletarius, pellicar(ius), pelliparius, pellius, peltarius, pelter, pelterer. Dealer in animal skins, or one who treats animal skins.

pellage collector. Person employed to collect an ancient duty or tax on animal skins.

pen grinder. Grinder of pen nibs in a factory. This was considered menial work for working class girls.

pencil maker. Originally a manufacturer of a small brush used by artists for laying on of colour. (Not to be confused with penicil maker).

penicil maker. Manufacturer of an early form of wound dressing pad. (Not to be confused with pencil maker).

penny gaff house owner. See gaff shop owner.

penny pane maker/seller. Supplier of small pieces of window glass which cost one penny each.

penny peepshow man. See under peepshow man.

penny pie man. Also called simply a pie man. His cry was 'Penny pie, toss or buy'. This referred to the customer's option of tossing a coin rather than buying a pie. The pie man always made the call. If he won, the customer paid a penny without obtaining a pie. If he lost, the pie man gave away the pie free.

penny pie shop man. The penny pie shops began in mid to late Victorian times in opposition to the itinerant piemen. As the shops were open all day, and the city piemen usually operated only at night, it was not long before the piemen almost disappeared from the streets. Countryside piemen survived much longer.

penstock contractor. Man who constructed and maintained wooden water mill troughs and floodgates.

pepperer. An early name for an English retail grocer as opposed to a grossier, who was a wholesaler.

pepperminter. In the early 1800s street vendors had a double tapped barrel selling 'peppermint water' and 'strong peppermint water'. The strong version contained alcoholic spirit. This was very much an illicit trade, but widely practised.

perambulator maker/seller. Someone who deals in children's prams.

perambulator mounter. Someone who bolts pram bodies to the wheel assembly.

perchemear. Parchment maker.

percher. One who works in the finishing processes in a textile factory.

percher manufacturer. Candle maker who specialised in perchers, a particular kind of large wax candle.

peregrin(ator). Travelling salesman. Sometimes a travelling worker.

perfum(i)er. Maker/seller of perfumes and powders.

periwig maker. Same as peruker.

pernance officer. Person who was employed by a land or property owner to collect rents which were paid in a kind rather than in money.

perpetual curate. A vicar or rector in his own right, as opposed to an ordinary curate who assisted a vicar or rector.

person(a). Parson.

peruke maker. Manufacturer of periwigs and caps designed as hair-pieces.

pesarius. Weight inspector.

Peter(man). Fisherman (in a fishing boat).

petticoat maker. Maker of undergarments (generally of cotton) which when in the form of the 'dress-petticoat' (made of quilted satin etc) were intentionally on show beneath the main dress.

pettifogger. Colloquial name for an unscrupulous lawyer.

petty. Used as a prefix to infer 'common'.

petty chapman. Same as chapman.

petty constable. A constable (i.e. not a High Constable).

pew opener, pewman. Officer in some churches who attended worshippers by opening the doors to pews.

pewter beater. Craftsman who makes trays and other objects by hand from sheets of pewter. Sometimes also called a swager.

pewterer. Craftsman who made kitchen utensils etc from the metal pewter.

phaeton hirer. Someone who hired out a small 'phaeton' carriage.

phantasmagorian. Man who made his living from magic-lantern shows.

pharmacopola. Pharmacist/druggist.

pheliparius. Uncertain. Possibly a dealer in fancy/decorated clothing or second hand goods.

philosophical instrument maker. Maker of microscopes or other scientific apparatus.

phonogram room worker. In the early days of telegram transmission, telephonists would direct all requests to send a telegram to a specialised worker in a phonogram room, set aside for the purpose.

photogravure printer. Printer of pictures using small dots engraved upon a flat surface.

Phrygian. The 'Phrygian Art' in old texts is supposed to refer to needle work or lace making.

physic. Doctor/physician (see also under apothecary).

phytologist. Scientist who studies and is versed in the knowledge of plants.

pibroch player. Musician who plays the pibroch otherwise known as a bagpipe.

piccadil(ly) seller. Person who sold ruffs and high collars.

piccage man. Person employed at a fair to collect the ground rent for stalls etc.

picker. Various trades. Someone who sorts or picks out items. Also shuttle caster in a cotton mill. Also same as a linter. Also a worker in a stone quarry who opens up a rockface with a pick, ready for work by the sawer. Also a fruit picker.

pickler. Someone who soaks something in a solution. The term is used widely in the food trade (e.g. pickled onions), the jewellery trade and the leather industry.

pickthank. Either someone who was over-officious or someone considered a parasite on society.

pictaciarius. Cobbler.

pictor. Painter.

piece goods salesman. Seller of cotton material woven to a standard length for sale as a piece, rather than for cutting from a roll.

piece worker. Anyone paid by the quantity produced (usually in manufacturing).

pieceman. Someone who was paid by results.

piecemaster. A kind of unofficial union representative.

piece(meal) seller. Seller of remnants/or remainder stock.

piecer. Same as patcher.

piecer(na). Mill worker who joins broken threads.

pieman. Seller of hot pies (usually itinerant). See also under penny pie man. See illustration.

pier glass maker. Manufacturer of mirrors designed to be fitted in the space between two windows, or between a fireplace and ceiling.

An old illustration showing children flocking round a pieman. Piemen were in their heyday in the time before every house had its own oven. The novelty of hot pies, particularly at fairs and country gatherings made for a ready sale.

pierage officer. Man appointed to collect a toll from ships and boats using a pier.

piercer. Low skilled factory job piercing holes in pen nibs. See also bead piercer.

pierrot. Seaside entertainer. They travelled in groups, often with white faces and pointed clown hats.

pig (bed) moulder. Iron industry worker who either makes moulds in sand or directs iron into the moulds to make blocks known as pigs. The name comes from the way the small moulds are laid out in rows like tiny pigs feeding from their mother.

pig food maker. A worker (generally for a city council) who converted treated household food waste into pig food for re-sale.

piggin maker. Carver of a kind of small wooden drinking vessel called a piggin.

A pikeman.

pigmaker. Iron moulder. Also a crockery worker/dealer.

pigman. Crockery dealer or iron worker.

pikelet baker/seller. Maker/seller of pikelets, a kind of crumpet filled with holes cooked from batter.

pikeman. Miller's assistant. In military context a pike carrier. Also a person who collects tolls. (See illustration.)

piker. Vagrant.

pileo. Hat maker.

pillboxer. Pottery trade worker making pill boxes.

pillion maker. Manufacturer originally of small cushions or pads, but later of small saddles designed to be placed on a horse, behind the rider, for a woman to ride as an additional passenger.

pillow lace maker. Maker of lace by hand.

pimp(er). Someone who controls or looks after one or more prostitutes and lives off their earnings.

pin maker. The art of pin making involved 25 separate processes each involving a different workman. Few had separate trade titles except the head spinner (see entry).

pin seller. A pedlar specialising in pins and needles. See illustration.

pince-nez supplier. Maker or seller of eye spectacles which clipped on to the bridge of the nose.

pincerna. Butler.

pinder. An official in charge of the city, town or parish stray animal pound.

pinfold (keeper). Same as pinder.

pinner. Maker or carder of pins.

pinner up. Dressmaker's assistant. Also a sheet music seller (see also wall song seller).

pinsor. The word means 'pounder' or 'crusher', probably of stone or herbs.

pintar. Painter.

pioneer. Originally a military term used for a soldier who went before the full army in order to prepare the way.

pipe maker. Originally a clay pipe maker (for smokers). Clay pipes for carrying water etc were referred to as conduits.

piriger. Pear grower or worker in a pear orchard during Anglo-Saxon times.

pirn maker. Bobbin maker.

pirogue hirer. Someone who hired (and usually made) canoes for pleasure boats. Pirogues were made from a single scooped out and shaped log of wood.

piscar(ius). Fisherman/fish-seller.

piscator. Fisherman.

piscenar(ius). Fish seller.

An 18th century illustration of a pin seller plying his trade. New pins were constantly required in the days before stainless steel pins came on the market. Because of rusting, they had a short life and in addition, many more items of clothing required the use of such fastenings. Because of this, pin sellers found a ready trade for their products which they purchased (or made) singly before threading them through the thick blue strips of paper in which they were sold. The above illustration from the 1700s shows a pin seller going about his work. In his left hand is a strip of paper containing pins, whilst under his other arm is a box containing further supplies.

pistor. Someone involved with flour, generally meaning a baker or miller.

pit brow lass. Same as buddler.

pit captain. Person in charge of a clay pit in the china clay industry.

pit digger. Sexton or grave digger.

pit lad/lass. Boy or girl who worked in a mine physically dragging wooden tubs or carts full of coal or ore along a railway line. See also pony lad/lass.

piteo. Maker of soft felt from animal skins.

pitianciary. An abbey clerk in charge of petty cash where no specific book-keeping was involved.

placeman. A 19th century government officer.

placer (miner). Alluvial miner.

plaid weaver. Weaver of tartan cloth.

plaider. Same as plaid weaver.

plain worker. Ordinary sewer who does not sew decoratively.

plaisterer. Plasterer.

plaitcher. Same as platcher.

plaiter. Weaver of straw into cords in order to make straw objects (e.g. hats and shoes).

planker. Hat making worker.

planisher. A person who polishes or smoothes something, usually in the metal working industry.

planographic printer. Printer of pictures or designs using a variety of mediums, all based on the idea that grease and water do not mix. (E.g. a picture painted in grease on a stone, and then coated with water based ink will reproduce the design when printed.)

planter. A Protestant living in Ireland. Many were massacred immediately prior to the English Civil War.

plantifene, plantifex. Forage seller.

plasher. A weaver, usually of sticks as in fence building. Also used colloquially for the operator of a 'coble' fishing boat in the North of England. The coble was also called a plasher.

plasmer. One who uses a plasm (mould or matrix). Used in a number of industries.

plaster face. Colloquial name in Elizabethan times for someone who dealt in, or applied cosmetics, dyed hair and/or bleached teeth.

plastic sculptor. A sculptor who moulds figures from wax, concrete or any mouldable substance. (See also glyptic sculptor.)

plastographer. Someone who produces carved or moulded figures and figurines from plaster.

platcher. Hedge maker.

plate doubler. Tinplate worker in a factory.

plate-maker. Engraver/maker of printing block plates. Also another name for a plater.

platen operator. Operator of a printing press. Sometimes used in reference to other kinds of press.

plater. Welder of metal plates in the shipping industry for boilers, ships' sides, etc. Also person in a large restaurant or on a cruise ship (e.g. the *Titanic*) carrying dirty plates to the washer-up or clean plates from the washer-up for re-use.

platter. Same as strawplaiter.

platter maker. Potter who specialised in producing dining and other plates.

playder. Same as plaid weaver.

pleacher. Same as platcher.

plebanus. Church minister (rural dean).

plebianus. Commoner (i.e without arms regardless of wealth or other status).

plebius. Common worker/labourer.

pledgehouse keeper. Keeper at a debtors' prison.

pledger. Pawnbroker.

plosher. Yorkshire fisherman fishing from a small 'coble' boat.

plough mixer. Brickworks worker.

plum duffer. Seller of a hot plum dough pudding containing raisins, treacle and spices and sold in slices.

plumassier. Dealer in or processor of bird feathers (usually for decorative use on clothes or hats).

plumbago worker. Graphite worker (e.g. manufacturing pencils).

plumb(bum) worker. Same as plumber.

plumber. Originally a lead worker. See illustration.

plumer, plummasier. Dealer in or dyer of ornamental feathers.

plush weaver. Weaver of a shaggy type of cloth called plush, (usually with hairy or velvety nap).

plyer. People such as coachmen, publicans etc who for a fee conducted couples to marriage houses to be married around the mid 18th century. (See also marriage house keeper.)

pockwood dealer. Dealer in particularly hard type of wood called pockwood.

poetaster. A petty poet who sold or read his own work in exchange for small amounts of money.

poieiner, poietes. Poet.

point maker. Same as a pointer. Also person who makes the seal on the end of laces.

point seller. Seller of laces.

pointel manufacturer. Maker of specialist pencils and styluses for industry.

pointer. The person who put points on needles, nails etc.

pointman. Same as point maker.

pointsman. Railway worker.

poldave worker. Maker of poldave, a coarse fabric.

polder man. Dyke patroller and repairer.

polderer. Rural working in marshy or coastal districts who drain land and/or build and maintain dykes.

pole lathe turner. Woodworker.

poletarius. Poultry keeper/seller.

polimitarius. Craftsman specialised in staining techniques.

A team of 18th century plumbers at work. Plumbers have been in existence since the earliest times. This was largely due to the fact that lead (plumbum in Latin) was easy to melt and to work. It was largely used for waterproofing of roofing, construction of water containers such as public baths, the laying of water conduits and of course, lead water pipes. One record survives of the destruction of Guisborough Priory due to the carelessness of the plumbers working in the roof-space. Evidently, at the end of their day's work, one of the workers had not put out the fire which was being used to melt the lead. The result was a devastating fire which burned the monastery down. The scene in the above picture illustrates working practices which were common from the 12th to the 19th century. Lead is being melted in a ladle over an open fire. The man on the left carries large coils of 'lead wire' over his shoulder, whilst the man on the ladder is holding a large roll of lead sheeting.

poling worker. Early form of scaffolder who would erect frameworks of wooden poles to assist in the construction of buildings.

pollard. Rural worker who was employed to cut off animal horns and antlers. Also used in the sense of chopping off tree branches. Sometimes called a poller.

pollarder. Similar to a coppice man but cutting wood back to about six feet in height, rather than to the ground.

poller. Hair cutter.

polygraph operator. Originally a person who operated a machine which could produce multiple copies of a document, i.e. an early form of duplicator. In more modern times the person who operates an electrical lie detector.

polyphonist. Ventriloquist.

pomade manufacturer. Maker of perfumed ointments used mainly for hairdressing purposes. Also called a pommatum maker.

pomar(ius). Literally apple seller but also applied to general fruit sellers.

pommacer. Worker who crushes apples to make cider. Also called a pummacer.

ponderator. Ancient market inspector of weights and measures.

pontibus. Person in charge of a bridge, usually collecting tolls.

pontifex maximus. The chief official of the old (pagan) religion of ancient Rome.

pontiff. Originally the same as pontifex maximus.

pontonier. Bridge constructor or one in charge of a bridge.

pony driver. A pit pony manager in a pit (often a child). Also a horse and cab proprietor.

pony lad/lass. Boy or girl in control of a pit pony. Sometimes used as an alternative for a pit lad/lass who dragged the coal without the assistance of a pony.

Poor Clare. A member of the 'Order of Poor Clare', a band of nursing nuns which was active during monastic times.

Poor Law Guardian. A (usually high status) person who sat on a committee dealing with the poor and workhouse inmates.

pop man. Pawnshop owner, or at least one who would pawn goods from his home.

popinjay. Same as jackadandy but also someone who dresses outrageously.

popish priest. A term used to distinguish Roman Catholics from other priests at a time when the term 'priest' was used to describe all clergymen.

poppet maker. Home worker who knitted or made small inexpensive dolls.

porcar(ius), porcator. Pig keeper.

porcelain button man. Someone who made and sold hand-made shirt buttons from broken porcelain crockery. This was a lowly occupation and considered a form of begging.

porcorum emptor. Pig dealer.

porringer. Plate and eating/drinking vessel maker.

portable soup manufacturer. Maker of dried soups.

portarius, porter. Carrier of various goods/door keeper/bag carrier. In an abbey a fairly high office with staff. He was the abbey's security officer in charge of inspecting visitors, goods, animals etc as they arrived and left.

porter driver/cartman. Man who delivered supplies of porter (ale) to public houses i.e. a kind of drayman.

portitor. Carrier of goods.

portionist. A priest who shared a parish.

portman. Anglo-Saxon town official, equivalent to a modern town councillor.

portram. Porter or door keeper.

portreeve. Chief magistrate of a port.

portress. Female gate or door keeper.

posset seller. Street seller of posset which was a kind of cheese, being milk curdled with wine.

post (cart) driver. A person employed to carry letters and parcels to and from railway stations.

postboy. Someone who travelled with a coach carrying the mail. Also a boy learning to be a postman.

poster. A fence builder. Also a quarry worker who broke up rocks.

posternkeeper. Keeper of a small door or gate, often the back entrance to a large building or castle walls.

postiller. Person who was employed to make marginal notes in a book.

postillion. Someone in charge of changing the horses at stagecoach stops. Also the rider of a horse which pulls a carriage (i.e. he sits on the horse, not on the carriage itself).

postman. Deliverer of letters. Also someone who erects fences. (See illustration.)

Even before the days of the 'Penny Post' uniformed postmen were paid to deliver and collect letters.

posturer. Acrobat.

posy woman. Same as bouquet seller.

pot boy/man. Washer-up of pots, pans, bottles etc.

pot burner. A pottery worker.

potale dealer. Person who bought waste from distilleries and breweries and sold it on for the fattening of swine.

pot luck victualler. Owner of an inexpensive eating house without a menu where diners would eat what was available at at any time from the pot. This is the origin of the modern term 'pot-luck'.

pot(ter) presser. A potter who makes objects using moulds.

pot shop owner. A person who sold but did not make pots.

pot thrower. Maker of pots using a potters wheel.

pot metal worker. Metal worker who made goods from 'pot-metal', an alloy of lead and copper. Also sometimes used to describe a worker in stained glass who used the same metal to hold the glass segments together.

potash maker. An early producer of potash using crude home-made equiment.

potato badger. Potato seller.

potato picker. Seasonal temporary farm worker engaged to follow a tractor picking up and bagging potatoes. In many rural areas children were employed and a special school holiday was created to allow the potato picking to take place.

pothawker. Itinerant seller (and sometimes maker) of pots.

potifex. Brewer.

pottage seller. Soup seller (usually a street vendor).

pottarius. Potter.

pott(er) carrier. Chemist.

potter. Someone who makes pots, but also a fisherman who catches crabs, lobsters etc in basket-like traps which replaced the ancient traps made of pot.

pouch maker. Leather worker who makes pouches and purses.

poulter(er). Poultry breeder or seller. In an abbey it was a high position in charge of business interests and staff concerned with poultry breeding.

pounce supplier. Manufacturer or seller of pounce, a fine powder used to sprinkle over freshly handwritten documents. Pounce was superseded by blotting paper.

pounder, poundkeeper. Same as pinder.

poverty knocker. A colloquial term for low paid or out of work mill workers in West Yorkshire. The term came from the sound the loom made when in action.

powder monkey. Ship's boy who assisted with the gunpowder used in the cannons.

powder watt. An 18th century street seller of washing powder and wash balls.

power loom operator. Mill worker.

powler. Hair cutter.

poynter. Lace maker.

practipedist. Foot care specialist.

praefectus. Officer.

pragmaticus. Solicitor.

prat(ellis). Unskilled agricultural worker who spent his time mowing meadows. (Origin of the word prat as a term for a person who professes knowledge or status that he can never achieve.) Sometimes known as an ellis.

prebend(ary). Ecclesiastic who enjoys a stipend granted to a canon out of the estate of a cathedral or collegiate church.

precentor. In Yorkshire an officer with responsibility for footpaths in ancient times. In an abbey he was a high ranking official in charge of choirs, musicians, robes, books, the abbey seal and the library.

preceptor/tress. School teacher.

prefectus. Local official e.g. reeve.

prelector. A lecturer.

Premonstratensian monk. Member of a strict order of monks with strong Cistercian beliefs. They were also known as White Canons.

prentice. Same as apprentice.

prepositor. Any respected scholar who was given the job of inspecting or examining other scholars.

prepositus. Manor officer similar to a reeve.

presbyter. Originally a village Elder who had authority over a community. Later a chaplain or priest.

presager. Fortune teller. Sometimes an advisor who will predict the possible result of certain actions, e.g. in a military capacity.

preserver. Someone who stuffs carcases of animals/birds for decorative purposes (taxidermist).

presser. A metal worker similar to a 'forger'. Also someone who operates machinery pressing out metal objects from thin sheet metal (sometimes called a 'stamper'). Also a laundry worker who presses clothing.

pressman. Someone who fits tyres to vehicles. Also a printer who rolls on the ink and takes a printed impression from the type etc. In modern times, someone who works for a newspaper.

prester. Priest.

prestidigitator. Stage magician.

prestigiator. Juggler.

preventative man. Early customs officer.

pricker. Many trades, including horticulture (pricker out). Also a horseman.

priest. Often used to indicate Roman Catholic clergymen (but not always). In the north, all clergy regardless of the church they represented, were (and still often are) referred to by this title. The common use of the term 'popish priest' illustrates that a distinction needed to be made.

primage agent. Man at a port who was responsible for paying the masters and crews of ships a small duty for their services in loading or unloading their own ship, as opposed to the port using its own workmen.

primogenial. The firstborn child in any family.

print librarian. Person once in charge of the finger print library at Scotland Yard in London.

prior. The man next in rank to an abbot in an abbey or in sole charge of a smaller monastery. He was the religious (rather than administrative and executive) head of a larger monastery (see abbot).

private monk. Someone who joins a religious order but does not join a monastery permanently. Often they were married and had similar status to a modern vicar.

privateer. Commander of a ship who was licensed by his own government to seize the ships/goods of the enemy. In effect he was a licensed pirate.

privatus. Private citizen.

privy attendant. Someone who looked after a public toilet.

probator. An examiner or approver, often in an official capacity.

process engraver. Printing block maker in the newspaper trade.

process worker. Used in many trades and industries to describe a worker who carries out part of the process but does not have a specific title.

proctor. An officer at a university, etc, responsible for maintaining discipline. Also a church lawyer.

procurator. An official who manages the affairs of others or on behalf of the state, e.g. Procurator Fiscal.

procuress. A 'Madam' in a brothel or a female pimp, i.e. one who organised and lived off the earnings of prostitutes but was not herself one.

profile cutter. Street artist who would cut profile silhouette portraits from black paper. He was also known as a 'shade cutter' and later (in the 19th century) a 'silhouette cutter'. The word 'silhouette' is said to come from a French government finance minister who decorated his home with these inexpensive portraits because it saved him money. Profile cutters generally worked in the street where a 'sitting' would take place. A portrait would be cut within minutes for a small amount of money. See illustration.

Two qualities of 'profile', 'shade' or 'silhouette'. Top left is an inexpensive type, whilst the second is a more complex, more artistic and more expensive version. Profile cutters, otherwise known as shade cutters were much in demand before the days of photography. The original purpose of the profile was to serve as an artist's basic model upon which to paint a portrait, but they soon became popular in their own right. Most profile cutters worked from a bench in the street with only scissors and black paper as their tools of trade, though some, especially if they were also artists, had the use of a studio.

prolucutor. Speaker or chairman at a gathering.

promarius. Waiter.

proof reader. Someone who reads a printed page for errors before it is mass produced for publication. Until recent times, most newspapers had a special department which employed a number of men to proof-read.

prop bobby. Colloquial term for a prop man.

prop man. Person in charge of pit props in a mine.

proper mariner. A highly qualified mariner fit for international navigation (as opposed to a common mariner - see under that entry).

proplasticator. Mould maker.

propola. Travelling dealer in small goods (of a general nature).

prothonotary. A chief notary or clerk of the court.

protocolist. Clerk or registrar.

proveditor. An officer or official in charge of procuring provisions, sometimes called a provedor. Also used occasionally for a purveyor of goods.

provisor. Salesman. The term is the equivalent of 'purveyor'. In a monastery or religious house, the person who was steward or treasurer.

provost. A kind of estate manager in manorial times. In Scotland a chief magistrate or burgh mayor.

provy man. Colloquial term for a credit broker who provided 'tickets' to instantly buy goods, to be repaid on a weekly part payment basis.

Prussian blue maker. Dye maker of a strong blue dye. Old boots bought from dustmen were used in the manufacturing process.

publicani. A tax collector similar to a farmer (see under farmer).

publicanus. Tax collector.

puddler. Miner for precious stones or ores/wrought iron worker.

puddling hand. Assistant in a works where wrought iron is produced.

puer supplier. Collector of puer (dog droppings) which were once used in the tanning industry.

puffer maker. Manufacturer of bellows.

puggera. Person who treads clay into a paste (often work for women and children).

pugging miller. Similar to puggera but using machinery to do the same job.

pugilist. Boxer (often working in a travelling fair).

puletarius. Poultry keeper/seller.

pulled linen stitcher. See under drawn fabric stitcher.

puller. Someone who rows a boat (e.g. ferryboat puller).

pulley maker. Maker of block and tackle devices for lifting.

pumbum worker. Same as plumber.

pummacer. Person who crushes apples in the cider making industry. Also called a pommacer.

pump maker. Maker of water or other pumps.

Punch and Judy man. Itinerant travelling entertainer who used puppets of the clown Punch(inello), Judy (Punch's companion) and other characters such as the Policeman, Butcher, Toby the Spotty Dog (or Bulldog), Crocodile, Baby, the Ghost, the Doctor, Jack Ketch (the Hangman), Beadle, Scaramouche, the Devil, Blind Man, and The Grand Senior. Children (and adults) were entertained using a portable theatre consisting of a decorated upright box and standard props such as miniature gallows, bells, ladders and a horse.

punchcard. (Punchcard machine operator, accountant, etc). Worker employed in many businesses to punch, or interpret information punched into cards. This was used for a variety of jobs, ranging from accounting departments to the operation of weaving machines and fairground organs.

punder. Same as pinder.

Fantoccini.

Punch and Judy men varied in standard from using makeshift wooden boxes to sophisticated side-shows such as this. Fantoccini boasted of being patronised by royalty. This sketch shows him in Pentonville, London in 1825.

puntil man, punty man. Assistant to a glass blower.

pupil teacher. An older and educated school pupil who assisted with teaching.

purl maker. Manufacturer of Purl, a 19th century medicated malt liquor.

putter. Hauler of coal tubs in a mine.

putter-in. Many trades. Worker who put something into a machine etc, as part of a process.

putter-out. Someone who would take on a job at a fixed price which he would 'put-out' to workers whom he paid himself, so making a profit.

putty maker. Originally a maker of a compound of lead and tin used in a similar way to modern glazier's putty.

pyrologist. A 19th century heating engineer or expert.

pyrotechnist. Firework manufacturer.

Q

quacksalver. Pretended or real doctor who continually boasted of his medical skills.

quadrel maker. Manufacturer of quadrel, an artificial stone made in blocks from compressed chalk and earth which was allowed to dry slowly.

quadriga racer. Person who appeared at fairs and festivals and would race for money using a two wheeled quadriga cart, used like a a chariot and drawn by four horses harnessed in a row horizontally across the front of the car.

quadrivium tutor. Teacher at a college, university or academy who taught the higher educational Quadrivium (the four subjects: arithmetics, music, geometry and astronomy).

quail piper maker. Manufacturer of small leather purses. Also a person who made whistles or pipes that imitated the call of quails and helped lure them into nets for capture.

Quaker gun maker. Manufacturer of wooden guns made to resemble real ones. These were mounted on ships alongside real cannons etc., to give the impression the ship had more defence capacity. The names came from the fact that Quakers, who opposed war, mounted them on their ships as a deterrent against attack.

quarrel maker. Arrow maker (in early times, a quarrel was an arrow with a square shaft). Later, the term was used for a manufacturer of small diamond-shaped glass panes called quarrels.

quarrel picker. Colloquial term for a glazier.

quarrerius. Quarryman or stone cutter.

quarrier. Quarry worker.

quartermaster. Orginally an army officer whose duties were to provide quarters, stores and provisions for soldiers, or on a ship, a petty-officer who was in charge of the stowage of ropes, signals, flags, etc.

quassillarius. Pedlar.

quaternion. One of four Roman solders given the task of guarding a prisoner overnight.

queensware potter. Manufacturer of a fine pottery involving a special process of suspending tobacco-pipe clay in water before using a complicated firing process.

querry. A groom.

questman. Churchwarden's assistant. Also called a sideman.

questuary. Someone employed to collect profits of any kind.

quiddany maker. Manufacturer of quiddany, a confection once made from quinces.

quidnunc. A news vendor. Also used to describe a person who pretended to know everything.

quiller. Textile industry machine operator.

quillwright. Wheelwright.

quilter/quiltress. Quilted cloth maker.

quister. Bleacher.

quitter. Person who delivered a document to another.

quizzing glass supplier. Maker or seller of monocle spectacle glasses for both men and women.

quoif maker. Manufacturer of caps and/or hoods.

R

rack maid(en). Female tin mine worker who sorted ore from rock.

racker. Medieval official torturer.

radknight. A tenant who was a good horseman and gave service as a horseman to his lord.

raddler. Hedge-maker using interwoven branches.

raff seller/man. Second hand goods dealer, particularly of a maritime nature.

raffia man. Maker of straw or grass goods.

rag (and bone) man. Person who collected and paid for rags and bones from householders (usually with a horse and cart).

rag cutter. Cloth or paper industry worker.

rag gatherer. Low grade cloth mill worker.

ragged school teacher. Usually a voluntary position, organising schools for poor children in the 1800s.

railer. Manufacturer of wooden rails for trucks and trolleys to run on in pits, etc.

railway carrier. Someone employed to deliver goods by road, either to or from a railway station.

railway guard. Person in charge of railway goods carriage who would also signal to the driver (with a whistle and flag) when it was safe for the train to leave the station.

railway porter. Railway worker, once employed in great numbers to carry the baggage of train passengers without charge.

raiser. Person who moulds the bodies of fountain pens in a factory.

raker. In the days before organised street cleaners, a raker was often employed to rake rubbish which had been left in the street into heaps. Often the heaps were simply buried in soil.

ramillie maker. Maker of wigs characterized by having a pigtail.

ramskin baker/seller. Person who baked and/or sold ramskins, a kind of cake made from pastry and cheese.

ramson seller. Someone who collected and sold wild garlic.

rand maker. Manufacturer of thin shoe inner-soles made from cork etc., and called a rand.

rapper. Someone in industrial areas who had the job of waking shift workers by knocking on their doors.

rapperee. An Irish plunderer.

raree show man. Street entertainer who carried a miniature show around in a box.

rashling. A term once used to describe a person who was always expected to act rashly.

rat catcher. General term for a person who would rid houses, etc. of any vermin. He often used a ferret for this work.

rattler, rattlewatch. Town crier.

reader. One of a department of men and boys in a newspaper office who occupied the reading room and had the job of reading the first print of the newspaper to check for printing and spelling errors. The trade began to die out in the early to mid 1960s.

reaper. Someone who harvests crops or cuts grass, generally with a sickle or scythe.

rebroccator. Shoe repairer.

rector. In Latin manuscripts means 'guardian' and virtually the same in modern English. As a clergyman, the rector received tithes of one tenth of all crops grown in the parish.

rector regis et regni. Regent (literally 'Guardian of the King and Country').

red herring curer. Someone who smokes fish (but not herring) to be sold as 'red herrings'.

redsmith. 'Red gold' craftsman.

redware maker. Potter who makes plain undecorated baked pottery for household/industrial use.

reeder. Collector/seller/ manufacturer of common ditch weeds for various household purposes.

reedmaker. Maker of reeds for musical instruments. Also a tapestry worker.

reeler. Used in many trades particularly textiles.

reeve. Overseer of the manor. Originally a lowly position but later developed into a powerful one.

refa. Anglo-Saxon official who acted as warden or sheriff. The title developed into the word reeve meaning an overseer of lands.

refectioner. In an abbey a kind of head waiter/master of ceremonies. In charge of staff who handled crockery and catered for ordinary meals and special occasions.

regardant villein. A special kind of villein who was permanently linked to one manor.

Regina. Queen (used also for 'Queen of the May' at Maytime celebrations).

register keeper. Keeper of marriage registers, who was often a marriage house keeper. (See under that entry.)

registrarius. Registrar.

regrater. A person who bought and sold provisions in the same market.

regular canon. A canon who lived in a religious house like a monk, but still carried out duties attached to a cathedral (see also canon and secular canon).

relict. Usually signifies 'widow', less commonly 'widower'.

renderer. Someone who made dripping from raw animal fat. Also applied to anyone who performed any service.

renter(er). Specialist sewer who repaired or restored valuable cloth such as in tapestries by stitching edges together without turning them over to form a risen seam.

rentier. Also known as a 'tenant in chief'. He was a powerful leaseholder of land who lived off the rents of his tenants.

repousser. Decorative metal worker.

representative. An agent (usually a travelling salesman).

reredos builder. Builder of a primitive type of fireplace from large flat stones, particularly in Scotland.

rereward. A guard who defends from the rear (e.g. a soldier at the end of a column).

restio, restionius. Rope/string maker.

retainer. Same as vassal.

revelus. Pedlar.

Reverend. Used for all clergy in early records (even nonconformist ministers). When in conjunction with Mr. (Magister) or Dr. (Doctor), this often indicated that the clergyman was a college graduate.

revolus. Pedlar.

Rex. King.

ribbon man. Itinerant ribbon seller. Also a member of an Irish Roman Catholic society.

ribbon weaver. Worker who operated a machine making silk ribbons.

rick man/stacker. Builder of hay ricks (hay stacks).

rickmaster. Cavalry officer.

riddler. Sifter or sorter (used in many trades).

riding officer. A Customs and Excise officer who patrolled on horseback, sometimes with the assistance of mounted dragoon soldiers.

rifter. Agricultural worker.

rigger. Ship worker dealing with the rigging. Also block and tackle operator.

rigging monkey. A ship's boy who climbed the rigging carrying out various tasks.

Rightboy. Same as 'Leveller'.

ring spinner. Cotton machine worker.

rip maker. Basket weaver who specialised in rips, small wicker baskets for the carrying of fish.

ripator. Reaper or grass cutter.

ripery worker. Worker in the cheese making industry. See illustration.

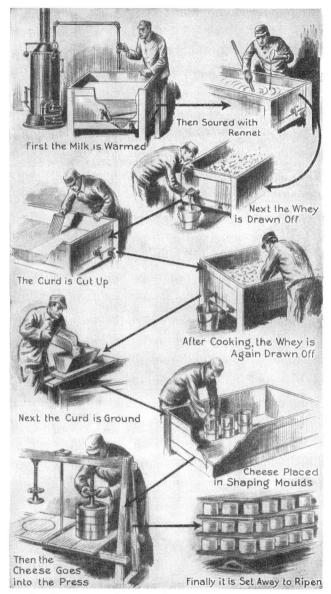

First the Milk is Warmed

Then Soured with Rennet

The Curd is Cut Up

Next the Whey is Drawn Off

After Cooking, the Whey is Again Drawn Off

Next the Curd is Ground

Cheese Placed in Shaping Moulds

Then the Cheese Goes into the Press

Finally it is Set Away to Ripen

Ripery worker. The process of making cheese was once all completed by hand. The ripery worker was employed in the final stages when cheese was 'set away' to be ripened. The full process from warming the milk to ripening is shown in this old illustration dating from around 1920.

ripper, rippier. Fish seller.

river finder. Same as mudlark.

rivet hammerer. Part of a two man team who rivets large steel girders together. The other team member being the 'holder-on'.

robot, robut. Production worker in a fruit canning factory (probably the origin of the word 'robot').

rock maker. Manufacturer of long sticks of a hard confectionery with letters which appear all through the bar.

rock salt miner. See under salt miner.

rocker. A nursery maid.

rockman. User of pneumatic drill in a quarry.

rodder. Fish processing industry worker who places a metal rod through rows of fish.

rogatorius. Beggar. (The word 'rogue' comes from this word.)

rogue. Officially defined as 'a person wandering about without being able to give good account of himself'.

rogue spotter. Someone in a bottling plant that watches the filled bottles on a conveyor belt and extracts any 'rogues' (i.e. badly filled or damaged ones).

roller mill worker. A factory worker in the early days of the mechanisation of flour production.

rolley man. Same as rully man.

rollway man. Mine worker.

roman cement worker. Worker in a fine cement factory.

root beer seller. Someone who sold beer made from root ginger, dandelions or other crop roots.

root seller. Street vendor of root vegetables, etc.

roper. Rope maker/net maker. See illustration.

ropery owner. Same as ropewalk owner.

rotar(ius). Wheel maker.

rotocraft pilot. Pilot of an autogiro or helicopter.

rotularius. Official notary.

rouper. Auctioneer.

A ropemaker of the 18th century. Ropers such as the one in the picture above, were self employed, often working with other members of the family to supply ropes to local farmers etc. Some were farmers themselves, often working in a spare field or paddock, whilst others performed the work as a secondary means of income. In coastal areas where more rope would be required, quite large roperies, or rope-walks were established. These provided employment for local men. Though the remains of the old roperies are now largely untraceable, some towns retain the name 'Ropery', 'Rope-walk' or 'Ropers Walk' in the names of modern streets.

rover. Wool trade worker. Also a merchant seaman or gypsy.

rubber presser. Specialised work as carried out by a presser in a metal works or factory. (Once used extensively in motor part manufacture.)

rubber seller. An 18th century branch of the haberdashery trade. The rubber seller sold brushes and leather rubbers which were used to rub up the raised fibres or nap on velvet hats and clothing.

rubber up. Generally a cab driver deprived of his licence who made a casual living by polishing the brass on other cabs and cleaning their upholstery. Also known as a buckman or buck giver as the use of a wet leather was known as 'giving out buck'. The American expression 'to earn a buck' may derive from this expression. (See also buck.)

rubbler. Quarry worker.

rulley man. Driver of a flat wagon or dray used for delivering heavy objects such as barrels, blocks of stone etc. (See also drayman.)

rumourer. A reporter of news (but not via a newspaper).

runner. Policeman (see under Bow Street Runner). Also a Victorian refuse collector who worked in a team using one cart. Also a messenger (see bookies runner).

running dustman. See under runner.

running patterer. Also known as a flying stationer. A street salesman of paper products who was continuously on the move.

running repairer. A fitter or mechanic who carries out minor repairs whilst the machinery is still in service, particularly such a worker in the tramway industry.

rupetra. Roper maker.

ruptarius. A freeman who sold his skills as a mercenary soldier.

rush gatherer. Collector of rushes for carpeting, weaving or for use in rush lights.

rush light maker. A blacksmith specialising in making holders for rushes soaked in fat or oil and used for lighting purposes when candles were expensive, absent or scarce.

rusk maker. Baker of rusks, a very light type of biscuit.

rusticus. Country dweller.

S

sabre-tasche maker. Leather worker who specialised in making or stitching little bags which were suspended from the sword belt of cavalry soldiers (particularly officers).

sacbut player. Player of a wind instrument which was an early form of trombone.

sacerdos. Priest.

sack collector. Same as bag collector.

sack sewer. Home based worker sewing hessian etc into sacks with stout string.

sacrist. Same as subchantor.

sad ironer. A maid who ironed clothes using an old fashioned heated smoothing iron which was also known as a 'flat iron'.

saddle tree maker. Specialist carpenter who made frames for saddlers to build saddles upon.

saddler. Saddlemaker and leather worker.

sadware man. Craftsman using 'heavy' pewter. (See also hollow-ware man and pewter beater.)

safernman, safroner. Grower/seller of saffron spice plants.

sagger maker. Maker of a fireclay container for use in the pottery industry.

sagger (bottomer). Pottery worker who put saggers in the bottom of kilns.

sagittar(ius). Archer.

sailor. In directories this generally applies to a labourer on a ship doing manual duties but in general parlance was used to describe any person under officer class who sailed the seas.

sailorman. Labourer on a ship or in the ship building industry.

sailor's woman. Colloquial term for a prostitute.

saintier. Norman-English term for a bell-founder. Also spelt santer, senter, etc.

salamander. A 'fire eater' (street or stage performer).

salarius. Same as salter.

sallet maker. Manufacturer of a light head piece similar to a balaclava or helmet.

salmagundi seller. Tradesman who sold salmagundi, a mixture of chopped seasoned meat and other ingredients.

saloop seller. Someone who sold hot soup from a stall in the early 1800s. These stalls gradually gave way to coffee stalls as coffee became much cheaper.

salt boiler. Salt maker (often by boiling sea water).

salt-junk dealer. Specialist butcher or provision dealer who sold dry salted beef, often for use on ships' voyages.

salt miner. Miner involved in obtaining rock salt which because of its discolouration (usually red/brown from iron deposits) was used mainly for salt brine in the chemical industries. Cheshire was once famous for its rock-salt deposits.

salt panner. Salt worker who pumped salt brine into large open pans to be evaporated.

salter. Salt dealer/maker. Also (infrequently) a roof mender.

saltstone wheeler. Someone who crushed salt (or sand) from larger pieces using a large stone or stone wheel pulled by a horse.

salvage sewer. Same as silker.

samite(re). Maker of a heavy smooth cloth similar to silk.

sanctioner. Accountant.

sandman. Someone who collected and sold river or beach sand.

sandwich board man. Man who walked round with advertising boards strapped to his front and rear.

santer. See under saintier.

saponar(ius). Soap maker/seller.

sarcinet weaver. Silk weaver.

sarne seller. Street (or sometimes shop) seller of thick slices of cooked meat (origin of the word sarny meaning a sandwich, and alternative origin of the word sandwich itself, i.e. sarne wedge).

A sandman and his donkey – from an old illustration. The sandman was always on call to supply river or beach sand for pathways, roads and building projects. Seaside areas naturally had more people carrying on this trade because of the abundance of free beach sand. However, those who could obtain river sand generally obtained a higher price and were considered a higher class of tradesman by their potential customers.

sarrator. Sawyer.

sartor. Tailor/dresser.

sateen weaver. Imitation satin maker.

satirist. 18th century writer (generally for a popular magazine which commented on local celebrities). Also a group of political painters which included artists such as Thomas Rowlandson 1756-1827 and James Gillray 1757-1815.

saucer. Same as salter.

sauser. Salt worker, dealer or carrier.

Savigny monk. Member of the Savigny order which was so similar to the Cistercians that its religious houses merged with them. The Savignies survived very briefly under their own title.

saw doctor. Sharpener/repairer of saws.

sawbones. Physician.

sawer. Person who saws stone blocks in a stone quarry. Sometimes erroneously used also in place of the term sawyer (a worker who saws wood in a wood shed).

sawney man. Colloquial expression for a bacon seller. An alternative explanation (other than that it was invented by Lord Sandwich) to the origin of the word 'sandwich' relates to a wedge of sawney (bacon) between sliced bread (i.e. sawney wedge).

sawyer. Wood shed worker involved in sawing wood.

say weaver. Tablecloth or sheet weaver (say being a type of cloth).

scabbler. Manual worker who uses a kind of pick known as a scabbler.

scaffolder. Someone who erects scaffold prior to building or repairing a building.

scagiol maker. Maker of imitation marble.

scaifer. Various spellings. A dry stone wall constructor.

scale wiggler. Anyone who gave short measure in the course of trade. Also called a wiggler.

scaler. The person who scaled and measured stacks of timber in the logging industry, especially in 19th century Canada. Also known as a culler.

scaleraker. Rubbish collector or street cleaner.

scallion. Same as scullion.

scantler. Low paid manual worker in a number of trades whose job was to break up something into small portions.

scappler. A stone mason or stone worker who smoothed rough stone to a flat surface. (See illustration.)

scarifier. Doctor or unqualified person involved in the ancient practice of blood-letting for medical purposes.

scarlet grain dealer. Dealer in dyes obtained from a specific female insect (possibly cochineal). Also known as a kermes dealer.

scatch maker. Manufacturer of a special kind of horse's bit for

An 18th century stonemason at work with his two scapplers. A scappler was a stone mason's assistant. If the illustration above is correct, then stonemasons and their scapplers were extremely well dressed. In reality this is unlikely and the wood block was probably engraved by someone who had never seen stonemasons at work. As a city dweller he would probably assume that everyone dressed in the normal attire of that time.

a bridle. Also a manufacturer of wooden stilts used by workers in muddy areas or fenlands.

scavelman. A cleaner of waterways.

scavenger. Rubbish collector/nightsoil man.

scenographer. Artist or draftsman who specialised in drawings/ paintings, using perspective.

scholar. Used on censuses to indicate someone who attended school (usually but not always, a child between 3 and 15).

scholiast. Specialist writer of explanatory notes. Also a commentator.

school attendance officer. Same as school officer.

school officer. Colloquially termed the kidcatcher (see under that entry).

schumacker. Shoemaker.

sciagrapher. Originally someone skilled at finding out the time by the shadows cast by the sun. Later, a person who drew buildings etc., as a black-filled outline, sometimes showing windows or other features but otherwise devoid of detail.

scindifaber. Maker of blades for tools and weapons.

sciolist. Name given to a teacher or tradesman who had a smattering of only superficial or imperfect knowledge about many things. Today called a Jack of all trades

sciomancer. Someone who made predictions or told fortunes from the way shadows fell.

scioptician. A pretentious name used by itinerant operators of magic lanterns at fairs and other gatherings. Also known as a scioptrician.

scissor. Hairdresser. Also used to describe a tailor (both used shears or scissors).

scold. An official name given to a nagging woman, who could once be charged for the offence.

scot collector. Collector of parish tax payments known as 'Scot and Lot', hence the expression 'Getting off scot free'. Also called a shot collector.

Scotch draper, Scotchman. Door to door salesman of goods who took part-payment on a weekly basis.

scourer. Leather trade worker.

scout. Colloquial term for a male college servant at Oxford University. Also someone sent out by an army or other group to search ahead of the main party.

scoveler. One who cleaned large ovens (as a chimney sweep would clean a chimney) using a mop known as a scovel.

S.C.R. Used in universities to indicate someone who was a fellow or tutor who was entitled to dine at the 'high table' and used the Senior Common Room as opposed to the under-graduates and junior research students from the J.C.R. (Junior Common Room).

scrap man. Scrap metal dealer. Also a seller of punched out and embossed illustrations called 'scraps' which were collected by children for pasting into books etc.

scraper operator. Coal mine worker operating automatic machinery.

scratch (wig) maker. 18th century wig maker.

scratter. A beachcomber who specialises in 'scratting' (digging with his hands) for coins in areas where they are known to gather by the action of waves on public beaches.

screener. Mine worker who sorts ore or coal.

screever. Person who made a living writing letters for those who could not write themselves. (See also slum scribbler.)

scriba. Clerk.

scriba aerarius. Bank clerk.

scribe. Writer or secretary.

scriber. Dock worker who marks goods or containers.

scribler. Reporter or writer. Also a wool mill worker.

scribus. Writer or secretary.

scriever. Shipyard worker who assists with the framework of the ship/boat by marking in the position of parts. (See also screever.)

scrimmer. Specialist plaster who would soundproof film-making sets using plaster and a material called scrim.

scriever-in. Same as scriever.

scrip maker. Usually a home worker in a leather or cloth manufacturing area who would make scrips (small purses, bags and wallets) out of scraps left over from the manufacture of larger items.

scriptor. When found usually means 'the writer of this'. This may be an official scribe, but not necessarily. See illustration.

scripture reader. Lay preacher.

scrivener. Professional record keeper who draws up bonds. Also colloquially used for a secretary.

scrutiner. Checker of accounts or vote counter.

scrutoire. A writer or clerk.

scudder. Leather trade worker.

A scriptor in a monastery. Scriptors were to be found both in and outside of monasteries. The word scriptor *means 'writer' or 'writer of this' and is to be found on many old documents. Many monastic houses had a scriptorium where a number of monks would be engaged in writing and copying documents and books.*

scuffler. Agricultural or horticultural labourer employed to use a hoe.

sculler boatman. A waterman who operated a boat rowed by two men.

scullery worker/maid. Low grade worker who washed laundry, washed up and cleaned.

scullion. Male counterpart of a scullery maid.

scummer. Someone whose work entails skimming the surface of a liquid to remove impurities (e.g. in a jam factory).

scurio. Stable worker.

scurtionist. A title once given to amateur cockle collectors by those who did it for a living.

scutcher. 18th century flax worker who beat the flax with a large blade.

sea-coal gatherer. Person who collected and sold coal gathered from beaches.

sea cook. Ship's cook.

sea-pieman. Baker who specialised in pies used aboard ship and often made of ingredients, particularly dried meat and paste boiled together, that would keep in good condition on short to medium term voyages.

seal presser. Glass industry worker.

seam worker. An underground miner.

seamstress. Sewer of cloth (originally by hand, then by machine).

seaplane pilot. Pilot of an aircraft fitted with floats for landing on the sea.

sear cloth manufacturer. Maker of cloths (or plasters) to be used for the dressing of wounds.

searcher. Customs and excise man.

seaweed gatherer. Person who collected seaweed in a cart to be sold as fertilizer to farmers etc.

second. An assistant, especially in combat (e.g. in fighting a duel).

secretarius. Scribe or secretary.

secretary. In an abbey it was another name for the subchantor (see under that entry).

secular canon. A canon who served more than one church or cathedral.

sedan (chair) carrier. Carrier of a 17th/18th century form of carriage in which two poles were used to carry a passenger chair (sometimes covered), with two men carrying, one man being at the front and one at the back. See illustration.

seether. Kitchen assistant who attended to the boiling of meat, broths, etc.

seggar. Pottery industry worker.

seiner. Fisherman aboard a boat using a large seine net.

seinter. Saddler/leather strap and girdle maker.

selectman. A member of the parish select vestry.

self acting minder. Spinning machine watcher.

self service store owner. Owner of one of the earliest forms of

Sedan Chair Carrier. An old cartoon showing the chaos caused by the large number of sedan carriers plying for trade in city centres. Sedan chairs were a relatively cheap and common form of transport during the 17th and 18th centuries. They acted as the equivalent of the modern day taxi cab and would gather outside theatres, public houses and in city squares. Generally they were intended to carry only one passenger, though two-seat sedans are known to have existed.

supermarkets, where a basket was picked up at the door and slid along wooden rails around the outside of the store in a similar way that trays are slid along wooden rails in a cafeteria. The customer picked up items as she went along and paid for them at the end.

sellarius. Salter (of meat, fish etc). Also a salt dealer.

seller. A term often used by tradesmen who sold different goods at different times (e.g. oranges one day, apples the next).

selvage edger. Cloth industry worker involved in the finishing process of cloth, usually by weaving an edge or border. Also called a selvedge weaver.

semi lorer. Leather worker.

sempster. A sewer of cloth (i.e. a seamstress).

sempstress. Same as seamstress.

senator urbanus. Alderman/councillor.

seneschal(us). A steward with jurisdiction over several manors. He was often also sheriff and/or High Constable.

sengel. Saxon solitary signalman.

senter. See under saintier.

septessarius. A general merchant or grocer.

seraphine player. Musician using a seraphine, being a wind instrument with a keyboard and a wind chest operated by bellows.

serf. An agricultural worker, who though not the property of any man, was a virtual slave because of his ties to his lord's lands. The official line was that though not a slave, they were 'unfree'.

Medieval serfs being directed in their work (from an old illustration). Though serfs were virtual slaves, they were not actually owned by their masters. The political situation of medieval times meant that in effect they were tied to a job which they could not leave. The official description of serfs was that they were not slaves, merely 'unfree'. In effect this was true because if a serf was badly treated he could not be punished for leaving his master's service. In reality, unless he had received a previous offer to work elsewhere, he would have to become a vagrant with all the dangers and penalties this might bring in the Middle Ages.

serge maker. Specialist candlemaker who manufactured very large candles such as corpse candles or serges.

sericulturist. Breeder of silkworms.

serifaber. Locksmith.

servant agent. Someone who operated a job agency for servants.

servant mover. Similar to or same as a servant agent.

serviens. Servant (usually holding land in exchange for a service to his lord).

serviens ad legem. Law officer.

servitor. General term for someone who 'serves', ranging from a maid to a public servant. Also a commoner university student who received part of his income from assisting gentleman commoners (see under those entries).

servus. Manual worker or servant.

set maker. Maker of road or paving stones.

setter. Mason who places the stones in their final position when building.

setter-on. A person in a cock-fighting pit who would set one fighting cock to face the other, immediately before fighting commenced. They acted as 'seconds' do in a boxing match.

setting schooler. One of a number of textile workers (usually women and children) who would work together on their own doorsteps in a 'setting school', setting teeth into leather straps for use in the factory.

settle maker. Woodworker/carpenter who specialised in making bench seats with high backs.

sewer hunter. Sewer cleaner or one who searched sewers for valuables.

sewer rat. Sewer worker.

sexton. A man in charge of digging graves and related churchyard jobs.

shade cutter. See profile cutter.

shadowgraph projectionist. Specialist worker in a motor car production plant who would use a machine which highly magnified screw threads etc., for examination and testing purposes.

shaft sinker. Someone who dug shafts (for mining etc) or wells.

shag weaver. Weaver of a coarse rough woolly and hairy cloth.

shagreen (case) maker. Leather worker.

shaker. Stone quarry worker who drives wedges into a newly cut stone block and drives a heavy iron bar into the cracks in order to 'shake' a block of stone loose before lowering it or lifting it with chains and a crane to the quarry floor. Also a member of a religious group that made shaking movements as they worshipped.

shako maker. Manufacturer of a kind of military cap known as a shako.

shale oil worker. Production worker in producing oil from heated shale rocks. Common in Scotland in the mid 19th century, but also elsewhere.

shaloon weaver. Maker of a closely woven lining cloth.

shambler. Butcher. (Rows of butcher shops were known as shambles.)

shammoyer. Leather worker who prepared soft leather using oil.

shanty singer. A street musician who would earn coppers by playing or singing sea shanties.

share-fisherman. A boat fisherman whose income is based on a share of the catch.

shaveling. A monk or friar.

shaver. A barber. Also a young man. Also a robber. Also a colloquial term for someone of sharp intellect whether funny or criminal (all 19th century terms).

sheafmaker. Agricultural worker who made up sheafs of wheat etc by hand at harvest time.

shear grinder. Knife sharpener.

shearer. Sheep shearer. Also a term for a metal worker.

shearing machinist. Operator of a machine to cut woolcloth which first came into use in the early 1800s.

shearman. Cloth cutter. Also a sheep shearer. Also a metal cutter.

shears operator. Person who operated machinery used for lifting heavy weights, also spelt sheers.

sheath manufacturer. Someone who made scabbards.

shebeen(er). Owner of an illegal brewery, distillery or drinking house.

shedder. Worker in a number of industries involved in the pouring of a liquid or molten metal.

sheer-hulk worker. Man who worked in a shipyard aboard a hulk specifically fitted out to remove the masts of other ships.

sheer-leg man. Operator of a derrick used for drilling for water, oil, etc.

sheerer. Shipyard worker.

sheet smoker. Rubber industry worker who smoked sheets of rubber to make it dark brown in colour.

sheldrake. Street cleaner or rubbish collector.

shellac worker. Someone involved in the production of shellac, a resin produced by the 'lac' insect, found on trees in India etc. It was once widely used to make sealing wax, inks, varnishes and gramophone records as well as adding to the mixtures involved in other products ranging from fireworks to chocolate.

shepherd. Though strictly a herder of sheep, the term shepherd was often given to anyone looking after a herd of animals (e.g. goats or mixed cows and sheep).

shepster. Sheep shearer.

sheriff. Originally the most important official in any county but later their powers were restricted (see also seneschal). The shire reeve, as the original title was styled, was the Monarch's representative in each county. The modern English equivalent is the Lord Lieutenant.

sherman. Cloth cutter or tailor.

shether. Medieval maker of sheaths and scabbards.

Shillibeer. Shillibeers were the original London horse-drawn omnibuses (named after the owner). Thus Shillibeer driver or Shillibeer conductor indicates that the person worked on London transport. Shillibeers first came into service on 4th July 1829.

shingler. Maker/repairer of wooden roof tiles.

ship's chandler. Originally a supplier of candles and lighting requisites for ships, then a general ship supplier of fittings.

ship's-husband. Person who is hired to look after a ship when in port, attending to repairs, obtaining provisions, etc.

ship's master. See master mariner.

ship-wright. Skilled ship builder.

shire mote official. An officer in ancient times who worked for the equivalent of the County Court.

shire reeve. Sheriff.

shirr stitcher. Worker who constructed shirr, an elasticated cloth made by stitching elastic between two sheets of ordinary cloth.

shiver. Slate worker who slit the slate into thin pieces.

shoddy weaver. Weaver of coarse cloth from recycled bits of cloth.

shoddy worker. Someone who dealt with rags and old fibres.

shoe black. Man who works in the streets cleaning shoes of passers by for a fee. In Victorian London and other cities, the job was often a cover for a prostitute's 'pimp'.

shoe seller. In medieval times, the shoe seller, the shoemaker and the leather cutters would all be found in the same street, either working as a team or as individuals.

shoebinder. Female worker in a factory who sewed the tops of shoes to the base.

shoer. Horse shoer/blacksmith.

shoesmith. Same as shoer. Also a cobbler.

shore. A term used in coastal districts to distinguish a tradesman who worked only on shore (e.g. a shore carpenter as opposed to a ship's carpenter).

shorer. Shipyard worker.

short night man. A cab driver who only worked in the dark, as opposed to a long night man who worked through the night and on into the daylight hours.

shot collector. See under scot collector.

shot firer. Quarry worker who sets the explosives used to blast stone.

shot maker. Manufacturer of lead shot for guns.

shotgun. (Australia/U.S.A) A driver's mate. Dates back to stage coach days when two drivers were employed; the one not at the reins carried the gun.

showmaker. A shoe maker.

showman. Someone who travelled around the country with a fair or circus.

shrager. Tree trimmer/pruner.

shrieve(r). Sheriff.

shroud layer. Rope worker making a rope consisting of four twisted strands.

shroud maker. Manufacturer of heavy duty covers for protection from the weather, particularly when at sea.

shuffler. General farmyard worker.

shunter. Railway goods engine driver.

shuttle maker. Maker of wooden shuttles for use in textile factories.

sickleman. Reaper of grass or crops.

side(s)man. Churchwarden's assistant. Also called a questman.

siderographist. Steel engraver.

sifker. Maker of sieves and riddles for sifting earth.

sifter. In Victorian London, a woman whose job entailed sifting through the material gathered by dustmen to retrieve useable and saleable objects.

sightsman. Musical term given to anyone who could quickly read a sheet of music and commit to memory instantly so as to be able to play the tune without further consultation of the written notes.

sign crester. Specialised blacksmith or metal craftsman who

Boiling bundles of silk. Silk dresser was a title given to a number of process workers involved in silk manufacture. In the above picture, silk dressers are seen boiling bundles of silk to remove the gum. The picture was taken in 1928.

would make scrolled wrought iron decorations for signs, signposts etc.

signal box man. Railway signalman.

signalman. Anyone who operates a signal device but generally applied to a railway signal box operator.

silentiary. Court official with the task of keeping those in court quiet. Also anyone sworn not to divulge state secrets.

silhouette cutter. See profile cutter.

silk dresser. Someone who prepares silk in a silk factory. See illustration.

silk engine worker. Silk industry worker.

silk mercer. Seller of silk fabrics and clothing.

silk reeler. Silk factory worker who reeled off the silk from cocoons.

Silk manufacture in 1929. In the production of natural silk, process workers who thicken silk threads by twisting one or more together are known as silk throwers, throwsters or yarn winders. This picture shows the throwing room in a well equipped silk works.

silk thrower. Natural silk process worker who thickens silk by twisting one or more threads (see also throwster). Also a silk yarn winder. See illustration.

silk twister. Same as silk thrower.

silk warper. Highly paid and skilled silk industry worker who drew together the threads of silk which would form the 'warp' in the weaving process. These were gathered together and wound onto a machine called a warping mill.

silker. Sewer of fabrics to prevent fraying edges.

silkmaker spinster. Woman silk spinner/thrower.

silkmaker throster. Male silk spinner/thrower.

sillabub seller. Street salesman of a liquor made from milk curdled by the addition of wine or cider.

silversmith. Maker of silver goods/jewellery.

simpler, simpleton. Gardener/herb seller.

sin eater. Lowly but professional funeral attender who for payment would ritually 'eat the sins' of the deceased by accepting food at the funeral meal, thereby giving the departed a 'clean soul'.

sinecure. Someone who received a salary for a high position which involved no actual work.

singing bread maker. Maker of church communion wafers.

single stick(er). Singlestick was a form of combat fencing, using a stick. Men often offered themselves for combat at fairs, offering a prize for anyone who could beat them.

sink maker. Manufacturer of kitchen or industrial sinks.

sinker. Well or shaft digger.

sinker maker. Maker of lead weights for weighing down the hooks on a fishing line. Generally a home based, part time industry.

sinterer. Metal worker who uses metal powders which are melted into moulds to form solid objects.

Sir. Used in early records to indicate knights and later members of the clergy.

sisal spinner. Someone who made sisal, a cheap quality rope or twine, by hand.

sister. Originally a woman who attended to the sick and washed their clothing. It was considered a low grade position. In later years the term sister came to mean a senior nurse in charge of others. Also used as a general term for a nun.

Sister of Mercy. A nun belonging to a religious order.

sizar. In a university, same as servitor (see under that entry).

sizer. Person who applies size in order to stiffen cloth, etc. Also someone who sorts goods by size.

skainer, skaner. Skane is an old Scandinavian word for 'shoe' (see mussel ska(i)ner).

skeel maker. Wood turner specialising in bowls.

skelper. Beehive maker. Also someone who trims the top off something (e.g. hedges).

skep maker. Maker of beehives from plaited straw.

skepper. Same as skep maker.

skilling contractor. Person who specialised in building skillings (cottage extensions, barns, etc., in rural areas).

skin dresser. Cleaner of animal skins for making into clothing etc.

skin professor. 19th century specialist tattooist.

skinner. Dealer in pelts, skins and furs.

skip-kennel. Young footman or any other young male servant.

skip maker. Manufacturer of medium to large containers of various kinds.

skipper. Person in charge of a boat or ship.

skiver. A person who split sheep skins to be used in bookbinding.

skivvy. A washerwoman or general cleaner.

slamkin. An old extremely derogative term for a woman, equivalent to the modern word 'slut'.

slap(p)er. Pottery clay worker.

slapjack. Street seller of hot pancakes.

slate maker. Manufacturer of school writing slates and slate-pencils. Rarely used as another term for a slater (roofing slate maker).

slate man. Anyone who sold goods on credit.

slater. Slate worker and roofer.

slatt layer. Roofing specialist who used thin slabs of stone in place of slates.

slatter. Person whose job was to prepare thin wood strips known as slats, lats or laiths in a wall, ready for the plasterer to begin work.

slattern. An untidy woman.

slave. The word derives from the Slavs who were once widely enslaved because of their hard working abilities and loyal temperaments. Though in some societies, slaves were roughly treated, in many they were treated well and some achieved later high status as free men and women. Some authorities believe that Slavian slaves were used to build the pyramids.

slay maker. Maker of wooden combs for weaving.

sled builder. Specialist woodworker who made industrial wooden sleds for towing by oxen or horses to carry heavy goods. (See also sledder.)

sledder. A carrier of goods uing an animal and a wooden sled. Also called a sledman. (See also sled builder.)

sledgeman. Industrial worker who transports goods using a wooden sledge.

sleymaker. Same as slaymaker.

slicker. Someone who finishes off in the treatment of raw leather or finished leather goods.

slipper. Production worker in a pottery who coated the pots with 'slip'.

slitter. A production worker in a pen factory who has the job of splitting the pen nibs.

sliver drawer. Mechanised rope factory worker.

sliverer. Cloth industry worker. Also worker in wood processing.

sloop owner. Owner of a small ship which was hired out for the carriage of goods etc.

slop shop keeper. Same as slopseller.

slop tailor. Someone who made new clothes from old ones or repaired them for resale.

slopper out. Lowly worker who empties dirty liquid containers.

slopseller. Human urine buyer/seller in the alum trade's 'slop-shops'. Sometimes a seller of old clothes i.e. 'sloppy clothing'.

slubber. Cotton spinning industry worker.

slubber doffer. Spinning industry worker who was responsible for putting on and taking off bobbins of thread.

sluggard waker. Minor church official who was responsible for getting people to attend church.

slum-scribbler. Low class poorly educated scrounger who made pocket money from writing letters etc for his neighbours. (See also screever.)

slungshot maker. Manufacturer of a special kind of shot for heavy guns or cannons, consisting of a normal shot with a loop or strap attached. This was used to carry ropes etc., long distances (i.e. for rescue or in battle).

small clothes taylor. Trouser manufacturer.

small man. Refuse collector who worked for a great(er) dustman.

smallcoal seller. Street seller of coal dust in the 18th century.

smallholder. Subsistence farmer with a very small area of land to cultivate.

smallware maker. Maker of small cloth, wood or metal items.

small-wear seller. Street seller of tapes, cotton reels and similar items.

smatter hauler. Small time criminal who specialised in stealing silk handkerchiefs from people's pockets.

smelter. Iron trade worker who extracted the raw metal from the dross in a furnace.

smitt manufacturer. Person who in rural areas would make and sell balls of clay ore used for the marking of sheep.

smock-frocker. Manufacturer of a coarse linen cloth (or the completed smock made from it) used by labourers and farmers.

smock maker, smocker. Person who made the traditional smocks once always worn by country men.

smoke house proprietor. Someone who preserves fish or meat for human food consumption.

smoke jack maker. Manufacturer originally of spits used for turning meat and driven by the current of air drawn up a chimney. Later, the manufacturer of cowls for the top of chimneys, which when blown by the wind would turn against it, so preventing smoke going down the chimney.

smoke sheet worker. See under sheet smoker.

smoker. Person who owned a smoke-house for smoking and preserving fish, meat, etc.

smugsmith. Colloquial term for a smuggler.

snake catcher. Woodman employed to catch adders or vipers. One New Forest snake catcher was Brusher Mills, who was still carrying out his trade in 1896.

snarer. Animal hunter using string, rope or metal snares.

snipper. Colloquial 19th century term for a tailor.

snob, snobscat. High class boot repairer.

snood fisherman. Sea fisherman using a line with other baited lines branching from it.

snow-man. Operator of a cargo boat known as a snow, being a vessel equipped with two masts like a brig and with a third mast at the back carrying a trysail.

snow warden. Official in charge of clearing streets of snow.

snuffer manufacturer/seller. Someone who deals in candle snuffers.

soap boiler. A skilled trade as a soap boiler had to know the correct mixtures and ingredients to make a variety of industrial and household soaps using fats, oils, quick-lime, soda and potash as well as the art of perfumery. Soap was once heavily taxed and soap boilers had to inform the excise officers 24 hours before making soap.

sock manufacturer. Originally the maker of a kind of very soft shoe often used by actors. Also, in the 19th century, a maker of ploughshares or a maker of short stockings.

socman. Same as sokeman.

sofett maker. Manufacturer of a piece of furniture shaped like a sofa, but much smaller.

soft potter. A potter who made earthenware items fired at a comparatively low temperature.

soft worker. Victorian criminal parlance for someone who passed forged notes.

sojourner. Travelling salesman. Also used to describe any visitor.

sokeman. A free landholding tenant who had the right to have his disputes heard in a court of law.

soldier monk. See under Templar and Hospitaller.

sole (press) cutter. Worker who operates a machine in a shoe factory.

solutus. Bachelor.

somnipathist. Usually a doctor, but sometimes a non-medical practitioner of mesmerism (hypnotism).

son in law. In census returns and other records, this may indicate a step son, or adopted son.

songsheet seller. A seller of self penned songs, often of a humorous or satirical nature. The songsheet seller was considered almost a beggar.

soper. Soap manufacturer.

sophomore. Colloquial term for a second year student at university (particularly in U.S.A.).

soror. Sister (usually meaning nun).

sorter. Cloth worker, also sorter of goods in other trades.

sortor. Same as sorter. Also a tailor.

sounder. Stone quarry worker who sounds cut stone with a pebble or a piece of iron to check that the piece of stone is sound throughout before it is cut. If it is declared unsound then the stone block is cast aside as waste.

sour wine dealer. Vinegar dealer.

souter. Shoemaker.

sow gelder. Unskilled street trader who sounded a horn (in the 18th century) to announce himself available for the castrating of pigs and other animals.

spa attendant. Same as spaw attendant.

spallier. Low grade light metal worker.

spar. A boxer.

spatterdash maker. Manufacturer of a kind of covering for the legs so as to protect from mud, etc.

spaw attendant. Attendant at a medicinal spa where visitors would 'take the waters' during the Victorian period especially.

Special Officer. Voluntary police officer who assists the main police. Also a member of the former Special Irish Branch of the police (formed around 1883 to deal with the 'Irish problems'). It later became Special Branch.

speciarius. Dealer in spices.

specksioneer. Crewmember of a whaling ship (and possibly other ships) in the early 1800s. (See also lose harpooner and fast harpooner.)

spencer. A person in charge of the spence (buttery or larder).

sperviter. Sparrow hawk trainer.

sphragist (ician/ologist). Scientific historian who specialised in dating old documents from the type of seal upon them.

spicer. Trader/dealer in spices.

spinner. Any cloth spinner.

spinster. Spinning wheel/loom/machine operator. (Anciently used in similar way to 'housewife'.)

spit (man/boy). A servant whose duty was to cook meat and continuously turn the spit over an open fire.

spittle man. Keeper of a hospital/hostel.

spleget maker/seller. Sewer of small cloths known as splegets, used to wash sores and treat wounds.

splitter. Slate quarry worker. Also a biscuit maker who splits pairs of biscuits that have been handled by the moulder and the stamper and passes them on to the chucker.

spokesman. Same as spokester.

spokester. Maker/repairer of wooden spokes for wheels.

sponsa. Housewife.

sponsus. Husband or householder.

spooler. Textile thread manufacturing worker.

spooner. Spoon maker.

sportarius. Maker of basketware.

spotter. A specialist worker at early dry-cleaners who would take out any stains left, by hand, after the dry cleaning process. The spotter's job was a skilled and qualified one. Also a military name for a lookout.

spout operator. Dock worker who loads grain onto ships using a large funnel.

sprag(ger). Person in charge of watching a cart, machinery or container to ensure it does not run away (i.e. down a slope). His task was to sprag the wheel or cogs by sticking a wooden spoke in and so stop the wheel or cog turning. (Hence, the term to 'sprag on someone' or to 'put a spoke in the works'.)

spurrer. Spur maker/mender.

spurrier. Same as spurrer.

squire. Gentleman with land.

stabular(ius). Stabler.

stacker. A stone quarry worker. Also a general term in factories for someone who stacks any sort of goods.

staddle maker. Maker of crutches for medical purposes. Also used generally for people who made pit and other types of props.

stage rigger. Same as stager.

stager. Man who erects staging on a building site, in a shipyard etc.

stagnator. An old term for a tin miner.

stagno. See under stango(e).

stainer. Glass dyer or wood stainer.

stallarius. Horse groom.

stallumius. Stall holder.

stamin supplier. Supplier of stamin, a kind of woollen material used for stuffing furniture etc.

stammel dyer. Dyer of a woollen cloth called stammel, which was coloured red with a dye of the same name.

stamper. (Many trades.) Anyone who stamps or impresses anything, e.g. leather. (See also under presser.)

stang maker. Pole maker.

stango(e). Someone whose duty it is to clean a pond, stock it with fish, etc. Also known as a stagno.

stanhope hirer. Hirer of a light two-wheeled carriage without a top and designed for only one person.

stannar(ius). Maker of pewter goods.

stapler. Merchant adventurer who dealt in wool. Also a wool sorter. Also dealer in basic foodstuffs, hence a 'staple' diet.

starcher. Person in the clothes manufacturing or cleaning businesses who stiffened cloth, using starch.

starter man. Man in a hunting party who handled the starter dogs whose purpose was to startle game such as pheasants, etc. (Sometimes called a startle man.)

station porter. In the days of steam railways, someone who would wheel passengers' luggage to and from trains free of charge.

stationer. Dealer in writing materials, paper etc.

stationmaster. In charge of a railway station.

statist. Politician.

statuary. Sculptor specialising in carving or manufacturing free standing statues. Statues were classed by size, the largest being 'Colossuses' (e.g. the Colossus of Rhodes).

stavemaker. Maker of wooden strips for constructing barrels. Also a fence post maker. Also a walking stick maker.

stay maker. Maker of stays for women's underclothing. Also (rarely) a stout rope maker.

steam coal merchant. Specialist dealer in a high grade industrial coal which was very hard and burned with great heat, producing very little smoke or ash.

steam engine driver. Railway train driver.

steam lorry/wagon driver. Driver of a road vehicle propelled by steam.

steam navvy driver. Operator of a large steam driven machine used in quarrying operations, particularly in the chalk industry.

steam still manager. Furnace/still manager in the early petroleum industry.

steam tram driver. Driver of a tram drawn by a separate steam engine (which looked like a gypsy caravan with a long funnel). The last one is believed to have been scrapped in Birmingham in 1906.

steamer driver. Driver of any early steam propelled vehicle.

steel fixer. Building industry worker where steel is used in the construction.

steening building. Specialist builder who built the steening, (brick or stone wall lining for cesspools, vats, etc.).

steeper. Someone who soaks a product in liquid during its processing. (See flax steeper.)

steersman. Same as coxswain.

steganographist. Someone who compiled, encrypted or decoded coded messages.

stelographist. Specialist stonemason who inscribed characters and writing on pillars.

stenographer. Writer in shorthand.

stenter operator. Operator of a cloth stretching machine.

stenterer. Same as stenter operator.

stentor. Any person with a powerful voice. Often employed to address large gatherings before loudspeakers were invented.

step lad/boy. A youngster employed to assist passengers up and down from coaches.

stereocromist. Specialist wall painter using a method which was supposed to supersede fresco painting. The method, using murals, proved unpopular and was short-lived.

stereotyper. Maker of printing plates known as stereotypes. The method became virtually extinct in the 1970s due to the production of more modern methods of printing.

stereotypographer. A printer who used stereotypes.

steriliser. Worker in the meat industry involved with the sterilising of tinned meats or potted meat in jars.

sterquill man. Manual worker in charge of a dung hill.

stevedore. Docker.

steward. High manorial officer responsible for transactions and record keeping. In modern usage, a person who attends to passengers on a train, plane, boat etc.

stickler. A sidesman in duelling contests who inspected the swords etc. before the fight to ensure all was in order for a fair contest.

stiddy man. A blacksmith, particularly, but not exclusively, a horse shoeing smith. Also called a stithy man.

stigweard. Anglo-Saxon steward.

stingo maker/seller. Manufacturer or seller of any renowned strong pungent beer or liquor in the 19th and early 20th centuries.

still room maid. General maid who made tea, washed up, laid the table and sometimes carried tea to the rooms.

still room worker. Tea maker in a large household or hotel. Sometimes a worker in a distillery.

stillier manufacturer. Maker of balance scales.

stink trap maker. Generally a carpenter or plumber who specialised in fitting valves or other devices to 'soak-away' type cess pits under dwellings (on order) to prevent the smell of sewage returning into the dwelling.

stinter. Any worker who was allowed to go home as soon as his task was finished as part of his employment rules.

stipendiary. Any person who received an annual payment for services given, especially, but not exclusively, a clergyman.

stirrup maker. Maker of horse-riding stirrups. Also a maker of pumps for pumping water.

stithy man. Same as stiddy man above.

stoaker. Person employed to stop or choke off water, gas, etc., in any industry.

stock and foil tallyman. 15th century accountant who kept accounts by notches on a 'stock' of wood. This was then split giving a counter 'foil'.

stock maker. Skilled worker in the gun making industry.

stocking weaver. The first woven stockings were produced in England in 1564 by William Rider who had brought the idea back from Italy. Prior to this they were sewn from pieces of cloth. Machines to weave stockings from wool etc began to appear generally towards the latter part of the 16th century.

stockin(g)er. Maker of stockings. Also a framework knitter or weaver using a machine.

stoker. Someone who shovelled fuel into a boiler.

stone banker. Someone who dresses stone blocks.

stone crusher. Unskilled labourer in a stone crushing plant where rocks were treated for putting on roads etc.

stone cutter. Stone worker who cut large slabs of stone. Sometimes just a stonemason.

stone dresser. Stone quarry worker.

stone glasser. Stoneworker who polishes stone surfaces (especially marble).

stone picker. Labourer who picked and removed stones and rocks from a farmer's fields.

stone planer. Quarry worker.

stonehand. A printer who sets loose type into pages.

stoneman. Any man responsible for highway maintenance (often a stonewarden).

stonewaller. Dry stone wall builder.

stonewarden. An official position with responsibility for road maintenance.

stoneworker. Quarry worker.

stoomer. Person in the wine industry that induced a second fermentation (called stooming), generally using bags of herbs or other substances of which often he alone knew the composition.

stoup(e) maker. Manufacturer of flagons for holding liquids. Also a stonemason who specialised in making church fonts.

stover man. Agricultural worker responsible for cattle fodder known as stover.

A wire rope factory in 1929. Strand closing was one of the many operations entailed during the making of wire ropes. In the above scene, a strand closer can be seen operating the strand closing machine in the centre of a wire rope making factory. Around him in the large factory are machines carrying out other processes which were involved in the making of the final product.

stowyer. Someone responsible for packing something away (e.g. luggage or nets).

strake fitter. Wheelwright who put the 'strake' or metal band around the wheel.

strand closer. Operator of a machine making steel ropes. See illustration.

stravaiger. A tramp.

straw hat maker. Specialist manufacturer of straw hats from ready plaited or braided straw ribbons. He earned less than the strawplaiter who provided him with his raw materials.

straw joiner. Roof thatcher.

straw yard officer. Officer of a refuge for the poor and homeless.

strawplaiter. Maker of objects from straw. Also manufacturer of woven straw ribbons used by straw hat makers.

Though the straw-plaiter in this picture was photographed in Florence, Italy in the early 1900s, the contraption and techniques she is using were carrried out in Britain and indeed throughout Europe on a widespread basis until the days of World War I.

stray. See under waif.

streaker. Someone who 'laid out' dead bodies and prepared them for burial.

street crier. Any one of the once numerous street sellers who would walk the streets of large towns and cities crying out what wares they had for sale. See illustration.

The following is an extract from an article that appeared in the *Spectator* magazine of 18th December 1711:

'There is nothing which more astonishes a foreigner, and frights a country Squire, than the Cries of London. My good friend Sir Roger often declares, that he cannot get them out of his head or to go to sleep for them, the first week that he is in town...

The cries of London may be divided into Vocal and Instrumental. As for the latter they are at present under a very great disorder. A Freeman of London has the privelege of disturbing a whole street for an hour together with the twanking of a Brass-Kettle or a frying pan.

The Watchman's thump at midnight startles us in our beds, as much as the breaking-in of a thief. The Sowgelders horn has indeed something musicle in it, but this is seldom heard within the Liberties...

Vocal cries are of a much larger extent and indeed so full of incongruities and barbarisms that we appear a distracted city to foreigners, who do not comprehend the meaning of such enormous outcries.

Milk is generally sold in a note above *E la*, and in so exceedingly shrill that it often sets our teeth on edge.

The chimney sweeper is confined to no certain pitch. He sometimes utters himself in the deepest base and sometimes in the sharpest trebble, sometimes in the highest and sometimes in the lowest note of the gamut.

The same observation might be made on the retailers of small-coal, not to mention broken glasses or brickdust. In these therefore, and the like cafes, it should be my care to sweeten and mellow the voices of these itinerant tradesmen, before they make their appearance in our streets, as also to accomodate their cries to their respective wares; and to take care in particular that those may not make the most noise who have the least to sell which is very observable in the vendors of cardmatches...

Some of these last-mentioned musicians are so very loud in the sale of these trifling manufactures that an honest splenetick Gentleman of my aquaintance bargained with one of them never to come into the street where he lived: But what was the effect of this contract? Why, the whole tribe of Card-matchers which frequent that quarter, passed by his door the very next day in hopes of being bought off after the same manner...

I must not here omit one particular absurdity which runs through the whole vociferous generation, and which renders their cries very often not only incommodious, but altogether useless to the publick. I mean that idle accomplishment which they all of them aim at of crying so as not to be understood. Whether or not they have learned this from several of our affected singers, I will not take upon me to say, but most certain it is, that people know the wares they deal in rather than by their tunes

"SHINE YER BOOTS"

"LARGE SILVER EELS"

"FRESH FISH"

"MYRTLES AND ROSES"

Street criers. The term street crier was applied to any street seller who cried out what they were selling to passers by. Most trades had their own particular cry, though there were many variations. Some were varied so much that they were unintelligible. However, they acted as a trade mark for the particular seller and drew customers to him or her. Here is a selection of street traders with their usual 'cry'.

"FINE STRAWBERRIES"

"ANY NEEDLES AND THREADS"

"OLE CLOSE"

"FINE LARGE CUCUMBERS"

"LIVE GEESE- LIVE GEESE"

than by their words, insomuch that I have sometimes seen a country boy run out to buy apples of a bellows mender, and ginger-bread from a grinder of knives and scissars.'

street Italian. A Victorian street salesman, generally but not always Italian in origin, who sold fine art and quality pictures.

street orderly. 18th century organised street cleaners who dressed in uniform and were armed either with a brush and dust-pan or a sweeping brush and barrow.

street urchin. Same as urchin.

street ward. Officer once in charge of streets and responsible for ensuring others kept them clean and safe.

streetman/boy. Street cleaner.

stretcher. Fabric industry worker.

striker. Same as a corn striker. Also a blacksmith's assistant. See illustration.

stringer. Stringer of bows (for bows and arrows).

strip roller. Tin plate worker in a factory.

stripper. Wool trade worker. Also a trade description used in various trades.

strosser manufacturer. Manufacturer of close fitting trousers used as underclothing in the 16th century.

strouding weaver. Weaver of a coarse cloth called strouding.

structor. Builder or constructor.

stuckler. Farm worker with the job of stacking sheaves of corn together.

stuff gownsman. Junior barrister (colloquial).

stuff weaver. Weaver of coarse flax.

stupe supplier. Person selling bandages medicated with warm herbs or drugs.

sty keeper. Pig man. Often this term was used because of superstition (see under grunter man).

subaltern. Any inferior or subordiante worker or officer.

subchantor. A high position in an abbey. He was assistant to the chantor. He ordered such things as vestments, candles etc and was in charge of the abbey bells, abbey seal and the cemetery. He presided at funeral services. He was also known as the secretary or sacrist.

sub porter. In an abbey, assistant to the porter. He was generally the abbey gatekeeper.

sub prior. In effect he carried out all of the duties of the prior, keeping a watch on the conduct of the abbey's inhabitants. It was a very powerful position as for all intents and purposes he was in charge of the abbey except in cases of emergency or when major decisions had to be taken.

substitute. Official title given to a person who had been sent in place of another selected by ballot to serve in the militia.

A Striker at work

16th century woodcut showing a striker at work. Even in medieval times, weights and measures were strictly enforced. The job of the striker was to fill round standard measures with corn (or other grain). This would then be packed down and levelled off with a tool provided for the purpose. Once this had been done, sacks would be filled and sealed with an official mark before being sold to the purchaser. Though of ancient origin, this method of measuring grain was used on an unofficial basis right up to the 20th century. The container used to measure the grain was known as a bushel. Unfortunately until the standardising of measurements under the modern 'Imperial Standards', bushels were of different sizes in different counties. Sacks were standardised under Edward III to contain 26 stone (364 pounds). Sack measurements stayed the same until World War I, when they were reduced in size to allow women workers to carry them. This was of course due to the shortage of manual labour.

succentor. Choir members who sings bass.

sucksmith. Smith specialising in making plough-share blades.

sudatory attendant. Attendant in a sweating bath or sudatory (similar to Turkish baths).

suffragette. Member of an actively political women's movement who fought for the right of women to vote.

sugar boiler. Boils sugar in the confectionery trade.

sulky hirer. Hirer of sulkys, a light two wheeled carriage which carried a single person.

summer merchant. Builders' merchant who supplied summers, large stone or timber supports or beams.

summus judex. Chief magistrate in medieval times.

sumner. Legal officer.

sumpter(man). Carrier of furniture and sometimes clothing by horse.

Sunday school teacher. Someone who gave religious instruction to children for one or two hours each Sunday. Sunday schools were sometimes formal, sometimes a form of entertainment with games etc being mixed with religious teaching. Teachers ranged from clergymen to local volunteer housewives.

sunn merchant. Supplier of a material similar to hemp, used for making canvas and ropes.

super. Abbreviation for either superintendent or supernumerary.

supercargo. Merchant ship officer in charge of cargo.

superintendent. The person in charge or an overseer.

supernumerary. A worker who is over and above the normal number of people employed for any work purpose. Once used extensively in the theatre industry as a substitute for the modern term 'extras'.

surface man/boy/woman. Someone in the mining industry who worked above ground.

surrogate. Deputy judge, especially an ecclesiastical one.

surtout maker. Manufacturer of overcoats (surtouts or surcoats).

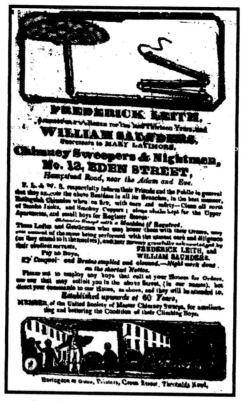

A rare surviving poster for a chimney sweep and nightman. The above poster advertised the Sweep and Nightman services of Frederick Leith and William Saunders of 12 Eden Street, Hampstead Road, 'Near the Adam & Eve', London. Though the poster isn't dated, it is believed to date from the mid 1800s. Leith and Saunders took over the business of Mary Latimore claiming that the service had been 'established upwards of 60 years'. The wording of the poster says: – "F.L. & W.S. respectfully inform their Friends and the Public in general that they execute the above Business in all its Branches, in the best manner, Extinguish Chimnies when on fire, with care and safety – Clean all sorts of Smoke Jacks, and Smokey Coppers; clean cloths kept for the Upper Apartments, and small boys for Register Stoves. Chimnies swept with a Machine if required. Those Ladies and Gentlemen who may honor them with their Orders, may rest assured of the same being performed with the utmost care and diligence (as they attend to it themselves), and their favours gratefully acknowledged by their obedient servants, FREDERICK LEITH, and WILLIAM SAUNDERS. Pay no boys, Cesspools and Drains emptied and cleaned – Night work done on the shortest notice. Please not to employ any boys that call at your Houses nor any that may solicit you in the Street, (in our names), but direct your commands to our House, as above, and they will be attended to. MEMBER of the United Society of Master Chimney Sweeps, for ameliorating and bettering the Condition of their Climbing Boys." *The poster was printed by Bevingdon & Gunn, Green Street, Theobald's Road, London.*

Surveyor of Highways. Equivalent to the modern County Surveyor.

sutler. Supplier of provisions, especially to an army on the move.

suttor. Stitcher (usually of shoes, i.e. cobbler).

suttor pannarius. Stitcher of cloth.

suttor vestarius. Stitcher of clothing i.e. a tailor.

suzerain. A feudal lord.

swager. Craftsman who beat sheets of pewter on a metal pattern (a swage) covered with soft leather. (See also pewter beater.)

swailer. Corn miller.

swain. A youth (e.g. a country swain).

swale. Corn miller.

swamper. Labourer who drains/clears swampy ground. Also someone who wipes down tables in a bar.

swealer. Corn miller.

sweep. Chimney cleaner. See illustration.

sweeper (out). Manual worker employed to sweep out a factory or other floor.

swellmaker. Maker of shallow baskets.

swell-mobsman. A criminal in Victorian England.

swineherd(er). Originally an official position to oversee local pigkeeping income from abbey farms. Later a common pigkeeper.

swineyard. Same as swineherd.

swing rioter. Also known as a machine breaker. Member of an organised band of protestors in the agricultural riots of 1830 when farm machinery, hay stacks and threshing machines were burned or destroyed. Farmers received threatening letters signed 'Swing' indicating that they would be hanged. Many of the ringleaders were caught and hanged themselves, though others were transported.

switchboard operator. Telephone operator who connects callers to each other. See illustration.

Switchboard operator. Staff at Faraday House Telephone Exchange, London in 1932. International operators at a London telephone exchange can be seen manually connecting calls using a system of plugs and sockets. Standing behind them are senior operators who are ready to step in if any problems occur.

sword cutler. Maker of swords.

syndicus. General term for a legal officer or official such as a burgess or legal advocate.

syther(ator). Harp player.

T

tabbinet mechant. Merchant who dealt in tabbinet, a kind of fine damask fabric made from silk and wool.

tabby mixer. Dealer or supplier of tabby, an old-fashioned type of concrete made from a mixture of shells and gravel.

tabby weaver. Weaver of tabby, a kind of wavy-textured cloth usually made of silk, but also of other fabrics.

tabellarius. Letter carrier.

tabellio. Official notary or witness to legal documents.

tabernar(ius). Shop or tavern keeper.

tabernius. Tavern keeper.

tabler. Someone who takes in lodgers. Occasionally used for a lodger.

tabor player. Drummer who plays with one hand whilst playing a pipe with the other.

tabularius. Keeper of an archive and/or a public notary.

tacket maker. Manufacturer of small nails with a large head called tackets, now called tacks.

tackle maker. Used in many industries to describe someone who makes or fixes equipment, but especially used in a shipyard or on a ship.

Tabor player.

tackler. Mill overseer.

tackling agent. Supplier of sails, ropes and ship's furniture. Usually employed to fit out a ship.

tag rag. Equivalent to the modern term 'tow-rag' meaning a low class, despicable or worthless person.

tail. Tail males and tail females were those who were determined as people who could inherit freehold land under an 'entail' inheritance which limited the persons who could become heirs.

tail end Charlie. Colloquial term for a rear gunner in a plane of the Second World War.

talliator. Tailor.

tallier. A tally man. Anyone who counts or checks by number or weight, originally using two tally sticks cut with notches, one being the tally foil, the other the counter foil.

tallow chandler. Candlemaker. He was subject to the same taxes and excise restrictions as the soap boiler.

tally shop owner. Owner of a clothes shop where those with good credit could obtain goods and pay for them on a weekly basis.

tallyman. Inspector or a counter of something (e.g bags of coal onto ships). Also a credit salesman.

tam(kin) maker. Worker in an armoury who made tams or tamkins (stoppers for cannons). See also tampion maker.

tammy (taminy) weaver. Weaver of a woollen cloth called tammy (taminy).

tamper. Worker who flattens down something, often used in road construction, e.g. hand tampers and machine tampers (who used a machine for the purpose). Also the person who puts explosives in a hole bored in a quarry. Also a small time wheeler-dealer in the 1800s.

tampion maker. Manufacturer of cylindrical wooden stops for cannons and guns. See also tam(kin) maker.

tan yard man. Labourer at a leather works. See illustration.

tankard bearer. An official who tested water supplies or the quality of beer etc.

tannarius/tannerius. Leather curer.

tannator. Same as tannarius.

tanner. Leather curer.

tap man/woman. Seller of beer etc straight from the barrel.

taper maker. Someone who made tapers used for lighting lamps, tobacco pipes etc.

Tan yard workers in a 1920s warehouse. Tan yard man is a general term given to anyone who worked in a leatherworks who was not directly involved in the production of the leather. In the above picture, tan yard men are seen working in the warehouse stacking finished hides using electric lifting gear.

taper weaver. Candle wick weaver.

tapetiarius. Carpet maker/seller.

tapiser. Tapestry maker/upholsterer/carpet maker.

tapley. Barrel worker (various jobs).

tapper. Publican. Also a wheel tapper.

tapping table worker. Worker in the chocolate industry who would tap the full moulds to release trapped bubbles of air.

taproom attendant. A man or woman employed in a public house to draw the customers' drinks from barrels.

tapster. Same as tap man/woman.

tar. A common sailor, often known as a Jack tar.

target maker. Manufacturer of targets, usually out of straw for the use of bowmen.

tasker. Reaper or thresher.

tatau artist. Early title for a skin tattooist, tatau being the original Tahitian word for skin decoration.

tatter. Collector of rags and bones, old jam jars etc. Also someone skilled in tatting, a form of making lace from knotted string etc.

tattie picker. (Pronounced tay-tee picker.) See under potato picker.

tauromacher. A 19th/early 20th century English term for a bull-fighter.

taverner. Inn keeper.

taw maker/seller. Early manufacturer of taws, small round clay balls with which children played the game of marbles. This was generally a subsistence form of employment for those who were disabled or otherwise unable to carry out normal work.

tawer. White leather maker/worker.

taxidermist. See preserver.

tazzler. In the textile industry, a woman who would make tassels on shawls etc by hand twirling the wool.

teacher. Quite often this indicates a nonconformist church minister.

teamer, teamster. Cattle/horse team driver.

teasler. Cloth industry worker.

teazle. Teazle growers, pickers, sorters, stackers, balers etc were all concerned with the provision of teazle plant heads used in the textile industry for raising the nap on textiles.

tector. Plasterer.

teemer. Ladle pourer of molten metal in a foundry.

teetotum maker. Small-time manufacturer of a children's toy resembling a spinning top with squared off sides. Sometimes also used for gambling in the form of 'put and take' spinners which carried a message on each side such as 'put one', 'take one', 'all put', 'take two', etc. referring to coins in the centre of the table.

tegularius, tegulator. Bricklayer or tile layer. Tegul is Latin for tile.

teinoscope maker. Manufacturer of an early optical instrument which used prisms.

telegrapher. Operator of radio telegraph equipment for sending messages.

telephonist. Someone who worked in the old telephone exchanges, connecting calls and answering enquiries. Also called an operator or telephone exchange worker.

teleprinter operator. Originally an operator of a typewriter which electronically printed out a message on strips of paper tape at a distant office. These were used for sticking on telegrams which were then delivered by a telegraph boy, also known as a telegram boy, on a bicycle.

tellarius. Tailor.

teller. General term given to someone who counts something, ranging from a bank teller who counts money whilst dealing with customers, to a parliamentary teller who counts the division of votes.

telonarius. Tax collector.

temperer. Metal worker who tempers metal to a specific degree of hardness.

Templar. Member of the Knights Templars who were set up in medieval times to fight a religious war in the Holy Land. They were greatly involved in the monastic movement, many of them being termed 'soldier monks', combining religious fervour with military and political might. They became over-powerful and finally suffered persecution, being eventually banned. Secret meetings continued and their followers are said to have developed into modern 'secret societies' such as the Freemasons.

tempse bread baker. Supplier of a superior kind of bread made from extra finely sieved flour, supplied to the rich. (A tempse was a sieve.)

tenant in chief. In ancient times, a high ranking landowner, directly below the monarch, who would in turn have his own sub-tenants. (See also rentier.)

tent maker. Apart from those connected with making tents for camping purposes, the term was also used before the 20th century by manufacturers of bandages made from rolled lint or linen, used especially in warfare, to press into gaping wounds to staunch the flow of blood.

tenter. Cotton or cloth worker. Also same as a tenter hooker.

tenter frame maker. Maker of frames for bleaching or drying cloth, sails etc in the open air.

tenter hooker. Someone who hangs cloth out for drying on tenter frames.

Teutonic Knight. A member of a branch of knighthood organised in Palestine around 1192 which invested its knights with the honours of the Knights Templar and Knights Hospitaller. It was officially abolished by Napoleon in 1809 but is said to have continued in secrecy.

tew contractor. General contractor who through a chain of contacts would supply anything required for any purpose, the word 'tew' signifying 'anything' but literally meaning a chain used for towing purposes.

tewel maker Manufacturer of tubes, pipes and funnels used for conducting smoke, heat, etc.

textor. Weaver/ textile maker.

thacker(ey). A thatcher.

thane. Old English high ranking position similar to gesith.

thatcher. Thatcher of house roofs with straw.

thegn. Same as thane.

theologus. Preacher/theologian.

theow. Anglo-Saxon convict or slave who had no rights.

thesmothete. A legislator or law-giver.

thill maker. Shaft maker, particularly of shafts for horse carriages.

third-borough. Ancient law officer with the rank of under-constable.

thole maker. Specialist smith who made metal pins for use in boat rowlocks, fixing blades in tool handles, etc.

thrall. Slave.

thresher. Farm worker who threshed the corn (first by hand, later by machine). Also known as a flailer.

thredonist. Musician/writer of thredonies, songs of lamentation prepared for (often important) persons' funerals.

throster. A silk worker/silk thrower (generally male).

throstle maker. Early 20th century spinning machine manu-facturer. The throstle was named from the fact that it made a sound like a thrush, a bird also called a throstle.

thrower. Potter or pottery worker.

throwster. Silk thread winder who thickens thread by twisting it. The word comes from the Anglo-Saxon 'thrawan' meaning to twist or turn.

tibialis confector. Knitter using a knitting frame.

tibialis factor. Same as tibialis confector.

tick (bed) maker. Bed mattress maker who manufactured a tick bed consisting of a kind of case or cover containing feathers, wool or other soft loose materials. Also called a ticken maker.

ticket of leave man. A transported convict who through good conduct and hard work obtained a 'ticket of leave' to enter paid employment outside the confines of his imprisonment.

tickneyman. Travelling pot seller.

tic-tac man. Bookmaker on a racecourse.

tide gauger. A guide who checked tides for those travelling over the seashore or a causeway. Also a tide waiter.

tide waiter. Customs inspector/harbour official who boarded ships entering and leaving 'on the tide'.

tideman. An earlier title for a tide waiter.

tie maker. Used in many trades but usually someone who made wooden railway joints.

tied tenant. In a public house, a publican who must sell only one brewery's products. On a farm, a labourer whose home is provided by his employer only as long as he works for that farm.

tignar(ius). Carpenter.

tille thecker. Tiler of house roofs. See also thecker.

tiller. Gardener, horticulturalist, farmer or ploughman.

Tiller Girl. Member of a once famous group of high kicking stage dancers known as the Tiller Girls.

tillier. Anglo-Saxon farmer.

tillman. Same as tiller.

tilt boat operator. A waterman carrying luggage and passengers in a boat of 15 tons burthen (especially between Gravesend and London Bridge). These were strictly regulated. Any tilt boat operator whose passenger drowned because of overcrowding of his vessel was liable to transportation.

time and motion man. Someone employed by a company to obtain the most cost effective production techniques by studying the workers on the job, timing their work operations etc.

time keeper. Person responsible for ensuring workers arrived and left on time.

timocrat. A ruler who was also a member of the aristocracy.

tin boiler. Worker who boiled tins of food after sealing in order to sterilise them.

tin dresser. Surface worker in a tin mine who broke and washed the ore.

tin man. Same as tinner.

tinning worker. Worker in a factory producing tinned food.

tin plate worker. Manufacturer of metal items from tin plate, a flat metal sheet consisting of iron coated or sandwiched with tin.

tinctor. Dyer.

tinker. Travelling salesman dealing in tin pots and pans.

tinner. A tin miner, worker or whitesmith. See illustration.

A tinner at work, mending a pan for a visiting housewife. A tinner was sometimes known as a tin man. As well as working with tin, he also used other light metals in his work of manufacturing and mending such items as tin baths, pans, bowls, toilet pans, etc. If in his work he also enamelled the tin objects, he would be known as a whitesmith.

tinter. Paint mixer or someone who coloured photographs and prints by hand.

tippet maker. Manufacturer of a kind of narrow scarf used as a shoulder covering which fastened round the neck.

tippler. Publican.

tipstaff. Warden or constable.

tipster. Man who made his living at race-courses selling slips of paper with the names of horses he 'knew' would win because of so called inside knowledge.

tireman/woman. Costumier or someone who dealt in some way with dressing people (attire-er).

Tiron monk. Member of a little known order of monks with only a few religious houses in Britain.

tirret maker. Specialist blacksmith, often attached to an army or prison, who would make handcuffs, manacles, etc.

tissue weaver. Weaver of a decorative cloth interwoven with coloured, silver or gold threads (19th century).

tithe protector. Official who called to collect farming tithes in the 19th century, particularly in Ireland.

tithingman. A constable.

tobacco grower. British growers of tobacco were once common following the naturalisation of the plant in Southern Britain and Ireland by Raleigh and others. They were stamped out by the time of Charles II as it interfered with import revenues being received from the new American colonies.

tobacco roller, tobacco spinner. Cigar maker.

tobacco twister. Woman who operated a machine to twist tobacco into ropes before steaming it to make it turn black.

tocsin man. Person responsible in any work situation for sounding or ringing an alarm.

tod(d). Animal hunter (especially vermin).

tofter. Someone who owns a building with a small amount of land used as a small-holding (see also cottager).

toftman. A cottager, i.e. someone who owned or occupied a building with a small toft of land.

toggery proprietor. Clothes shop owner.

toiler. Lace maker.

toilet seller. Seller (often at fairs, etc.) of small cloths made from toilinette, a fabric of wool or linen and cross woven with silk or other threads. These were known as toilets and were used to cover dressing tables, etc.

toison dealer. Dealer in sheep fleeces.

toller/toll keeper. Someone who collected fees to use a road, bridge etc.

tolonarius. Collector of tolls, fees and taxes.

tommy, Tommy Atkins. Soldier. Colloquial name given by the British to their own soldiers in both world wars.

tommy shop keeper. Keeper of a building providing food and beer for labourers and railway workers. The workers' contract often included a clause that they should only use the tommy shop for refreshments. Hence the employer received some sort of payment and prices were always higher than elsewhere.

tonellar(ius). Cooper.

tonite manufacturer. Pronounced 'toe-nite', tonite was a form of explosive made from pulverised gun-cotton in the early 20th century.

tonsor. Barber (not a barber surgeon).

tool helver. Same as helver.

tooth cutter. A specialist watch or clock maker who cuts the teeth in the wheels of the timepiece.

toothdrawer. Someone such as a blacksmith who would also offer his services to pull out a bad or painful tooth.

top sawyer. Same as topman.

toparch. The principal person in any government or country regardless of rank or title.

tophet keeper. Gaoler. Tophet literally means hell, but was generally used to decribe gaols. The name became corrupted in later years to hoppet.

topman. Timber sawyer with a long saw requiring a 'top man' and a 'bottom man'. Also the man in a crow's nest on top of the ship's mast.

topper. One of the jobs in a spinning mill.

topsman. Foreman, especially when droving animals.

torque maker. Manufacturer of bracelets etc from twisted metals.

totter. A collector of recycleable items for resale (especially on waste tips).

tower wagon driver. Same as overhead wagon driver.

town bellman, town crier. Public announcer who used a bell or rattle to draw attention to himself.

town husband. Nickname for an old parish officer whose job was to collect maintenance for illegitimate children.

town traveller. Travelling salesman.

town waiter. Customs/excise official.

townsman. A kind of mobile shop that delivered from a town shop to customers in the country, selling from a van or cart.

toxophilite. An archer, particularly used in sporting situations.

traditor. Term used in the late 19th century for both a delivery man and a traitor.

trafficker. General term for a tradesman of any kind.

trail bearer, train bearer. A servant who would walk behind an important person carrying the end of a trailing cloak or dress to stop it being soiled by mud and dirt.

trambler. Tin ore worker who washed the ore using a frame and a shovel.

tram(m)el fisherman. Professional sea trawler fisherman whose boat has a framework at the stern to lift and lower the nets.

tramp(er). Vagabond. Also a trampler. Also an out of work wool-comber in search of work at other establishments. It was the custom to provide a bench at wool combing shops for these tramps. If no work was available the man 'on the tramp' would be given a penny from a special fund contributed by workers.

tramp owner. Owner of a ship chartered to carry cargo. It operated under an agreement called a charter party. The owner placed the ship at the disposal of a charterer.

tramphouse manager. Someone who managed an establishment giving aid to vagrants.

trampler. Cloth worker/washer/dyer who walks on cloth in a liquid. Rarely used for a lawyer.

tranqueter. Hoop maker.

transrotulator. A medieval customs clerk.

tranter. Travelling pedlar with horse and cart.

trapanner. Animal trapper, i.e. a hunter.

trapezita. Banker.

traunter. Same as tranter.

travers. Toll collector.

trawler man. Professional fisherman working from a boat which drags its nets along the sea bottom.

treadmiller. Convicted criminal sentenced to work on a 'labour machine'.

treasurer. In an abbey he was the bursar.

treen dealer. Dealer in wooden objects.

treenail maker. Manufacturer of specialist copper nails for horticulture, forestry and shipbuilding. Also, maker of wooden pegs used in place of metal nails in shipbuilding.

trencher maker. Specialist baker who made trenchers (edible plates from bread dough). Later carpenters who made wooden trenchers.

treowe. Old English colloquial title for a well respected servant or retainer. The word actually means faithful.

trepanner. A surgeon specialising in opening the skull. Also a brush maker who used the 'trepanning' method to manufacture quality hair and other brushes by securing each set of bristles with wire drawn through a channel and knotted through a hole.

tribunus muiles. Army captain.

tributer. Cornish tin miner who received a 'tribute' (a share of the value of tin mined, rather than a wage).

trigiter. An entertainer, usually a juggler. (Various spellings such as trujedeter, trijetta, etc.)

Trinitarian. A member of a minor religious order with only ten religious houses in Britain. It followed the Augustinian rule.

tripe dresser. Someone who scrubs and boils the lining of animal stomachs, which were once served regularly as a cheap delicacy with vinegar or onions.

trivia (trivium) master. Grammar school schoolmaster after the Reformation who taught what was then the equivalent of the modern Three Rs (reading, writing and 'rithmetic). At that time the 'trivium' or 'threefold course' consisted of the subjects Latin grammar, rhetoric and logic, though in reality other subjects were also taught.

troll(er). Fisherman employing a method of catching fish using a circular movement of his boat to trap the fish in his net.

trolley man/driver. Driver of a tram or trolley usually guided by (originally) tracks in the road and later overhead electric wires.

tron(er). Person in charge of an official weighing machine.

trone worker. Steelyard worker. Also a person who clears drains.

trooper. Though used to describe any soldier, the term originally meant a cavalry member of a private army.

tropist. Academic who interpreted texts of scriptures in a rhetorical or non-literal sense.

trouper. Travelling player, actor or musician.

troubadour. Later name for a trouver(e).

trouver(e). Travelling singer of ballads.

trucher. Same as trucker.

truck driver. Driver of a heavy goods carrying vehicle.

trucker. Originally an interpreter. Also, a merchant who traded using the barter system (19th century). Later, a truck driver.

truncheoneer. Guard, watchman or army member armed only with a wooden truncheon.

trunk-hose manufacturer. Maker of 18th century breeches that were wide, short and gathered in at the knees.

trunk maker. Maker of boxes, travelling cases, buckets and all sorts of containers from wood and leather. Strong leather buckets were used in fighting fires and the trunk maker usually supplied these on a regular basis.

try worker. Worker in a try-works where blubber from the whaling industry was converted to oil.

tryfer meat seller. Seller of meat killed in the Christian fashion (as opposed to kosher meat killed in the Jewish fashion). Tryfer meat sellers were usually only referred to as such when they traded in a Jewish quarter of a city.

tub maker. Maker of wooden bath tubs (usually a side-line of barrel makers).

tub thumper. Colloquial name for a street corner preacher or speaker.

tubber. Same as tub maker. Also a mine worker (tubbing worker) responsible for building and maintaining the lining of mine shafts.

tucker. Cloth cleaner/finisher. Net or muslin maker. A manufacturer of rapiers.

tuft. A nobleman's son. The name derives from a tuft once attached to his cap to distinguish him as such at university.

tuft-hunter. British university slang for ordinary students who sought out the company of the wealthy fellow students who wore caps with gold tassels or 'tufts'. The wealthy students were known for their excessive drinking, gambling and cock fighting activities.

tugman. Operator of a river tug-boat.

tumbler. An acrobat.

tumbrel man. A man who operates a dung cart.

tupant. Medieval term for a person whose work involved excavation.

turf cutter/seller. Rural tradesman who would cut and dry squares of grass turf or moorland peat for use as fuel or roofing material.

turgeman. Ancient interpreter (originally between the Greek and Hebrew languages. Also called a meturgeman and a drago(man).

turncock. Man with the responsibility for turning a water supply on or off. Also known as a waterer.

Two very old printing blocks which were used as trademarks by early printers. Moveable type was used on the continent long before it found its way to Britain. Originally each page of a publication would be printed separately by hand using large presses as shown in the woodcut blocks above. Each letter of type would be set in a 'galley' ready for producing a page. A piece of paper would be laid upon it and the heavy press pulled down to create an impression. As paper was very expensive, there was little room for making mistakes during this time-consuming printing process.

Building up the layers of rubber on a tyre. When car tyres were made by hand, the tyre moulder would build up the layers of rubber before the tyre was cured in hot water. Next, holes would be punched for the valves and the valves inserted. Finally the laps of rubber would be sealed with rubber and the 'lap seams' would be vulcanized.

turner, turnarius. Wood or metal worker.

turnkey. Warder in a prison.

turnover. An apprentice of any trade who has been transferred from one master to another.

turnpike man. Collector of fees to use a turnpike road.

turnspit maker. Manufacturer of various contraptions for turning a spit for roasting meat over an open fire.

turribus. Specialised builder of towers.

tussore seller. Seller of imported Indian silk produced from the tussah moth and not the silk worm.

tuteler/tutelary. An official guardian, usually of a minor.

tutrix. A female guardian of a girl or young woman who may or may not also teach her.

tweeny. Young lower grade servant who acted as a general assistant to the other servants. Also a servant who worked both 'upstairs' and 'downstairs' in a household.

twigger. Low class basket maker using ordinary tree twigs rather than willow.

twisler. Operator of a weaving loom, usually in the silk industry. Also twister and twisthand.

tyler. One who laid roofing and other tiles.

tynker. Same as tinker.

type founder. Manufacturer of printer's type using melted lead and antimony and cast in moulds to form individual letters of the alphabet. (See also letter founder, letter cutter and letter caster.)

typesetter. Printing industry worker. Same as compositor.

typographer. Originally a printer, but later came to mean someone who designs a printed page using different type 'fonts' for the best effect. See illustration.

typographus. Printer.

tyre moulder. Motor car tyre maker (in a factory). See illustration.

tyre pressman. Someone who fits tyres to vehicle wheels.

tyreman/woman. Same as tireman/woman.

tyro. A new learner of any trade, often a boy.

U

umbrella maker. Originally (in Britain) this term was used for both umbrella and parasol makers as no distinction was made between the sun and rain varieties. Umbrellas (for rain) were considered originally as 'an excess only used by dandies'.

under butler. See footman.

under framer. Cleaner of the underneath of an engine or vehicle.

under salter. A medieval colloquial term for someone of inferior status (servants always sat below the salt cellar on a communal eating table).

under strapper. Term given to a middle man or inferior agent.

underbearer. Person employed to carry a coffin at a funeral. Funeral bearer.

underletter. Old property term to describe a tenant who legally sublets all or part of his property.

unlettered surgeon. Unqualified but respected person who acted as a local doctor, surgeon or dentist.

upholder. Upholsterer. Also a second hand goods dealer.

upstairs maid. Higher class maid who worked with the family of the house directly as opposed to a downstairs maid.

urchin. Dirty child (usually a beggar or from a poor family).

urigenator. Polisher of metal or armoury.

urinator. Professional diver.

userer. Money lender, usurer (forerunner of the banker).

usher. Someone who shows people to their seats (especially in church) and attends to visitors. Also a term for an assistant master in 18th century boarding schools.

usufruct tenant. Temporary tenant.

uxoricide. Legal term for a wife killer.

V

vaccarius. Cow keeper.

vagabundus. Tramp.

vagina maker. Same as shether.

vaginarius. Same as shether.

valet. Male servant responsible for the master's wardrobe, bathing and shaving needs and other personal services.

valet shop owner. Valet shops sprang up in the 1920s to press the clothing of customers. They developed into the modern dry-cleaners.

vallancy maker. Manufacturer of a particularly large type of wig that shaded the face.

valletus. Same as valet. Also a farmer with his own land, i.e. a yeoman.

vamper. Person who repaired old things to make them look like new.

van driver. The driver of a small horse-drawn delivery truck. Later a small motorised vehicle for carrying goods.

van man. Same as van driver.

van soldier. A vanguard soldier who led the other troops in an army.

vapulator. Person who gave the punishment of flogging on a ship or in a gaol.

vassal. Someone who had taken an oath to follow a leader and in exchange received his protection.

vat man. Someone who looks after the vats in a factory (e.g. a brewery, cloth or paper factory).

vault owner. Someone who ran a wine and/or spirit selling business (usually direct from the barrel for take-away sales) known as a 'spirit vaults'.

vavassor. Similar to a knight. He was a free tenant just under the status of a baron.

V.D.M. 'Verbi dei minister'. A nonconformist church minister.

vectigalis. Taxer (i.e. tax collector).

vedette. An army watchman on horseback, usually employed to keep watch over an encampment.

venator. Hunter.

venator con canis. Hunter who uses hounds.

vendor. Means 'seller of' with the commodity usually following.

venter. Public speaker or publisher who distributes information.

venur. Same as venator.

verbi dei minister. See V.D.M.

verderer. Originally a royal officer in charge of the King's forest. Later a petty constable.

verge maker. Specialist clock/watch part maker.

verger. Originally a lowly worker in charge of a yard or paddock known as a virga. Also, a clergyman or church/procession official.

verrier. Glass worker/glazier.

verser(er). Poetry seller/reader/compiler.

versificator. Poet.

vesica maker. Same as shether.

vestiar(ius). Clothing manufacturer/dealer.

vestryman. Member of a local (church) parish council.

vexil carrier. Flag carrier or standard bearer.

viaticus. Tramp (sometimes traveller).

vicar. As well as its use for a clergyman, the term was also used in the 19th century for a deputy or other authorised person.

vicar general. Ecclesiastical officer whose duties later became combined with those of the chancellor of a diocese.

vicarius. Vicar.

vicecomes. Viscount/sheriff/shire reeve.

viceroy. One who governs as a sustitute of the sovereign.

victor. Uncertain, probably a soldier or a victualler.

victualarius. Same as victualler.

victualler. Food shop keeper. Also inn keeper who also provides meals.

vidulator. A musician who played an instrument similar to a fiddle.

villanus. Common worker.

villein. A common worker. Unfree but above the status of a slave with a much restricted lifestyle (similar to a serf).

villein in gross. Same as a villein but could be transferred as a property to another owner.

villicus. Steward.

vinarius. Grape grower/wine seller.

vinerator. Grape grower.

vinero(o)n. Grape grower.

vini mercator. Wine merchant.

vintner. Wine merchant or dealer.

viper catcher. See under snake catcher.

virgiferens. A verger (church attendant) or procession official.

virgin (light keeper). Girl or young woman who was responsible for lighting the church candles.

virginal maker. Musical instrument maker.

viridarius. Grass cutter or hay maker.

viro. Boatman.

vitarius. Glazier.

vitellarius. Inn keeper who also provides meals.

vitillarius. Same as vitellarius.

vitrar(ius). Glass blower/seller or glazier.

vitrolite worker. Worker in a factory that made 'vitrolite' (rolled coloured glass).

viverrarius. A kind of medieval rat and pest catcher who used ferrets.

vocabulist. Compiler of dictionaries.

Workers in a rubber factory, vulcanizing car tyres. Before modern manufacturing processes, car tyres and other rubber objects would be strengthened by being vulcanized in large vats in which sulphur had been added. The workers in the above photograph taken around 1935 are lowering moulded tyres into the 'vulcanizer'. Between 12 and 35 tyres would be vulcanized at once.

votaress. Used to describe nuns, but strictly any female devoted to a particular form of worship or way of life.

votarist. Male equivalent of votaress. Also votary.

vulcan. Blacksmith.

vulcan rubber worker. Worker in a rubber factory.

vulcanizer. Rubber industry worker who hardened rubber by adding sulphur during the manufacturing process. See illustration.

W

wabster. A weaver.

wadding maker. Manufacturer of wadding for stuffing furniture (often using old rags).

waeg(e)nwyrhta. Saxon wagon builder. Equivalent of the more modern wainwrights, someone who made or repaired wagons.

wafer maker. Maker of church communion wafers.

wafter boatman. Owner or operator of a passenger carrying boat.

wagon examiner. Inspector of railway rolling stock.

wagon greaser. Railway worker who greased the wheels of carriages etc.

wag(g)oner. Carrier or horse and wagon operator.

wagonette driver. Driver of an open four-wheeled horse-drawn wagon fitted with long seats to carry four, eight, or ten passengers.

waif. A homeless person. As opposed to a 'stray' who had a home but was away from it.

wailer. Person who discards impure rocks in a coal mine.

wain-bote man. Driver of a heavy timber carrying horse-drawn carriage.

wain house proprietor. Owner of a building where wagons and carts could be stored or parked for a fee.

wainius. Ploughman.

wainman/waindriver. Driver of a cart e.g. a haywain.

wainwright. Wagon maker/repairer.

waister. Man stationed in the waist of a sailing ship between the quarter deck and forecastle.

wait(man). Night watchman who guarded the gates of a city wall and marked the hours by playing a note on a musical instrument or bell.

waiter. A carrier of any sort of goods including meals in a cafe. Also a customs official (see under land waiter, town waiter, tide waiter, King's waiter etc).

wakeman. Night watchman.

waker. A night watchman or person employed to 'knock up' workers from their beds in time for early morning work.

waldglas manufacturer. A ancient maker of green or 'forest' glass in small quantities. (See also under forest glass maker.)

walker. Cloth worker who walked on cloth during treatment. Also, an ancient forester.

wall song seller. Also known as a pinner-up. He sold large song sheets for communal singing etc.

wall stenciller. A kind of sign writer who uses stencils.

wallah. A term imported from India (during British rule) meaning servant (e.g. tea wallah), later came to mean any worker with a specific job (e.g. guard wallah for a train guard, etc).

waller. Same as a setter, but also someone who builds walls of any sort (sometimes a salt maker).

wallet maker. Manufacturer of a type of knapsack used for carrying workers' tools etc.

Walloon. A Flemish (Dutch or Belgian) person, many of whom came to England in the Middle Ages and later.

wallpaper printer. Small printer who printed only rolls of wallpaper in the days before factory production.

wang maker. Manufacturer of small fastenings, especially buckles for shoes.

wantcatcher. Same as warp catcher.

wapp & wanty dealer. Salesman of straps, nets, ropes, etc., for tying and securing goods. Wapps are ropes used to tighten other ropes together, especially on ship's rigging, 'wanty' being a kind of heavy leather strap used for securing loads on wagons and beasts of burden.

wappet. A watchman. The name comes from an identical term for a watchdog.

ward. See under watch.

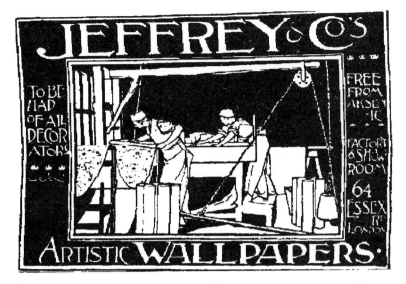

Wallpaper printer.

ward holder. Scottish land holder who held his land in exchange for a promise of providing war service when needed.

wardcorn. Watchman armed with a horn for sounding the alarm. He was generally in charge of a castle's security in medieval times.

warden. Part of the Civil Defence system during World War Two. Each warden was responsible for about 100 people. Five or six wardens would work from one central wardens' post. They were responsible for ensuring no lights were showing during the 'black-out' and for sounding the air raid warning siren and co-ordinating activities after a bomb attack.

warker. Specialist builder of walls, embankments and embattlements.

warp catcher. Mole catcher (moles were known as mouldi-warps).

warper (and beamer). Textile industry worker who places the warp upon beams. Warper is also a boat mover.

warrener. Keeper of a rabbit/hare warren in medieval times.

warriner. Same as warrener.

wart curer. Usually a secondary occupation whereby for a fixed fee, the wart curer would touch warts with nitric acid in order to remove them.

wart rubber. Person who was known as a healer of warts, but who often acted as a general untrained country doctor using plants and other natural medicines.

wase weaver. Home worker who made wases, small wreaths of straw used by milkmaids, water carriers and other workers as a padded cushion when carrying buckets or items on their heads.

wash miller. Process worker in the cement industry.

washerwoman. A person who 'took in' other people's washing into her own home for a fixed fee. As opposed to a laundry woman who did the same job in a commercial establishment.

washman. Tin worker.

wassailer. Woman who would call at houses at Christmas carrying a model of Jesus in the manger and singing Christmas carols. She would be paid by the householder as a sign of Christmas cheer. The term was also used for carol singers in general.

wasteman, waster. Refuse disposal man. Also a mine worker who checks for gas etc.

watch. Somebody appointed to guard at night (as opposed to a ward who carried out the same duties in the day).

watch finisher. Clock/watch assembler.

watcher. A 18th century night nurse.

water bailiff. Originally a customs boat search officer in ports, now an officer mainly in charge of preventing salmon poaching.

water boatman. Operator of a small river boat used for carrying cargo.

water carrier, water carter. Someone who sold fresh water from a travelling cart. Also someone who sprayed roads, and flushed drains etc for the local council.

A London water cartman at the turn of the 20th century. Water cartmen were of two types, those who carried water for general sale to the public and businesses, and those who were employed by town and city councils to water the roads. The above rare picture of one such water cartman in London shows him on a dusty un-made road which he is no doubt spraying from a tank in the back of the cart. Generally, the rear of the cart contained a tin tank or other container connected to a spraying system which was operated by a lever at the side of the driver.

water cartman. Someone who collected and sold fresh water (using a horse and cart) in the days before public supplies. See illustration.

water-crane operator. Man in a railway goods or maintenance yard who was responsible for filling locomotives with water.

water crease girl. Same as water cress girl.

water cress girl. Seller of watercress in the street or at a market.

water gilder. Water bird trapper.

water leader. Same as water carter.

water loder. Same as water carter.

water policeman. See under marine policeman.

water ram operator. Operator of a hydraulic ram.

waterer. Man with the responsibility for turning a water supply on or off. Also known as a turncock.

waterguard. Customs officer.

waterman. Boat or barge worker.

wattle hurdle maker. Fence maker.

waulk miller. Same as walker.

waulker. Same as walker.

waver. Weaver.

waveson collector. Official or unofficial collector of floating goods following a shipwreck.

wax-scot/shot collector. Ancient minor official who collected wax for recycling. Later, a church official who collected money to provide for lighting a church.

waymaker. Surveyor/controller of highways. Also used sometimes for a labourer who builds roads.

wayman. Surveyor of highways. Also used to describe a shipwright and/or a platelayer who is working on a ship launch framework.

waywarden. Surveyor of highways.

weard. Watchman or warden.

weather cloth maker. Manufacturer of long thin tarpaulins and similar cloths used to protect people or goods from the weather.

weather machine operator. Worker who used a machine in early motor car construction specially developed to test fabrics, paint, etc., and to simulate years of weathering.

weather spy. Someone who predicted the weather by watching the skies.

webber. Person who used cloth webbing strips during a manufacturing process, usually of furniture. Sometimes, also a weaver of webbing.

webster. Originally a high ranking steward or bailiff. Later a female (then any) spinner/weaver.

weed hirer/outfitter Person who hired out weeds (mourning dresses).

weeder. Garden or farm labourer.

weel trapper. Fisherman who used a trap made from twigs or basketware.

weigher. Same as weigh(t)man.

weigh(t)man. Cargo weigher on a dockside.

weighter. Silk industry worker.

well-boat builder. Builder of fishing boats constructed with a central well or hold to store the fish as they are caught.

well sinker. A digger of wells.

wellmaster. A Court Leet officer with responsibility for local water supplies.

wellwright. Maker of winding and other well equipment/ accessories.

wet end(er) man. Factory worker engaged in the wet processes involved in manufacturing paper.

wet glover. Leather glove maker.

wetnurse. A woman who uses her own breast milk to feed the children of others (usually for a fee).

wetter. Glass worker. Also used in the printing industry.

wetworker. Leather trade worker.

whacker (in). Colloquial term for a driver of animals.

wharfinger. Docker or dock owner.

wheel cutter. Operator of machinery which cut cogs for clocks etc.

wheel tapper. Railway worker who checked the wheels of locomotives.

wheeler. Spinning wheel attendant. Also a wheelmaker. Also a pit pony attendant in a mine.

wheelwright. Wheelmaker/repairer. Wheels consisted of three parts; the 'hub' or centre, the 'spokes' and the 'fellies' which made up the outside rim. Many wheelwrights also made carts, carriages and wagons.

wheeryman. Rowing boat proprietor.

wherry man. Same as rully man. Also same as wheeryman.

whey cutter/drawer. Cheese industry worker.

whiffler. A person who went before an army or procession group, announcing their coming by the sound of a trumpet.

whig. Horse drover/driver (usually in Scotland). Also a member of a liberal political party.

whinyarder. Swordsman.

whipcorder. Maker of whips.

whipper. As well as the person inflicting punishment by whip, the term was also used to describe the man who hauled coal from the hold of a ship, either on deck or onto a quay.

whipper-in. Huntsman who controls the hounds.

whirlicote manufacturer. A maker of the earliest British horse carriages for the carrying of women.

whisket weaver. Basket maker.

whiskey driver. Driver of a light speedy carriage called a whiskey.

whit cooper. Same as white cooper.

w(h)itcher. Maker of wooden, woven or basketware chests or similar containers.

White Canon. See under Premonstratensian monk.

white collar worker. Colloquial expression for anyone in a clean job, usually an office worker.

white cooper. Maker of barrels and containers from tin or light metals.

White Friar. Member of the Carmelite order of friars.

white gold jeweller. A jeweller specialising in 'white gold' which is gold mixed with platinum or palladium.

white goodsman. Early name for tradesman dealing in fridges and similar appliances.

white limer. Painter of walls (with white lime).

white-meat dealer. 19th century dealer in dairy products (not meat).

whitear. Animal skin or raw leather cleaner.

Whiteboy. Same as 'Leveller'.

whitener. Same as a white limer. Also a cloth bleacher.

whitening roll maker. A manufacturer of whitening used by white limers.

whitesmith. Metal worker who deals in tin, light metals and white enamelled goods.

whitester. Cloth bleacher.

whitewing. Street sweeper.

whitster. Bleacher of cloth.

whitsul seller. Vendor of a dish made from milk, sour milk, cheese, curds and butter.

whittaker. Same as whittawer.

whittawer. Saddler/ harness dealer.

wicker. Lamp/candle wick maker.

widdy. Widow.

wide-awake maker. Manufacturer of a brimless hat known as a 'wide-awake'.

A scene depicting people in a medieval village. The molander (1) rides towards one of the abbey's water mills whilst talking to a local neatherd (2). His cattle pound is nearby. A boscar (3) can be seen chopping down trees as a hayward works behind him. Behind the little priory, a fur (4) runs out of the wood with a rabbit. To the left a hind (5) harrows the field whilst behind him on the road a rogator (6) and a mendicant friar (7) head towards the village with their hands out in a begging posture. A wain (8) ploughs the field with his oxen and looks towards the stocks where a common cursitor (9) sits. Along the river bank a haggard (10) calls to falcons on a nearby tree whilst his wife washes clothes in the river next to him.

widow. In the 1700s was often used to indicate a woman living alone on private means. At that time it did not always indicate that the woman had previously been married. Old records such as 'Widow Jane Smith, Spinster' can therefore be confusing.

wildfowler. A hunter of game birds.

willow plaiter, willow weaver. Basket maker.

winchman. Someone who operates a winch or pulley (usually in a mine).

wind cheater manufacturer. Maker of light weatherproof jackets (originally made of leather).

winder. Textile worker. Also same as a winchman.

windster. A silk industry worker who winds silk.

wing coverer. Aeroplane worker who covered old fashioned plane's wings with linen etc.

winkler. Collector of periwinkles (a kind of sea snail) from the shoreline to be boiled and sold as food. (See also cuvin collector.)

wire drawer. Maker of wire from thicker metals.

wire splicer. Maker of hand-made metal rope from wire. Also used to describe a ship rigger. (See also rigger.)

wiseman/woman. Unofficial but often respected herbalist who in rural areas acted as doctor/nurse/midwife.

wisket maker. Basket maker.

withy weaver/peeler. Basket-worker.

witster. Cloth bleacher.

wonkey-scooper. Person who operated a kind of scoop contraption with a horse.

wood reeve. Officer who was in charge of a forest.

woodbreaker. Wooden cask maker (sometimes from recycled wood).

woodcutter. Used to describe both a forest worker and an engraver of wooden printing blocks.

woodman. A woodworker or forestry worker.

woodranger. Same as woodman.

woodward. Same as wood reeve.

wool blender. Wool sorter in wool trade.

wool driver. Travelling shepherd who takes animals to market, or for shearing. Also a deliverer of wool to market.

wool factor. An agent or wholesaler in the wool trade.

wool grower. Sheep farmer.

woolpresser. Packer of raw wool into bales before transporting it to a factory.

wool sorter. Grader of wool in the wool trade.

wool stapler. Same as wool sorter but originally an export merchant in the 1500s who was a member of a group who had a monopoly on the export of wool.

wool weaver. Also known as dress goods room workers. See illustration.

wool winder. Wool trade worker who winds up the skeins/balls of wool.

A day in the life of a mill girl. Wool weavers were also known as dress goods room workers. It was usually a woman's job and involved the operation of weaving machines. A group of such workers are pictured above surrounded by all the complex machinery, bobbins etc.

woolcomber. Woollen mill worker who separates fibres.

woollen billy piecer. Wool mill worker who collects broken yarn and joins it.

woolman. General term for anyone in the wool trade.

woolstead man. Woollen cloth dealer.

worsted manufacturer. Wool cloth maker.

worsted shearman. Worsted cloth cutter.

wrangler. Originally someone who earned high honours (e.g. in an examination). Later associated with American cowboys.

wrap rascal maker. Clothing manufacturer who made a cheaply produced coarse overcoat called a wrap-rascal, used by the Victorian lower classes.

wreck-master. Official appointed to take charge of goods thrown on shore after the wreck of a ship.

wrecker. Unscrupulous coastal dweller who on dark stormy nights would put false lights on beaches and cliffs with the intention of causing a shipwreck and so looting the ship's contents.

wright. Worker with construction skills (e.g. wheelwright, shipwright etc).

wringer. Someone in industry who applied 'wring bolts'. Also the operator of a mangle in a large laundry.

writer. Originally a secretary or scribe.

writer to the Signet. High ranking Scottish law attorney who attended to royal documents. Also called clerk to the Signet.

wuzzer. A person who dried out wet wool in the weaving industry by whirling it round and round.

wyrtha. A worker (labourer).

X

Xylographer. Printing block engraver/maker.

Xylopola. Wood merchant.

xylopyrograher. Craftsman who engraved on wood using a red hot poker.

Y

yacker. Colloquial term meaning 'worker' (e.g. farm yacker).

yagger. Pedlar.

yardman. Farm worker. Also a railway yard worker.

yardmaster. Early term for a stationmaster or head yardman.

yatman. Gatekeeper or doorman.

yeager. Hunter of game. (See also jaegar.)

year man. Someone engaged at annual 'hirings' for a year's work (usually agricultural).

yellow book inspector. School inspector (used throughout Britain), so called from the colour of the report books.

yeoman. Farmer who farmed his own lands. He could serve on juries and had a vote. Also a ship's storeman.

Yeoman of the Guard. Originally one of the royal bodyguards.

yest maker. Same as barm maker.

youngling. A child.

younker. A young gentleman or knight of independent means.

yowler. Assistant to a thatcher. He held the yowles of straw and passed them to the thatcher (17th century).

Z

zeotrope manufacturer. Maker of an early form of cylindrical optical toy with slots which when looked through gave the impression of moving scenes, animals running, etc., as it was spun.

zigarius. Gypsy.

zincographer. Someone who engraved on, or printed from, zinc plates known as 'zinco's'.

zole collector. Tax man or toll collector.

zoographer. Someone who classifies species of animals.

zoolithologist. Scientist or student who studied or collected fossilised remains.

zootomist. Scientist who specialised in the dissection of animals.

zymotechnist. Scientist who studied the fermentation processes.

zythepsarist. Brewer.